AF560002

PERFORMANCE IN SCHOOL MATHEMATICS

By

Dr. D. Krishna Reddy

Principal

Sri Vidaya College of Education

Tirupati

DISCOVERY PUBLISHING HOUSE PVT. LTD.

NEW DELHI-110 002

Published by:
Tilak Wasan

DISCOVERY PUBLISHING HOUSE PVT. LTD.
4831/24, Ansari Road, Prahlad Street
Darya Ganj, New Delhi-110002 (India)
Phone: +91-11-23279245, 43764432
Fax: +91-11-23253475
E-mail: parul.wasan@gmail.com
discoverypublishinghouse@gmail.com
info@discoverypublishinggroup.com
web: www.discoverypublishinggroup.com

First Edition: **2011**
ISBN: 978-81-8356-808-1

Performance in School Mathematics

Printed at:
Shree Balaji Art Press
Delhi

Dedicated to my

Beloved wife Smt. B. Ravi

&

Children D.V. Santhisri &

D. Saandeep

Foreword

Mathematics plays a very important role, at the primary and secondary levels of Education. A strong foundation in mathematics is needed for the primary teachers; who enter into the profession, at the end of Intermediate Education. Also a strong foundation in mathematics at the secondary level functions as a link for those who opt for mathematics at higher level. Unfortunately majority of the students at the secondary level feel that mathematics is the most difficult subject, due to various factors, as is evident from the public examination results of X class every year. But if taught in a well plannedmanner, by competent, dedicaated teachers with proper positive attitute towards the subject, the study of mathematics can be made more interesting and easy. The author with his experience of teaching mathematics over a period of 37 years, at different levels, namely secondary, Intermediate, Degree and B.Ed and through his research on the influence of certain factors on the achievement in mathematics, attempted to find out the contribution of various factors in improving the performance in mathematics at X class level.

The findings mentioned in the book will go a long way in changing the attitute of teachers and the concerned people, to make the study of mathematics as easy as possible, by strengthening the positive aspects and by removing the negative aspects. I hope this book serves as an eye-opener and guide for Teachers, Researches, Parents, Educational administrates and students in knowing the factors which enhance the scores in mathematics and also develop positive attitude towards the mathematics.

Prof. N. Prabhakara Rao
Vice-Chancellor
S.V. University
Tirupati

Preface

In the present day global context, mathematics at school level forms the foundation for the future education, in the areas of science and technology. The standard of mathematics, received at secondary level, plays a lead role in the selection of higher education stream and performance in the future occupations. Keeping this in view, stress has been laid on the teaching of mathematics at secondary level. As a result, this has led to the creation of aptitude for the study of mathematics, in case of some students and at the same time, it also created a phobia for mathematics in case of majority of the students. Hence, there is a need to create a conducive environment at the school level for study of mathematics, without which a large section of the students would be left out to the other streams of education.

Recognizing this, myself being a mathematician for the past three decades, conceived a study to identify the bottlenecks and contributing factors in the performance of the students in mathematics at school level. The work has been arranged in six chapters namely, Introduction, Review of related literature, The present study, Method of investigation, Analysis and Interpretation and Summary, Findings, Conclusions, Recommendation and Suggestions.

The introductory chapter deals with the importance of mathematics, its relevance in the secondary school curriculum, views expressed by eminent educationists and its need in the present day context.

The second chapter Review of Related Literature, deals with the recommendations of various committees on mathematic education and presents an overview on earlier studies made relevant to the present study.

The third chapter states the statement of the problem, Objectives of the study, Hypotheses formulated, Variables included in the study and Limitations.

The fourth chapter deals with the tools used in the present study. i.e. construction Objective achievement Test and adoption of the tools namely, Self-concepts, HSPQ and Study Habits Inventory. It also describes the selection of the sample and administration of the tools on the sample.

The fifth chapter gives the rate of achievement in mathematics among different groups of students, influence of the various variables on the achievement and extent of contribution of variables on the scholastic achievement. The finding of the study in terms of factors contributing for the achievement of the mathematics will provide an insight into the minds of the teachers and curriculum framers to design an instructional strategy to make a study of mathematics interesting and joyful. For researchers it provides tips for further research.

I acknowledges my gratitude to Prof. B. Ramachandra Reddy, Department of Education and Prof. P. Adinarayana Reddy, Principal IASE, S.V. University Tirupati for their continued support and guidance in the present work. All the suggestions for the improvement of the book shall be thankfully received by me.

D. KRISHNA REDDY

Contents

Abbreviations

ANOVA	:	Analysis of Variance
BC	:	Backward Caste
CV	:	Coefficient of Variation
DDE	:	Directorate of Distance Education
DF	:	Degrees of Freedom
ERIC	:	Educational Resources Information Centre
EVS	:	Environmental Sciences
FES	:	Family Economic Scale
FIG/Fig.	:	Figure
HCF	:	Highest Common Factor
HSPQ	:	High School Students Personality Questionnaire
IASE	:	Institute of Advanced Studies in Education
K_U	:	Kurtosis
LCM	:	Lowest Common Multiple
M	:	Mean
Md	:	Median
Mo	:	Mode
MSU	:	Maharaja Sivajirao University of Baroda
N	:	Number of Sample Subjects or Number of Observations
NCERT	:	National Council of Educational Research and Training
NFE	:	Non-formal Education
NCTM	:	National Council of Teachers of Mathematics
NPE	:	National Policy of Education

OAT	:	Objective Achievement Test
OC	:	Open Category
PhD	:	Doctor of Philosophy
Q_1	:	First Quartile
Q_3	:	Third Quartile
QD	:	Quartile Deviation
R	:	Range
SC	:	Scheduled Caste
SD	:	Standard Deviation
SEM	:	Standard Error of Mean
SES	:	Socio-economy Status
SHI	;	Study Habits Inventory
S_K	:	Skewness
SVU	:	Sri Venkateswara University
ST	:	Scheduled Tribe
TLM	:	Teaching Learning Material
VN	:	Variable Number

1

Chapter

Introduction

Mathematics plays a very important role in the life of human beings. Without the knowledge of mathematics, it is difficult to learn other school subjects, more importantly science subjects. In the modern scientific world, mathematics occupies important place in the school curriculum. Hence, the achievement in mathematics is crucial for every pupil, studying in the schools. If the teacher teaches in a planned and methodical way it is expected that achievement of children is certainly going to be satisfactory.

Teachers, awareness of teaching methodologies and techniques of teaching are vital not only for an effective transaction of curriculum in the classroom but also for the improvement in standard of achievement of children. The Delors' International Commission on Education for the 21st century stated in its Report:

> "Improving the quantity of education depends on first improving the recruitment, training, social status and conditions of working teachers. They need the appropriate Knowledge and skills, personal characteristics, professional prospects and motivation, if they are to meet the expectations placed upon them" (Delors, 1996:142).

In the study of mathematics, the emphasis should be more on the development of general problem-solving ability rather than on finding a solution to a particular problem. Knowledge is useful, only when one is able to apply it effectively. The ability to apply it, in turn, needs power to think effectively. Therefore the pupil should attack problems logically in the spirit of discoverer.

The progress and improvement of scientific method and mathematics are linked to the prosperity of whole human civilization. To arouse and maintain the interest of students in mathematics, therefore, the elements of curiosity, motivation, imagination, novelty, originality, newness and usefulness are required. 'Interest' is a motivating force that arouses, sustains and regulates concentrated efforts. There is a need and accountability on the part of the teacher to arouse this 'interest' in pupils.

MEANING AND DEFINITIONS OF EDUCATION

There have been a lot of controversial statements about the meaning of education, beginning from Socrates and Plato to Dewey and Gandhi. If it is not completely impossible, it is rather very difficult to assess the real value of the term 'Education'

Education is nothing but a process, through which a child can have free, spontaneous and individual development. Education awakens those innate powers, which are there in a child. This process of awakening is nothing but 'Education'.

Education is a bipolar process in which one personality acts on another to modify the development of other. It is a process of development from cradle to grave. In this, we find all sorts of influences, like home, friendship, recreations, hobbies etc. Education is a long process, which is never ending.

Here under, we analize the various view points of various thinkers about the word 'Education'.

> Education is a process through which a child makes its internal, external.
> **Frobel**

The analysis of the word 'Education' clarifies the fact that a child possesses various internal capacities but these capacities are made external through the weapon of 'Education'.

> When Education works on a noble mind, it draws out to view every latent virtue and perfection
> **Addison.**

Education means bringing out the ideas of universal validity which are latent in every human being. **Socrates**

By Education, I mean an all round drawing out of the best in child and man-body, mind and spirit." **Mahatma Gandhi**

Education is complete development of individuality of child, so that it can make an original contribution to human life according to the best of its capacity. **T.P. Nunn**

Education is defined as natural, harmonious and progressive development of one's innate powers. **Pestalazzi**

Education is the creation of a sound mind in a sound body. **Aristotle**

"Plants are developed by cultivation and men by Education." **Locke (1969)**

In a world based on science and technology, it is the Education that determines the level of prosperity, welfare and security of people. **Kothari Commission (1964-66)**

IMPORTANCE OF EDUCATION IN HUMAN LIFE

The importance of Education in human life can best be seen from Educational values. The Educational values are individual as well as social .

The Educational values have the following advantages for individuals' social life. They are:

- Development of a healthy and balanced personality
- Capacity to earn livelihood and acquire material prosperity
- Development of Vocational efficiency
- Creation of good citizenship
- Development of good character
- Adjustment with environment and its' modification
- Fulfillment of needs
- National integration and national development

- Promotion of social efficiency
- Preserving cultural values
- Utilization of leisure time

The above Educational values play an important role in human life. Through them one is able to lead his personal and social life successfully.

The overall development of a nation depends on the proper utilization of its natural as well as human resources. The opinion of the Planning Commission in the 7th Five Year Plan (1985-90) may be mentioned in this context:

> "Human resources development has necessarily to be assigned a key role in any development strategy particularly, in a country with a large population. Trained and educated on sound lines, a large population can itself become an asset in accelerating economic growth and in ensuring social change in designed directions. Education develops basic skills and abilities and fosters a value system conducive to and in support of national development goals, both long term and immediate".

Hence, the development of human resource is a must for any modern society. As M.S. Swaminathan remarks:

> "Human resource is the most valuable global resource and any short or long term development strategy should be oriented towards the continued well being of human race."

Education plays a significant role in the development of human resources.

> "If this change on a grand scale is to be achieved without violent revolution, there is one instrument only that is: Education."

Other agencies may help and indeed some times have a more apparent impact. But the national system of education is the only instrument that can reach all the people.

The school can help in manpower planning though, it has no direct role in the matter. It is a social agency and it has social accountability. Education is a social process and so it has a significant role in manpower planning in the light of individual as well as social needs.

In all the countries of the world, it may be seen that high per capita incomes are associated with high rates of literacy. Education is valued because, it contributes to a better life. Alfred Marshall emphasized the importance of education as a national investment – it is the most valuable of all capital, invested in human beings. Economic growth in any society is dependent on the existence of a high level need, for achievement among people in that society.

In a democratic country, education can be used for giving training in a good citizenship. It can produce leaders who are capable of independent thought, judgement, self-expression, originality and initiative emphasizing the importance of education. The Kothari Commission's report on Indian Education (1964-66) says:

> "In a world based on science and technology, it is the education that determines the level of prosperity, welfare and security of the people and the quality and number of persons coming out of our schools and colleges, will depend on our success in a great enterprise of national reconstruction, whose principal objective is to raise the standards of living of our people."

The development of a country is primarily determined by the quality of its human resources, which depend on the level of knowledge, skills, attitudes etc. Therefore, creating the right minds through the right process of education requires the top-most priority.

From the above discussion, it is clear that Education leads to the overall personality development (Spiritual, moral social, cultural, mental and economic etc). Therefore, 'Education' is a must for any invidividual and for the development of one's country.

MATHEMATICS – DIFFERENT VIEWS

What is mathematics? The term 'Mathematics' may be defined in a number of ways. It is an exact science which is related to measurements, calculations, discovering relationships and dealing with problems of space.

According to *New English Dictionary* 'mathematics - in a strict sense - is the abstract science which investigates deductively, the conclusions implicit in the elementary conception of spatial and numerical relations'.

In Hindi we call mathematics as *"Ganita"* which means the science of calculations. It is a systematized, organized and exact branch of science. It arises out of practical applications. We form certain intuitive ideas or notions known as axioms and postulates. These are self evident truths.

Mathematics is also called the science of reasoning. According to Locke:

> 'Mathematics is a way to settle in mind a habit of reasoning'.

Mathematics is an expression of human mind, reflects the active will, the contemplative reasoning and the desire for aesthetic perfection. It's basic elements are logic and intuition, analysis and construction and generality and Individuality.

Mathematics has always been regarded as a tool for sharpening the intellect. For this purpose one has to think systematically, logically and precisely.

Bramhagupta, the great Indian mathematician of eighth century said:

> "if you want to shine in the company of learned, propose mathematical problems and solve them".

Dr. Maria Montissori, T.P. Nunn etc. have advocated the importance of mathematics. In their view, the intellectual and cultural development of a person is not possible, without the study of mathematics.

Mathematics has its own language and symbols. The symbols in mathematics have, their own meanings and their own significance.

Mathematics is the creation of man, for his needs. It has been rightly said that:

> "Mathematics is the mirror of civilization." Natural phenomena follow mathematical principles.

As we move into the 21st century, there is consensus among the experts about the necessity for all the students to have string of mathematical ability. Majority of eminent educationists of the past as well as of the present including Herbert Froebel, Pestalozzi, Dr Maria Mantissori etc. have advocated, the importance of mathematics. In their opinion, the intellectual and cultural development of a person is not possible without the study of mathematics.

In several fields centred round human activity such as accountancy, banking, shop-keeping, business, tailoring, carpentry, taxation, insurance, Posts and Telegraphs and so on, there is the use of mathematics. It has become, the basis of the world's entire business and commercial system. Thus mathematics is an inseparable part of human activity.

Many a phenomenon of the universe can be predicted through mathematical calculations. There has been explosion of knowledge in every field of human endeavour including science and technology. Extension of research in science and technology resulting in several discoveries and inventions has changed the face of human society by providing things that make modern life happier and more comfortable than ever before. At the root cause of all these, we can not ignore the role of mathematics. Hence it is imperative that our educational environment provides opportunities to all students to do worthwhile and purposeful mathematical work.

HISTORICAL DEVELOPMENT OF MATHEMATICS

Mathematics is a study of relationships among quantities, magnitudes, and properties of logical operations by which unknown quantities, magnitudes and properties may be deduced. In the past mathematics was regarded as the science of quantity, whether of magnitudes, as in geometry, or of numbers as in arithmetic or the generalization of these two fields, as in algebra. Towards the middle of 19th century, mathematics came to be regarded increasingly as the science of relations, or as science that draws necessary conclusions. This latter view encompasses mathematical or symbolic logic-the science of using symbols to provide an exact theory of logical deduction and inference, based on definitions, axioms, postulates, and rules for transforming primitive elements into more complex relations and the theorems.

This brief history of mathematics traces the evolution of mathematical ideas and concepts, beginning in pre-history.

Indeed mathematics is nearly as old as humanity itself. Evidence of a sense of geometry and interest, geometric patterns, has been found in the design of pre-history pottery and textiles and in cave paintaings. Primitive counting systems were almost certainly based on using the fingers of one or both hands, as evidenced by the predominance of numbers 5 and 10 as the bases, for most number systems today.

Throughout the centuries, mathematics has been recognized as one of the central stands of intellectual activity. From the very beginning, mathematics has been a living and growing intellectual Persuit. It has its roots in every day activities and forms the basic structure of our highly advanced technological developments.

Mathematics, like every thing else, has been created by man, exists to fulfill certain human needs and desires. It is very difficult to say at what point of time in the history of mankind, and in which part of the world, mathematics had its birth. The fact that it has been steadily pursued for so many centuries, that it has attracted ever-increasing attention and that it is now the dominant intellectual interest of mankind, shows that it appeals powerfully to mankind. This conclusion is borne out by every thing that we know about the origin of mathematics. More than 2000 years before beginning of Christian era, both Babylonians and Egyptians were in possession of systematic methods of measuring space and time. They had the knowledge of rudimentary geometry and astronomy. This rudimentary mathematics was formulated to meet the practical needs of agricultural population.

Mathematics is something that man himself has created, to meet the cultural demands of the time. Nearly every primitive tribe invented words to represent numbers. But it was only when ancient civilizations such as the Summerian, Bobylonian, the Chinese and May on developed trade, architecture, taxation and other civilized contracts that the number systems were developed. Thus mathematics has grown into one of the most important cultural components of society. Our modern way of life would not hardly have been possible, without mathematics.

Since the times immemorial, Indians have been contributing significantly for the development of mathematics. The system of numeration and the concept of zero are a gift of Indians, to the world of mathematics.

IMPORTANCE OF MATHEMATICS

Mathematics has been made a compulsory subject of study at the secondary level, with the hope that it will inculcate some minimum basic skills to every future citizen of the country to ensure their future, a happy life.

But at present none of the consumer, the dispenser, or the producers of knowledge of mathematics education is satisfied with the students' achievements in mathematics. So we are directly or indirectly responsible for maiming our future generation by not providing them with proper mathematical knowledge at the secondary level. Jean Piagets (1973) revolutionary finding "Every normal Child is capable of learning mathematics" has put a greater responsibility on dispensers of knowledge of mathematics education, which they can not escape by passing the buck to the poor mathematical ability of the students.

Plato advocated the inclusion of mathematics in school education because mathematical reasoning disciplines the mind. He wrote over the portals of his academy:

"Let no one ignorant of geometry enter here."

The Kothari Commission (1964-66) emphasised the significance of mathematics in the school curriculum by stating:

> "One of the outstanding characteristics of scientific culture is quantification. Mathematics, therefore, assumes a prominent position in modern education. The advent of

automation and cybernetics in this century, marks the beginning of scientific and industrial revolution and makes it all imperative to devote a special attention to the study of mathematics. Proper foundation in the knowledge of the subject should be laid at the school level itself."

Mathematics has been considered as mother of all sciences. If our students are to function effectively at this time of extraordinarily and accelerating global changes, they must understand the fundamental and basic concepts and be able to use them in their personal and professional lives. There has never been a greater need to be mathematically literate than any other thing these days. Those who understand and are proficient in mathematics have, significantly enhanced their opportunities and options to open doors to productivity. Those who lack mathematical competence will find such doors and options closed.

Mathematics at the secondary level is the basic structure on which the whole super structure of mathematics, mathematical sciences and technology in technical institutions, rests. To quote Professor K.E. Brown:

"mathematics has become the basic fabric of our social order. The strength of that fabric, infact, the very survival of our nation may well depend upon the amount and kind of mathematics taught in our secondary schools. This is a great sobering responsibility for those who design and administer the programmes. If we take the responsibility lightly, our children will suffer the consequences of our foolish action."

In several fields centered round human activity, such as banking, accountancy, shop keeping, tailoring, carpentry, taxation, post and telegraphs etc. there is maximum use of mathematics, without the use of which, they cannot survive. The career and financial prospects of every individual depend heavily on his mathematical knowledge and learning.

Some of science subjects such as physics, chemistry and even biology can not be studied without making use of the fundamental principles of mathematics. Thus mathematics continues to occupy a prominent place in human life.

In this complex world passing through scientific, technological and rapidly moving towards computerization age, the importance of mathematics is going to be increasingly felt and recognized.

MATHEMATICS - ITS RELEVANCE IN SECONDARY SCHOOL CURRICULUM

Mathematics is living and flourishing branch of our culture. It is both a discipline in its own right and a service subject used in all the facets of life. It is a universal means of communication. It is a discipline that seeks understanding of patterns and structures of constructs of human mind. There is no end for its depth. As a subject, it is of great value - aesthetic, utilitarian and social. It plays an indispensable role in shaping our natural phenomena with human behaviour.

Many education commissions appointed by Government of India have stressed the need for strengthening mathematics teaching at the secondary level, leading to the introduction of mathematics as one of the compulsory subjects of study up to the secondary level, inspite of some criticism.

In spite of playing such a vital role in our cultural development as well as for individuals' progress, mathematics is not a subject of choice for so many students. Majority of students are afraid of mathematics and develop a phobia for mathematics. Our broad results of past few years, tell us the real story. Failures in mathematics are increasing day by day. Inspite of its great importance, students avoid mathematics. Students are getting irrationally impulsive and have started things at face value.

Mathematics is taught like a mechanical subject with no creativity and imagination. Students are trained to develop mathematical skills of calculation and construction. They are not encouraged to develop mathematical thinking, mathematical aptitude and problem solving approach.

Problem-solving in mathematics requires an ability to understand mathematical ideas and apply them in a variety of situations. It also requires a positive attitude towards mathematics, including confidence, enjoyment and perseverance. This is possible only when, mathematics is presented as a progressive body of knowledge as a whole and not as a fragmented set of skills. Students should be made aware of the wider relevance of mathematics including its aesthetic and humanistic role in the society. Teaching of mathematics should concentrate more on developing attitude, self esteem and confidence. School mathematics should not be considered as a tool for vocational aspirations but it must be considered as a subject, which is useful for all human beings, of all vocations and as a subject which has vide applications in other subjects, like physics, chemistry, commerce and even social studies. It is for the mathematics teachers to see that students at school level, realize the importance of mathematics applications for the scientific and technological development.

Kothari Commission (1964-66) has rightly observed:

> "Special attention should be given for the study of mathematics in view of the importance of quantification and advent of automation and cybernetics. The curriculum in mathematics need be modernized and brought up-to-date at all stages with necessary emphasis on laws and principles of mathematics and logical thinking. Methods of teaching mathematics should be modernized laying stress, on the investigatory approach and understanding of basic principles. The curriculum should be flexible that special needs of the gifted children may be catered."

There is a view that everybody needs some knowledge of mathematics in one way or other. But it is believed that mathematics is exceptionally a difficult subject, the study of which requires some special ability and intelligence. Hence everybody should not be burdened with the study of this tough subject. References are made to the low pass percentage in this subject.

But contrary to this view, educationists began to feel that at such an early age, it is difficult to know who is going to opt for mathematics in higher education and who is going to stop his education at secondary level. While making mathematics a compulsory subject of study, the interests of both types of students are to be safeguarded.

Hence, while framing the mathematics curriculum at the secondary level a great deal of clear thinking and careful planning is necessary in which, school teachers, university professors and educational administrators, have a significant role to play. Our object should be not to change the curriculum but to strengthen it and improve significantly, keeping in view, the present day needs and technological developments.

ROLE OF TEACHERS

The role of a teachers is extremely crucial in the context of education being the best instrument of change and nation building.

Teachers play an important role in moulding the lives and careers of students and through them the destinies of the Nation. It is they who develop in their pupils, the qualities to lead disciplined lives with a spirit of service. Reverence for teachers is a part of our tradition. Their responsibility is beyond imparting the knowledge and training the mind. A complete human being is the product of a good education, both in home and in school.

Teachers are saviours of the society and redeemers of the race. It is in this respect, the role of the teachers, acquires significance in shaping the society and in bringing revolutionary changes in the development of the country. So the teachers are held in high esteem and respect.

Dr Radha Krishnan, himself as a teacher said:

> "An ordinary teacher teaches; An average teacher explains; A good teacher demonstrates, but A great Teacher inspires."

Dr Radha Krishnan's life as a teacher inspired every one and he has been a shinning example to prove that a teacher can rise to the expected heights in life. A teacher should love his profession and develop right type of attitude and zeal towards the profession. Half hearted teachers are as bad as half baked bread. The paramount duty of a teacher is to disseminate learning and impart correct information to the students.

According to Louis Raths:

> a researcher, the main functions of a good teacher are explaining, informing, initiating, directing, administering, unifying the group, clarifying, diagnosing, learning problems, evaluating, recording, reporting, participating in school activities and in professional and civic life.

Another researcher Arthur W.Comb, says:

> that a good teacher can be characterized typically in the light of knowledge of his subject, his frame of reference for approaching problems; his perception of others; his perception of self; his perception of purpose and process of learning and his perception of appropriate methods of teaching

MATHEMATICS TEACHER

In this age of enormous growth of science and unexpected development of Technology, the role of a mathematics teacher in a secondary school is very crucial and important.

All knowledge acquired, skills developed and attitudes formed at the secondary level forms the basis for the student's growth at the higher level and be useful in his life. Every teacher has to acquire professional growth, during the entire period of his tenure as a teacher.

Professional growth, as given in the *Dictionary of Education* by carter V. Good, means:

> "increase in the subject matter. Knowledge, teaching skills, efficiency and insight into the educational problems with a concomitant increase in success as a teacher."

This means knowledge of subject matter, insight into the educational problems or subject area should increase with expertise in teaching skills too, is called the professional development.

A genuine teacher of mathematics must be interested in knowing why should every body learn mathematics, why should this subject be taught at all at secondary level. He must know the importance of this subject, in life and in school curriculum. He must be aware of the advantages of devoting so much of effort, time and money in teaching mathematics. He must feel convinced about the utility of this subject, so that he may be able to convince his students likewise. He should be able to explain to the learner why he needs to read this subject, that he will profit by its knowledge; and ignorance of this subject will keep him handicapped in several ways. Some thing in the personality of the child will certainly remain unrealized in the absence of study of mathematics. The knowledge of its values and aims will stimulate and guide the teacher to adopt effective methods, devices and illustrative materials. Adherence to these values and aims will make the teaching of mathematics purposeful. Mathematics learning results, in the development of a number of fruitful values for the students. However, these values can not be attained automatically by learning mathematics. Only a resourceful teacher of mathematics with his deliberate efforts and planning makes it possible for the students to attain these values. Hence the mathematics teacher plays a crucial role in making the students, realize the values of mathematics in life, and how useful it is in learning other subjects also.

VALUES OF TEACHING MATHEMATICS AT SECONDARY LEVEL

Those who teach any subject are confronted at the very outset by the question "what is the real purpose of and value of teaching this subject" A good mathematics teacher should know, not merely what to teach and how to teach but also why he teaches. It is the duty of every teacher to know as to why his subject is a part of the school curriculum.

According to Lim and Ernest (1997) there are at least six categories of values of teaching mathematics. However, these values of teaching mathematics can broadly be classified as:

1. Practical values,
2. Cultural values,
3. Social values,
4. Disciplinary values.

Mathematical facts have the same validity and truthfulness in any culture and civilization.

The service function of Mathematics cannot be ignored as some of the subjects like, physics and chemistry in the curriculum of secondary school, require the use of some basic principles of mathematics both in theory and practicals.

Only a resourceful and dedicated mathematics-teacher, with his deliberate efforts and planning makes it possible for the students to attain these values.

Problem-solving in mathematics is a fruitful exercise for the development of one's mental faculties, as the process of problem-solving involves the scientific method of thinking and reasoning. It emphasizes the originality of thought and reasoning rather than a mere reproduction of rules and formulae from memory.

The study of mathematics also helps the students to lead a well disciplined life, as it helps the students to imbibe the values like honesty, truthfulness, open mindedness, objectivity, self-confidence, self- reliance, patience, will power, and it trains the students in systematic and orderly habits, namely concentration, punctuality, neatness, hard work, orderliness, regularity and so on.

Mathematics has got other values like ability to form and use a symbolic language, ability to make independent discovery and forming the habit of self scrutiny.

From the above discussion, it is clear that it is important for every mathematics teacher to know the values of teaching mathematics at secondary level. Then only he can make the student to realize the importance and values of mathematics.

ATTITUDE OF STUDENTS AND TEACHERS TOWARDS MATHEMATICS

Why do students dislike mathematics? Is it because of apathy, frustration, lack of motivation or aptitude, hostility, scare due to difficulty and abstraction of this subject?

Obviously, different factors such as physiological, social,

emotional, intellectual and pedagogical, may cause 'maths-aversion' in the students and it is the duty of the mathematics teacher to identify and isolate these factors. Once the disease is diagnosed, the remedy might be easy and often it may require lot of effort, on the part of the teacher, in order to make the subject more fascinating, provide him with intellectual food to satisfy his curiosity and induce him to develop the habit of thinking, which is very essential for problem solving in his future life. Solving problem through mathematical games could be helpful in this area.

It is sad to observe that even today, educational system in India, remains essentially, examination oriented. Under this system, learners do not receive mathematics education. They mostly prepare themselves for passing the examinations. Such a situation not only damages the purpose of all education but also proves ruinous for mathematical education. If we want to make mathematical education more meaningful, this situation will have to be changed and the entire system of education will have to be reviewed and reoriented.

If we observe carefully mathematics classes, we find that the rate of progress is decreasing at all stages of school education.

Mathematics is also presented from a wrong point of view. It is presented as a matter of dead facts and techniques and not in terms of its true nature, which involves processes that demand thought and creativity.

Making students aware of strategies or principles, relevant to the problem solving, is one the goals of National Council of Teachers of Mathematics (NCTM). This can be best noticed while observing students do proofs in geometry, on basis of the model proofs presented by the teachers. Often this is done with a little thinking or no thinking on the part of the student.

It is, therefore necessary that only correct mathematics should be taught correctly at the secondary school stage.

There are some adverse comments on mathematics as follows:

"It is too remote from life to interest the students."

"Mathematics has outlived its usefulness as a subject of secondary school instruction."

"Mathematics is completely taught on theoretical grounds"

"It is more abstract in nature."

"Teaching is confined to the class-room and not related to pupils' life."

Obviously, the teachers assume monopolized responsibility to solve problems, one after the other and as many as could, in order to complete or 'cover' the heavy syllabus and examination requirements.

A dominant trend of 'haste' to proceed as fast as or as much as they could has been quite transparent and evident. Such an accelerated style, would, by implication, hamper sustained effort of the problem-solving stages and processes. With the result the students would acquire, rapid, but, mechanical drill type skills, resulting in the total loss of the thrill and creative problem solving processes.

Mathematics is not merely a 'product' but a process. It is not only a 'knowledge'; it is an activity also. Its 'static' part is important, its 'dynamic' part is even more vital. Not only mathematical facts are to be taught, method of arriving at these facts are also to be communicated. All these require a rethinking about the goals of mathematics education.

The progress and improvement of scientific method and mathematics are linked to the prosperity of whole human civilization. To arouse and maintain the interest of the students in mathematics, therefore, elements of curiosity, motivation, imagination, novelty, originality and usefulness are required. Actually interest is the motivating force that arouses, sustains and regulates concentrated efforts.

One old saying is :

"we can take a Horse to the water; but we can not make it drink".

This old saying can suitably be changed to suit the present day technological world as:

"First make a Horse feel thirsty; then it drinks."

Therefore, the mathematics teachers should make the students realize the present day importance of mathematics, motivate and inspire for learning the subject- then the students tend to learn, which reduces the burden of the teachers.

ACADEMIC ACHIEVEMENT

Academic achievement has been playing an important role, since formal education decides the level of learning of different students in different subjects all classes. Achievement can be defined as total marks or score obtained by a student in a particular subject. Achievement differs from student to student and from subject to subject. Factors for this difference also vary from person to person. Various factors play their role for this difference in the achievement. It has been observed that in subjects like mathematics, science and English, the achievement is considerably low; when compared to the other subjects, in the case of majority of students at secondary level, due to various factors.

Academic achievement is a multi-dimensional phenomenon and may be effected by three main types of factors viz. subjective, objective and personality factors. Subjective factors are related to the individual himself, his intelligence, learning ability, aptitude, self-concept, perception of school, study habits and level of aspiration; Objective factors lie with in the environment, socio-economic status, family traits, education system, system of evaluation, school situation, type of the school, number of students in the class etc. Personality Factors are related to the individuals' adjustment with the school environment, his attitude towards the subject, attitude towards the teachers, adjustment with his peers and emotional adjustment.

Academic achievement has raised several important questions for educational researchers. What factors promote achievement in students? How far do the different factors contribute towards academic achievement? Many factors have been hypothesized and researched upon.

Scholastic/academic achievement is of paramount importance, particularly in the present socio-economic and cultural contexts. Great emphasis is placed on achievement right from the beginning of formal education. A considerable number of students from schools go to the colleges and institutions of higher learning. It is very important to ensure that such students acquire the requisite competence so as to benefit more out of higher education. Setting the stage for achievement of youth is thus a fundamental obligation of the educational system.

In schools/colleges, great emphasis is placed on the achievement right from the beginning of the formal education. The school has its own systematic hierarchy, which is largely based on achievement and performance rather than ascription. The school/college performs, the function of selection and differentiation among students on the basis of their scholastic and other attainments and open out avenues for advancement, primarily in terms of achievement.

The central aim of all formal educational efforts is academic achievement, on the part of the students. Even though, it is desirable to have alround development as a goal of educational process, where academic achievement would be just one of the dimensions; but in most of the educational institutions, academic achievement continues to be the exclusive concern, narrowing down the very concept of educational process. Nevertheless it is important to note that achievement in curricular subjects is not an independent phenomenon. Rather, it is directly influenced by a number of factors, some of which are personal to the individual while many others are located in the environment in which learning process takes place. Thus in order to fully understand the concept, as well as, the process of academic achievement, it is imperative to identify and explore various factors related to the academic achievement

NEED FOR THE PRESENT STUDY

Scholastic achievement continues to be one of the most important variables held in high esteem, in all cultures, countries and times. Hence, the research related to the area of academic achievement is an ever growing concern of the researchers, educationists and administrators. Any enquiry into the previous works suggested that studies related to this area may be broadly classified into three categories.

1. Studies with sociological base.
2. Studies with psychological base.
3. Studies relating to both sociological and psychological areas.

Some outstanding studies conducted by curry (1962), Chopra (1966, 1967, 1982), Gupta (1968, 1982) and Raymand (1977) have focused their attention mainly on sociological factors related to the academic achievement. The main emphasis on those studies, were on the variables, like socio-economic status, parental aspirations, family environment and so on.

In contrast, some of the prominent researches by Entwistle Kundu and Chakravarthy (1997) and Pande (1978) have in their own right, laid emphasis on psychological factors like personality, intelligence, adjustment, anxiety, self concept, motivation and so on in relation to the academic achievement.

"The destiny of India is being shaped is her class rooms" (Education commission 1964-66). So there is a dire need for teachers to reflect, visualize, plan and act accordingly so that the children of today can become world class citizens of tomorrow. The cognitive growth and academic development of the individual has become a matter of concern for the psychologists, sociologists and educationists. Day-by-day achievement related problems are increasing. There is growing awareness of developing ways and approaches for improving children's scholastic achievement. **(Pathak 2007)**

Though there are considerable number of studies related to the sociological and psychological factors at primary and secondary levels, very few studies were found, particularly in the subject "Mathematics" and more particularly at "X class" level.

The achievement in mathematics, particularly at Xth class level has been chosen, keeping in view the fact that mathematics is a compulsory subject of study upto Xth class only and after Xth class, it is an optional subject. Those who develop interest and aptitude for mathematics will, only opt for mathematics after Xth class. Hence, it is felt that there is a need for research study to find out the influence of various Psucho-Sociological and personal factors on the achievement in mathematics, at 10th class level.

It is observed, more percentage of failures in mathematics than in other subjects in 10th class public examination. Majority of the students are not opting mathematics at higher education level. Hence, the investigator felt that there is a need to know various pscho-sociological and personal factors contributing for mathematics achievement at 10th class level, so that proper and suitable suggestions can be offered for mathematics teachers, working in secondary schools.

RESUME OF SUCCEEDING CHAPTERS

Chapter 2 deals with an analytical presentation of research work conducted so far in the area, in which the investigator is interested to investigate further.

Chapter 3 deals with present study, which includes: Statement of the problems, Need for the present study, Operational Definitions of various terms, Objectives of Study, Hypotheses to be tested, Variables included and limitations of the present study

Chapter 4 deals with tools employed, methods of collecting data, and statistical techniques employed in the analysis of data.

Chapter 5 deals with analysis of data, and a detailed discussion of results of the present study.

Chapter 6 deals with summary of investigation, major findings, conclusions, Educational implications, recommendations and suggestions for further research.

Chapter 2: Review of Related Literature

This chapter deals with the internal review of the literature. It is an attempt to discover relevant material published in the problem area under study. This covers the empirical research studies done previously in the problem area. The studies conducted during the last few decades in the field of achievement that are more relevant and pertinent to the present investigation are discussed in this chapter

PURPOSE OF RELATED LITERATURE

Review of related literature, provides a comprehensive understanding about what has already been known about a topic. It forms the basis for subscribing rationale for having chosen the problem for the study. Review of related literature allows the researcher to acquaint himself with the current knowledge in the field or area in which, he is going to conduct his research. It enables the researcher to define the limits of his study. It also helps the researcher to delimit and define his problem. The knowledge of the related literature brings the researcher uptodate on the work, which others have done and thus state the objectives clearly and concisely.

By reviewing the related literature the researcher can avoid unfruitful and useless problem areas. He can select those areas in which positive findings are very likely to result and his endeavours would be likely to add to the knowledge in a meaningful way. Through the review of related literature, the researcher can avoid unintentional duplication of well established findings. It is no use to replicate a study, when the stability and validity of it's results have been clearly established.

The review of related literature gives the researcher an understanding of the research methodology, which refers to the way, the study is to be conducted. It helps the researcher to know about the tools and instruments, which proved to be useful and promising in the previous studies. It also provides an insight into the statistical methods, through which the validity of the results is to be established.

The important specific reason for reviewing the related literature is to know about the recommendations of the previous researchers, listed in their studies for further research.

Good, *et al.* (1941) analysed the purposes of review of related literature as given under:

- To show whether the available evidence material solves the problem adequately without further investigation.
- To provide ideas, theories, explanations or hypotheses valuable in formulating the present study
- To suggest the research methods to the problems
- To locate comparative data useful in interpretation of the results
- To contribute to the general scholarship of the investigator

NEED TO KNOW ABOUT RELATED LITERATURE

For any worthwhile study in any filed of knowledge the research worker needs an adequate familiarity with the library and its many sources. Only then will an effective search for specialized knowledge be possible. The search for reference material is a time consuming but very fruitful phase of research programme. Every investigator must know what sources were available in his field of enquiry, which of them, he is likely to use and where and how to find them. (Sukia *et al.,* 1980).

According to Best (1959), practically all human knowledge can be found in books and libraries. Unlike other animals that must start a new life with each generation, man builds up accumulated and recorded knowledge of the past.

Availability of adequate information about educational thought and research does not by itself result in possession of its knowledge by investigator. The investigator may be very keen to possess uptodate information regarding his field, and may try hard to be posted up-to-date, and yet fails to get enough information due to non-existence of source of such information (Sukhia 1980).

In the field of education, as in the other fields too, the research worker needs to acquire up-to-date information about what has been thought and done in the particular area from which, he intends to select a problem for research. But it is found that generally the extent of important, up-to-date information regarding educational research and ideas possessed by educational workers, is very limited (Sukhia 1980).

The investigator should strive hard to be posted with necessary information, relating to his field of enquiry, basing on which, he has to build up his findings.

CONCEPTUALISATION OF THE PROBLEM

An objective of teaching mathematics should be, to make clear the nature of mathematics itself as reflected in the following characteristics:

Mathematics is a Dynamic Intellectual Enterprise: Mathematics is primarily an intellectual subject. It should not be presented as a collection of rules, which have to be applied mechanically to a large number of examples. The whole curriculum should be built round interesting and intellectually challenging problems. The student of mathematics is not simply a verifier of results but an explorer of new vistas of knowledge. Mathematics is considered as the Science of Sciences and Art of all Arts. Almost all subjects require mathematical knowledge to a great extent.

Mathematics is Logical: Logic is the essence of mathematics. Mathematics draws necessary conclusions from explicitly stated assumptions. The student must study a number of axiomatic systems. These may not be deep, but they must be logically correct. They must understand the nature of the proof. After a good mathematical training, the student must be able to detect faulty deductive reasoning and to differentiate between definitions, axioms, postulates and validly drawn theorems deduced from axioms.

Mathematics is a Study of Sets with Structures: Sets and structures are the basic unifying concepts in mathematics. At the school stage mostly algebraic and order structures are studied. The students must be clear about these structures for natural numbers, for integers, for real numbers and for complex numbers.

Mathematics is a Study of Patterns in Number and Space: The student must develop a sense for noticing patterns, when he comes across these. Number and space institutions have to be strongly built. A student must be able to exploit symmetries in number and geometrical patterns.

Mathematics Deals with General Structures: By seeing carefully a number of particular structures, the student should be able to perceive, a general structure with his intuition. He must feel how certainty of scientific results depends to a great extent on the use of mathematical methods.

Mathematics Deals with Abstract Structures: Abstraction is essential in mathematics. The school curriculum must be motivated by very concrete situations. The goal of abstraction must, however, not be given up and must ensure that the children can see the points of abstraction.

Mathematics Deals with Precise and Elegant Structures: The student must be able to make precise statements and should be able to detect loose statements, when these are made.

Mathematics is the numerical and calculative part of man's life and knowledge. It helps man to give exact interpretation of his ideas and conclusions in the form of a mathematical equation. On the other hand, describing the relationship between the qualified aspects of a phenomenon is not only exact but also brief.

Mathematics Deals with Deep Structures: The students must build up an ambition to study deep structures and derive pleasure out of them. The primary aim of teaching mathematics is, to enable the student to develop understanding and skills related to mathematical concepts, Principles, formulas and operations and to develop abilities to apply them to problem – solving situations.

Nagalakshmi (1995) studied the secondary school students of Hyderabad, on the their performance in solving problems at five stages of development, namely comprehension, Judging the adequacy of the data, given approximations drawing conclusions and making generalizations. She found that students were not aware of various stages and processes and were mainly concentrating on arithmetic operations rather than on the understanding of the process as a whole.

THE RECOMMENDATIONS OF VARIOUS COMMITTEES AND COMMISSIONS ON MATHEMATICS EDUCATION

In Indian schools, the present syllabus of mathematics has been modified in the light of changes suggested by Kothari Commission and the guide lines suggested by the N.C.E.R.T. (J.N. Kapoor, 1993)

The Commission has recommended that at the primary level, the courses in Arithmetic and Algebra be integrated and emphasis be laid on the laws and principles of mathematics and logical thinking. The syllabus should include the development of number system, systems of numeration and notation, equations, groups and functions. The Geometry course should be re-organised in a more rational manner.

At the high and higher secondary level, the mathematics syllabus, which at present, is divided in the traditional manner into Arithmetic, Geometry and Algebra, Trigonometry, statistics, calculus and coordinate Geometry, need to be revitalized and brought uptodate. The whole of Arithmetic course and also the basic operations in algebra can be so arranged as to be completed by the end of primary stage. Out-dated topics like simplification, factorization, L.C.M. and H.C.F. etc. should be deleted. Trigonometry should be relegated to Algebra and then, there will be no need to treat it as a separate subject. Much of the work on identities, solution of triangles, heights and distances can be cut down. The emphasis on memorising of theorems and exercises in Geometry should be given up. The approach to the teaching of Geometry should be based on axiomatic and systematic treatment.

Set language may be used in designing the basic terms in Geometry, and difficult portions should be gradually taken up in the next grades.

Earlier the Indian Education Commission (1966) clearly pointed out:

> "We can not overstress the importance of mathematics in relation to science education and research. This has also been so, but at no time, the significance of mathematics been greater than today. It is important that deliberate effort is to be made to place India in the world map of mathematics within the next two decades or so."

The National Policy of Education (1986) made the relevant observation as follows:

> "Mathematics should be visualised as the vehicle to train a child to thin, reason analyse and articulate logically. Apart from being a specific subject, it should be treated as concomitant to any subject involving analysis and reasoning. With the introduction of computers in schools, educational computing and emergence of learning through the understanding of cause-effect relationship and the interplay of variables, the teaching of mathematics will be suitably re-designed to bring it, in line with modern technological devices."

In this context NPE suggests that a multimedia approach for curriculum transaction should be adopted and Educational Technology should be extensively used. Accordingly mathematics educators recommended the development of instructional packages comprising the following.

- The textbook
- The supplementary problem books, consisting of additional material plus some challenging mathematical problems for high achievers and talented
- Enrichment materials for higher achievers and the talented for use in mathematics clubs in schools
- Teachers hand book, based on the above materials
- Models, charts, films etc.

According to the experienced mathematics educators, the implication of the policy (NPE 1986) statement for mathematics education, in the secondary level is as follows:

> "At the secondary stage, a beginning will be made to teach mathematics as a discipline in a suitable manner. Even then the concepts of essential learning outcomes, minimum level of learning and mastery learning are relevant and valid."

The NCERT publication 'Position of Mathematics in India' has listed the following objectives in the Indian syllabi (Kapoor 1993) at the secondary level:

1. To develop understanding of those mathematical concepts, facts, terms, procedures, symbols, relationships and principles, which are needed to solve every day problems,
2. To develop such qualities as
   (*i*) Working with speed, precision, accuracy and neatness
   (*ii*) Estimation and approximation and
   (*iii*) Capacity to apply mathematics to simple, concrete situations.

The UNESCO Project lists the following objectives at the secondary level:

- To make pupils learn modern developments in mathematics;
- To prepare pupils for advanced study of science and technology
- To develop powers of logical thinking, abstract thinking and generalisation,
- To acquaint the pupils with a systematised knowledge of mathematics,
- To enable the pupils acquire techniques of problem solving, and
- To develop an attitude for investigation and critical analysis.

Thus mathematics is essentially a programme of education, which fosters mental processes of questioning, reasoning, analysing, inducting, logical and reflective thinking of a very high order. Hence, the teaching of mathematics is of at most importance in any school curriculum, so as to make achievements in the subject satisfactory.

Academic Achievement in General

Academic achievement is of paramount importance, particularly, in the present socio-economic and cultural contexts. Obviously in the school/college level, great emphasis is placed on the achievement, right from the beginning of formal education. The school performs the function of selection and differentiation among pupils on the basis of their scholastic achievement and other attainments, which open out avenues for advancement in life.

The central aim of all formal educational efforts is academic achievement on the part of the students. Even though, it is desirable to have all-round development, as the goal of educational process, where academic achievement would be just one of the dimensions; but in most of the educational institutions, academic achievement continues to be the exclusive concern, narrowing down the very concept of educational process. Nevertheless, it is important to note that achievement in curricular subjects is not an independent phenomenon; rather it is influenced by a number of factors, some of which are personal to the individual, while many others are located in the environment, in which learning takes place.

Mathematics is one of the subjects included in the school curriculum, the achievement in which is the main concern of the investigator. The investigator wants to know various socio-demographic and psychological factors which influence the achievement in mathematics, which is considered to be one of the most important subjects in the school study. In this context, the investigator presents some of earlier studies made in this direction.

There are number of studies relating to the scholastic/ academic achievement done in the past. However only the literature pertaining to the independent variables used in the present study is referred in the succeeding pages

In general terms, achievement refers to the scholastic achievement of the student, at the end of an educational programme. It is to this concept that the term achievement is referred here. To maximise the achievement within a given set up, therefore is the goal of every educationist, a teacher or an educational administrator. Research has been to our aid, looking into what variables – personal, home, school etc. promote achievement and what are the determinants to it.

A glance at the related literature reveals that a number of variables have their impact on the academic achievement or in particular achievement in mathematics.

The present investigation took note of the above facts and attempted to treat some of the prominent intellectual and non intellectual factors as Psychological and sociological factors and coined it as psycho-sociological factors. The influence of certain psycho-sociological factors on the scholastic achievement in mathematics of 10th class students is investigated.

Under Achievement in Mathematics

"Human talent is our greatest national resource. Its conservation and development should, therefore, be a primary concern of every one. When human talent is wasted, every one is deprived, when it is rightly developed, every one is benefited" Harriot (1963).

The wastage of talent is mainly observed in under achievers. In fact, under achievement is a crucial problem that needs urgent solution, so as to enable the society, to derive optimum benefits from the system of education. Though it is necessary to identify under achievement at different stages, during the course of the students educational career, there is a strong view that it is unfair to label a youngster as under-achiever. For once he is labeled so, he remains such for ever and very often the label is erroneous in many respects. This is a misconception in students, where they are backward or dull. A child, who is lagging behind in class, is considered backward. On the other hand, a child who does not fair well in class, even though his level of intelligence is normal or even above normal, is also considered to be backward, only because his educational achievements are not satisfactory. In many eases the teachers are not able to distinguish one from the other, and label both these types of children under the category of "Dull children". Under such circumstances, even the child of normal intelligence becomes unable to exert himself, as he is made to believe that he is dull.

The under-achievers have restricted themselves opportunity for higher education. At the same time, they have difficulties in obtaining a job. Many times these under-achievers who could have been of great use to the society, misuse their potentialities and become a nuisance to the others. They can create tension in the society by their violent behaviour.

The studies have proved that the large number of drop-outs at school level is because of under-achievement, especially in mathematics. Mathematics is a single subject which has caused maximum wastage. Kothari commission (1966) while contemplating on the problem of under-achievement has observed:

> "The group of under-achievers who are not intellectually dull but are not at least of average and may even be superior ability. The failure of such children should be of great concern to developing country like India which can not remain indifferent to this loss of potential man power within the higher ability range. Several factors like physical, intellectual, emotional and environmental contribute to the failure of under achievers to come up to the level of their talent abilities."

Dr. Akre pointed out that there are 18.46 per cent of under-achievers in mathematics at secondary school level. It is a very serious problem, because of importance of mathematics in daily life. Especially in new vista of 21st century, mathematics is one of the important subjects to enable to fit oneself into a changing world and make one ready to adopt one self to new circumstances. Right from human civilisation, use of mathematics is very close for development of man. At the present 'competitive era', mathematics may be offered in various competitive examinations. It gets witnessed for 'all-rounder personality' of the child, one who knows mathematics.

Under-achievers are the lot of large students population of our country, who are just neglected and left unmotivated, thus causing a great loss to the society, collectively and individually. Hence it is our duty to attend these under achievers and challenge to our educators, psychologists and national leaders. Hence necessary steps are to be undertaken to find the root causes for this under-achievement so as to eliminate the problem of under-achievement, thus reducing the wastage of talent.

Some of the earlier studies conducted on the impact of various psycho-sociological variables on the achievement are presented in the following pages.

EARLIER STUDIES RELEVANT TO THE PRESENT STUDY

There are a number of studies relating to the scholastic/ academic achievement done in the past. However only the literature pertaining to the independent variables, used in the present study, is presented here under.

Achievement and Type of the Management

The type of the management of the school in which a student studies, may have some impact on the academic achievement in mathematics. Some of the studies conducted earlier in this direction are presented here under.

Jagannadhan (1983) investigated into the type of the school and academic achievement and found that pupils of V, VI and VII classes in government schools achieved the highest mean (58.50) academic achievement followed by Panchayat Raj (49.81), Private (45.99) and municipal (45.02) schools. The F test (17.17) revealed that the means differed significantly at 0.01 level.

Rathore, Jyoti (2000) revealed that the mean scholastic achievement of children (N=500) From Formal Primary schools in Science was better than children (N=500) studying in Non-formal education centres.

Panda, Manoranjan (2000) reported that the mean academic achievement of IX class pupils in the schools managed by SC and ST Development corporation, Government and Non-Government differ significantly from one another at 0.01 level. The achievement of pupils (N=370) in Non-Govt schools is better than the pupils (N=140) from Government schools. The achievement of pupils from Government schools is better than that of Pupils from (N=40) SC and ST development department schools.

Gnanasundaratharasu and Vincent De Paul (2002) found that due to video assisted instruction, there is no significant difference in the mean achievement scores in Social Science among the pupils of Government and aided primary schools.

Manjuvani and Mohan (2002) investigated that there is no significant difference in the academic achievement of

(*i*) adolescent girls studying in single sex (N=95) and Co-education (N=98) schools.

(*ii*) Adolescent boys studying in single sex (N=95) and co- education (N=101) schools.

(*iii*) Adolescent boys and girls studying in single sex schools and in co-education schools.

James, Anice and Marice (2004) investigated into the academic achievement in Science among XIth standard students (N=470) and found that students from Matriculation (N=196) Schools and state Board (N=270) schools have no significant difference in their achievement scores in Science.

Behera, Laxmidhar and Sushant Kumar Roul (2004) reported that type of the institution (coeducational and women) did not exert any influence on the achievement of BEd students.

Srinivasan and Arivudayappam (2004) reported that the achievement level of Aided Schools and Government Higher Secondary Schools is greater than Panchayat union Middle School and Government High Schools.

Achievement and Sex

In a male dominated society, girls are deprived in all aspects in the society. Pre-determined notion of parents, partiality in treatment, restrictions in their mobility, lack of freedom, social evils like dowry system, have been the biggest impediments in the progress of the girls in the field of education. Sex is one of the important variables in the academic achievement.

The following are some of the studies reviewed on this aspect:

Farquhan (1963) observed no significant relationship between academic achievement and sex of XIth grade high school students.

Pavithran and Feroze (1965) found that there is no marked difference between boys and girls in the scholastic achievement of tenth class pupils. Both are more or less on the same levels of achievement.

Nayar, Padmanabhan and Visweswaran (1966) found that there was significant difference between the achievements of urban boys and girls of tenth class. But however, they found that there existed a marked difference in the achievement of rural boys and girls.

Balasubramanian and Feroze (1966) found that there existed no significant difference in the achievement of boys and girls of urban locality, while there was some marked difference in the achievement in mathematics between boys and girls of rural areas of tenth class.

Gupta (1968) observed no significant differences between boys and girls of 9th class in three variables (i.e.) academic achievement, intelligence and economic status.

Gupta, Hargovinda (1968) observed that except, in the high intelligence group of class VIII pupils, a significant relationship between academic achievement and sex appears to exist in both the moderate and low intelligence groups.

Ramkumar, Vasantha (1969) found that there existed significant differences in the achievement of boys and girls.

Rangaswamy and Visveswaran (1977) found that there was no significant difference in the achievement of sports men and non sports men in SSLC class XI pupils examination. However they said that girls who participate in sports are better achievers than boys, sex difference is however not significant in case of non sports boys and girls.

Roach (1979) conducted a study on 206 boys and 212 girls from five urban elementary schools in Jamaica and found that the girls scored significantly higher than boys on a mathematics achievement test.

Dhalakia (1980) found no significant difference in the achievement of male and female teacher trainees.

Asudullakhanl et al. (1982) showed that sex of Pre-university students class XII was found to be not effective in bringing about any variation in the scholastic achievement.

Gupta (1983) found that girls on the whole, had better achievement motivation, than boys and had higher academic achievement than boys. The relationship between achievement motivation and academic achievement is positive and significant.

Jagannadhan (1983) reported that sex does not have any significant influence on the academic achievement of class V, VI and VII pupils.

Gopalacharyulu (1984) found no difference in the achievement levels between male and female teacher Trainees (TTIs).

Watkins, *et al.*, (1984) showed that there existed significant influence to sex, self-concept and intelligence on academic achievement of pupils.

Quraishi and Bhat (1986) conducted a study on 200 undergraduate students of M.S. University of Baroda and found that sex has a significant effect on academic achievement.

Ramaswamy (1990) observed no significant difference between boys and girls of high and low achievers.

Verma and Gupta (1990) revealed that class VIII boys belonging to the high environment group achieved significantly greater mean than boys belonging to the low environment group. However no significant differences were found in the case of girls of high, medium and low environment groups.

Panda, Bujendranath (1991) observed that 9th and 10th class boys of rural areas and urban girls were better in academic achievement than their counter parts.

Vijayalakshmi and Hemalatha Natesan found that class XI girls (N=50), (1992) have better mean academic achievement than boys (N=50) which is significant at 0.01 level.

Rao, Rama and Sinha (1993) reported that the performance of girls in examinations at all levels of higher education was much better than that of boys.

Gilson, Judith (1999) observed that large differences were not found in mathematics achievement, quantitative ability of 8th grade girls from single sex schools or girls from co-educational schools.

Sood (1999) in her study found that although girls achieved somewhat higher than boys, yet insignificant differences exist in their mathematical achievement.

Nestesan and Susila (2000) reported that there is a significant difference at 0.01 level in the scholastic achievement of fifth standard boys (N=300) and girls (N=300) in Environmental Science.

Reddy, Govinda (2002) found that sex does not have any significant influence on the academic achievement of DIET students. (N=600)

Panda (2002a) observed that V class boys (N=478) and girls (N=404) studying in Urban, Rural and tribal areas did not differ in their achievement in all the school subjects.

Suneetha and Mayuri (2002) reported that gender was found to be more important variable than IQ in deciding the high academic performance, as more girls were found among top ranking students of classes IX and X.

Gakhar and Aseema (2004) found no significant difference in the academic achievement of boys and girls of class X, in their Previous annual examination (Class IX)

Aggarwal (1974), Sharma (1976), Tiwari (1980) and Dubay (1982) have found that girls perform better than boys in all the school subjects.

Aruna, But (1981), Chanda and Sunanda Chandira (1985) have reported that boys had better achievement than girls.

Again Satyanandam (1969), Panchanathan and Shanmuga Ganesan (1992) found that sex had no bearing on the academic achievement.

Khayyer Mohammad and Philip R. Delaccy (2005) found that girls academic achievement was higher than boy's academic achievement.

Subramanyam, K. and K. Srinivasa Rao (2008) revealed that boys and girls do not differe significantly in academic achievement.

Pondey, SN, Md Faiz Ahmad: (2008) conducted a study on a sample of 621 students of standard XI (Male adolescents = 417 and Female adolescents = 204) from, Azamgarh (Dt), Bihar (State) and found that there is no significant difference between male and female adolescents on the measures of academic performance.

Paavola Sapiyonja (2008) stated that

A research group from Kellago school of management of North Western University headed by professor Paavola Sapiyonja conducted a study on the Proficiency in mathematics of boys and girls below the age of 15 years over 40 countries. The research group made a study on 2.70 lakhs students. The details of the study were given, by *"Daily Telegraph"*. As per the details given; in the worldwide average rate of efficiency in mathematics, girls average rate is 2 per cent higher than boys. In Britan girls, average rate of scoring is 0.7 per cent less than boys. Where there is no much encouragement for girls education, like in Tourkey, the girls average performance is 4 per cent less than boys. If equal opportunities are given, the difference in scoring between boys and girls can be reduced.

From the above observations, it is clear that a few studies have shown a relationship between sex and academic achievement and hence sex has been is eluded as one of the variables in the present study.

Achievement and Locality

This variable is a neglected one in educational research, particularly on the influence of locality on achievement in mathematics. As the investigator is interested in mathematics, locality is included as one of the variables in the present study to examine it's impact on the achievement in mathematics. Some of the earlier studies in this direction are presented below:

Pavithan and Feroze (1965) observed that, the scholastic achievement of urban students of class X, is significantly better than rural students in all the subjects.

Jagannadhan (1983) concluded that the Pupils of classes V, VI and VII from urban areas had better achievements than rural pupils.

Koteswara, Narayana and Ramachandra Reddy (1998) showed that there is the influence of locality on the reading achievement of high school pupils. Pupils in residential schools performed better than pupils in rural and urban. Among the three groups, pupils from rural areas were the lowest in their achievement.

Kumar, Salinm (1998) reported that locality has significant influence on the achievement in biology of secondary schools pupils (N=700) at 0.01 level.

Moorthy, Krishna (1999) found that locality has caused no significant difference in respect of academic achievement in History.

Prakash (2000) in his study concluded that urban students were better in their mathematical achievement when compared to the rural students.

Gupta, Naresh Kumar (2002) reported that the achievement of majority of V class pupils (N=946) in slum area schools has been observed to be unsatisfactory, not only in mathematics but also in all other subjects.

Ponda (2002a) revealed that class V rural students had shown better performance in all the school subjects, when compared to their urban and tribal classmates. (N=887)

James, Anice and Marice (2004) studied the academic achievement in science among XI standard students (N=470). Students hailing from rural (N=199) and urban (N=271) areas have the same type of academic achievement in Science.

Gakhar and Aseema (2004) found that class X rural students significantly achieved better in their annual previous examination (class IX), than the urban students.

Panchalingappa (2004) concluded that there is no

significant difference between rural and urban high school pupils of Devadasis in respect of their academic achievement.

Achievement and Age

Age of the students may have some relationship with their scholastic achievement. Some of the related studies are presented here.

Srivastava (1967) found that the relationship between the age and academic achievement is insignificant.

Gupta, Har Govinda (1968) reported that no significant relationship existed between the age of the pupils and their academic achievement.

Ulla, Asud, *et al.* (1982) revealed that the age of the pupils was found to be not effective in bringing any variation in scholastic achievement.

Vyas (1982) reported that age of B.Ed students was significantly related to the total marks.

Quraishi and Bhat (1986) found that there is no significant relationship between the age and academic achievement.

Dowson *et al.* (1999) observed that age is strongly related to the academic motivation and achievement.

Biswas (2001) investigated into the relationship between the age and academic achievement of distance education learners and found that age has no effect on their performance.

Reddy, Govinda (2002) found that there is no significant relationship between the age and total marks.

Suneetha and Mayuri (2002) found that age has significant influence on academic achievement.

Manchala (2007) found that age has significant influence on the academic achievement.

It is observed from the above studies that there are very few studies showing the relation between the age and academic achievement of 10th class students. Hence age is taken as one of the variables in the present study.

Achievement and Caste

In Indian societies caste system is special social evil, there are reservations in the name of the caste in educational institutions for making admissions and in the recruitment to the various posts in the government service. There are many associations in our societies in the name of the castes, for their upliftment.

Hence the investigator is interested in knowing the effect of caste on the achievement of marks in various subjects and particularly in mathematics at secondary level. Hence, caste is included, as one of the variables in the present study.

Some of the earlier studies made in this direction are presented here under:

Dubey and Mishra (1977) have reported that the school environment was significant predictor of academic achievement among upper caste, backward caste, the S.C and Muslim girls.

Jagannadhan (1983) observed that the academic achievement of forward caste pupils of classes V, VI and VII is significantly better than that of backward caste pupils.

Gopalacharyulu (1984) found that different castes of student teachers of TTIs had, same achievement of three variables, theory, practical and total achievement.

Kumaraswamy (1992) found that caste of the adult learners did not have any influence on their academic achievement in the case of reading, writing, arithmetic (3Rs) as well as total achievement.

Sing (1993), Mehata (1992) and Lidhoo and Khan (1990) have found that the academic performance of upper castes was significantly higher than that of scheduled castes, scheduled tribes and backward castes.

Naidu, Jayachandrama (1998) observed that the influence of caste is not significant on the academic achievement of learners N=300 of formal education; where as caste has significant influence on the academic achievement of learners

(N=300) of non-formal education and the total sample is (N=600).

Dubey and Mishra (1999) made a study to find the determinants of academic success of scheduled caste (SC), Backward castes (BC), Muslims (MS), upper castes (UC) and rural high school boys (N=400). Results suggest that there was no consistency in the predatory of academic success across the four groups.

Dash (2002) reported that ST students had the lowest percentage of passes in Higher Secondary Certificate (HSC) examinations in the State of Orissa. A considerable number of class X students of high schools, managed by Tribal Welfare Department, Government of Orissa were detained and were not allowed to take H.S.C. examination.

Reddy, Govinda (2002) found that cast is not significant on the achievement in Theory and total (theory and practical) achievement of DIET students (N=600)

Manjula (2002) revealed that the achievement of Tribal students was low, except in language and mathematics, which was only on border line of average performance.

Achievement – Birth Order

Birth order means, the child born first, second, third and so on. Birth order may have some relationship with the academic achievement of the students in mathematics. The investigator included Birth order as one of the variables in the present study. Some of the earlier studies are presented hereunder.

Jagannadhan (1983) found that the birth order of class V, VI and VII pupils did not have any significant influence on their academic achievement.

Panda, Bhujendranath (1991) found that birth order of class IX and X students did not have any significant influence on their academic achievement.

Reddy, Govinda (2002) revealed that the birth order of DIET students have significant influence on the academic achievement in practical and in total achievement.

Achievement – Size of the Family

It is assumed that the size of the family i.e. the total number of persons in the family may have some impact on the studies of the children and hence on the academic achievement. Some of the earlier studies are presented hereunder.

Panda Bhujendranath (1991) observed that class IX and X pupils coming from small families were better in their academic achievement, when compared to that coming from big families.

Naidu, Jayachandrama (1998) reported that family size has no significant influence on the academic achievement of learners from formal education centres (N = 300); whereas family size has significant influence on the academic achievement of total sample i.e. formal and non-formal education learners (N = 600).

From the above studies, it is clear that there were no much studies on the effect of family size on the academic achievement. Hence size of the family is included as one of the variables of the present study.

Achievement and Mother's Education

Educational status of the mother may have influence on the scholastic achievement of the students. If mother is educated, it would have an impact on the child's performance. Some of the studies reviewed are presented hereunder.

Pavithran and Feroze (1965) found that there is no significant relationship between scholastic achievement and educational status of the mother in the case of 10th class students.

Gupta, Har Govinda (1968) found that there is no significant relationship between academic achievement of pupils and their mother's education.

Sarma (1984) showed that mother's education is highly associated with the academic achievement of their sons and daughters.

Jagannadhan (1986) conducted a study on highschool pupils and found that mother's education is not associated with the achievement of the pupils whereas father's education has impact on the scholastic achievement.

Sethi, Vijaya Kumar (1990) revealed that the parents of high achieving students of all the four professional groups i.e. engineering, law, medicine and teaching are better qualified than those of low achieving students.

Panda, Bhujendranath (1991) concluded that 9th and 10th class pupils with college educated mother's are having better academic performance than illiterate or elementary class educated mother's.

Swamy, Ranga and Visveswaran (1977) reported that no definite pattern of relationship between the academic achievement of pupils and educational status of parents, is noticed.

Krishnamurthy (1999) revealed that there is significant relationship between academic achievement and education of mother.

Borbora, Rupa Das (2002) reported that backward classes children of literate mother's showed better academic achievement, than the children of illiterate mother's.

Chakrabarthi, Sharmistha (2002) observed that educational level of the mother's influenced female learners' literacy achievement attending the literacy centres.

Gnanasundaratharasu and Vincent Depaul (2002) inferred that due to video assisted instruction, there is no significant difference in mean achievement scores among the primary school pupils whose mother's qualification is below metric and those above metric.

Reddy, Govinda (2002) investigated that mother's education has significant effect on the academic achievement of B.Ed. students both in theory and total achievement.

It is noticed from the above studies that very few studies are found showing the relation between scholastic achievement of 10th class students in mathematics and mother's education. Hence, mother's education is included as one of the variables in the present study.

Achievement and Father's Education

Education of the father may have some influence in the academic achievement of the pupils. General assumption is that educated fathers would assist their children in their studies in the form of counseling and guidance. Hence there may be some relationship between the scholastic achievement and father's education. Some of the studies reviewed in this regard are given below:

Pavithran and Feroze (1965) found that there is no significant relationship between the scholastic achievement of 10th class pupils and the education level of the fathers or other members of the family.

Gupta, Har Govinda (1968) observed that in the case of all the three i.e. high, moderate and low intelligence groups of 8th class pupils, no significant relationship seem to exist between subjects academic progress and their father's education.

Fraser (1959) found that there exists significant relationship between academic achievement and father's education.

Sarma (1984) found that father's and mother's education is highly associated with the scholastic achievement.

Jagannadhan (1986) found that high school pupils academic performance and father's education are significantly related.

Sethi, Vijaya Kumar (1990) found that father's education has got much impact on the academic achievement of their sons and daughters studying in professional course (or) engineering, law, medicine and teaching.

Shamsuddin (1996) found that most of the secondary school male teachers were from families where fathers were not highly qualified, whereas most of the female teachers were from families with highly qualified fathers.

Krishnamurthy (1999) found that there is significant relationship between father's education and the academic achievement in history of second year higher secondary students. This gets support from earlier studies : Chatterjee *et al.* (1971), Khanna (1980) and Rajput (1985).

Grouws, *et al.* (2000) stated that there is a positive relationship between educational level of the parents and students' performance in mathematics. But there is a considerable overlap in the performance of students from different educational background. Infact many students whose parents had a high school education or less scored higher than students whose parents had a university degree. Students whose parents were university educated, performed about two-thirds of a proficiency level higher than those whose parents had no more than high school education. However there is one important nuance to add to this finding. Students whose parents worked in an occupation that required advance mathematics skill, infact, performed almost one proficiency level higher than students whose parents had similar education levels and income but whose occupation did not require advanced mathematics.

Reddy Govinda (2002) investigated that

1. Father's education and mother's education have significant influence on the academic achievement of B.Ed. students.
2. Brother's education has significant impact on the total academic achievement of DIET students.

Panda (2002a) revealed that 5th class pupils of college educated fathers had shown better achievement in mathematics.

It is noticed from the above studies that very few studies are found showing relationship between the scholastic achievement of 10th class students in mathematics and education of father. Hence father's education is included as one variable in the present study.

Barbara, Rupa Das (2002) reported that

1. Backward caste children of literate parents scored higher than the children of illiterate parents.

2. The academic achievement of first generation learners i.e. children of illiterate parents was found to be the lowest.
3. The achievement of girls was found to be comparatively better than that of boys.

Chakrabarthi, Sharmistha (2002) observed the education level of the family influenced female learners (N = 320) literacy achievement attending to literacy centres.

Gnanasundaratharasu and Vincent De Paul (2002) found that due to video assisted instruction, there is no significant difference in mean achievement scores in social science among the primary school pupils of parents with below metric and those of above metric.

Achievement and Occupation of Parents

Scholastic achievement of students may vary depending upon the occupation of parents. Some of the earlier studies are shown hereunder.

Pavithran and Feroze (1965) found that the occupational status of the parents highly accelerates the scholastic achievement of 10th class students.

Gupta, Har Govinda (1968) found no significant relationship between academic achievement and occupation of the father in the case of 8th class students, except in the case of moderate intelligent group.

Other research studies namely Fraser (1959), Alexander (1965) and Smith (1966) corroborate these results.

Dawson, Ford (1970) found that the employment of mother's had no effect on the achievement of children either in a positive or negative direction.

Rangaswamy and Visvesvaran (1977) reported that no definite pattern of correlation could be noticed between the academic achievement and occupational status of the family of 11th class students.

Jagannadhan (1986) found much impact of father's occupation on the achievement of students

Bhujendranath Panda (1991) observed that 9th and 10th class pupils (N=280) with skilled professional parents were found to be better in their academic achievement when compared with their counterparts. This finding is agreed with the findings of Jammar (1964).

Ayishabi and Moly Kuruvalla (1998) found that there is no significant difference between mean scores of achievement motivation of pupils of 9th standard of working and non-working mother's, for the total sample (N=871). The findings are congruent with the findings of Stein (1973) and Bal (1988) who found a positive effect of maternal employment on the achievement motivation of adolescent and college going children.

Naidu, Jayachandrama (1998) found that the influence of father's occupation is not significant on the academic achievement of learners from formal education (N=300); whereas father's occupation has significant influence on the academic achievement of learners from non-formal education (N=300) and the total sample is (N=600).

Goswami, Meenakshi (2002) found that children studying 9th class with working mother's were more achievement oriented than the children of non-working mother's. Boys with working mother's were most achievement oriented than girls with working mother's.

Reddy, Govinda (2002), reported that the employment of father, brothers and sisters have significant effect on the academic achievement of B.Ed students in practical work and practical examination (N=600).

Panda (2002a) investigated that father's occupation did not have any significant impact on the learning achievement of 5th class pupils (N=882) in rural, urban and tribal primary schools

Achievement and Religion

Cultural background of the students may have some influence on the academic achievement of the students. Community/ religion may also have some impact on the scholastic achievement. With this view, studies related to community / religion and achievement are presented hereunder.

Nair (1974) and Asudullakhan *et al.*, (1982) found that religion of pre-university students (XII class) was found not to be effective in bringing any variation in the scholastic achievement.

Radhamohan (1998) reported that there is significant difference in the high school student's academic achievement belonging to different religions viz., Hindu, Muslim and Christian.

Kobal-Palcic *et al.*, 1999 showed that French pupil's scholastic achievement was more, when compared to that of Slovenian pupils.

Moorthy, Krishna (1999) observed that there was no significant difference on the achievement, in History of second year higher secondary students (N= 455).

Regnerus, Mark's (2000), study indicates that respondents' participation in church activities is related to heightened educational expectations and these more intensely religious students score higher on standardized Maths/ reading tests.

Form the above shown studies, it is clear that there were no many studies showing the relationship between achievement in mathematics and religion. Hence, religion is included as one of the variables in the present study.

Achievement and Annual Income

Annual income of the family may have some impact on the scholastic achievement of students. Studies related to annual income and achievement, conducted earlier, are presented here under.

Gupta, Har Govinda (1968) found that except in the high intelligent group a significant relationship between academic achievement and their father's income, seems to exist, in the moderate and low income groups.

Fraser (1959) found higher correlation between income

and scholastic achievement (r = 0.44), than between income and IQ (r =0.35).

Wiseman (1964) did not find any significant influence of father's income on the brightness of the child in the school.

Rao, Gopal (1965) found a significant and positive correlation between economic status and scholastic achievement (r = 0.39).

Jagannadhan (1986) conducted a study on high school pupils and found that father's income had much impact on the academic performance.

Sethi, Vijayakumar (1990) observed that the parents of achievers of all four courses engineering, medicine, law and teaching were generally had better income than those of low achievers.

Panda, Bujendra Nath (1991) found that class IX and X students with high income parents were better in their academic achievement, than those of students with low income parents.

The studies of Chopra (1964) and Khanna (1980) strengthened the above findings.

Nadiu, Jayachandrama (1998) found that the influence of father's income is not significant on the academic achievement of learners from formal education (N=300), whereas mother's income has significant influence on the academic achievement of learners of non-formal education (N =300) and total sample (N =600).

Krishnamoorthy (1999) observed that the economic conditions of the family has caused no significant differences in respect of academic achievement in History of the second year higher secondary students.

Reddy, Govinda (2002) found that the family income has significant influence on academic achievement of DIET Students (N = 600)

Selvam and Sundaravalli (2002) conducted a study on 300 higher secondary students and found that the academic achievement has significant relationship with their economical, educational and vocational problems.

From the above observations, it is clear that there was no much previous study conducted on the significance of father's income in respect of academic achievement of 10th class students in mathematics. Hence income of the family has been included as one of the variables in the present study.

Achievement and Socio-Economic Status (SES)

Socio-economic status of a family plays an important role in different aspects of an individual's life. There may be some significant relationship between the SES and academic achievement of an individual. Some of the earlier studies made, on the relationship between SES and academic achievement of the students are presented herewith :

Pavithram and Feroze (1965) found that the relationship between economic status of the family and scholastic achievement of 10th class students is extremely low and almost negligible. There is no any conclusive evidence of either favourable or unfavourable influence of economic status of the family on the academic achievement

Rao (1965); Srivastava (1967), Bernstein (1968) Sudamma (1973), Ahuliwalia and Shyam (1975) and Sharma and Bhargava (1980) found very little and negligible impact of SES on the academic achievement.

Gupta (1968) revealed that the students of 9th class with higher economic status and mental ability were better in their scholastic achievement, compared to those with lower SES.

Anand (1973) observed the relationship of SES and academic achievement. He found that the relationship between the two existed even when the influence of intelligence of non-verbal as well as verbal types were partialled out. He revealed that there was some of impact of socio economic status of family on the mental abilities as well as academic achievement of students of classes VIII, IX and IX.

Mennon (1973), in his study revealed that over achievement and under achievement were influenced by socio-economic and demographic variables.

Rangaswamy and Visvesvara (1977) claimed that no definite pattern of correlation could be found between socio-economic status and academic achievement.

Ullakhan, Asud *et al.*, (1982) showed that SES of pre-university students (class XII) was found to be not effective in bringing about any variation in the scholastic achievement

Shakiba-Nejad *et al.*, (1983) observed a strong positive correlation between SES and academic achievement of the students.

Singh, Lal (1984) found that there is no effect of socio-economic status on the academic achievements of XIth class students (N =200), when the students have intellectual ability.

Jagannadhan (1986) conducted a study on a class V, VI and VII students and found that SES had got much impact on the academic performance

Quaraishi and Bhat (1986) conducted a study on 200 undergraduate students of M.S. University Baroda and found that socio-economic status has a significant effect on academic achievement.

Sood, Ramana (1990) found that there is no significant effect on academic achievement of Pre-Engineering students (N = 120) and their socio economic status.

Rossi (1950), Gopal Rao (1956), Washburne (1959), Saini (1968), Lincoln (19069) and Srivastava *et al.*, (1980) found significant relationship between academic achievement and socio economic status.

Thorndike (1952), Cattell *et al.*, (1966) Meller (1970), Ahuwalia and Deo (1978), and Venkaiah (1980) found either negative or very low correlation between academic achievement and SES.

Vijayalakshmi and Hemalatha Natesan (1992) found a positive relationship (r = 0.46) between academic achievement and SES of IX class students (N =100) which is significant at 0.01 level.

Marcon, Rebecea (1999) observed that SES was found to be an important factor in the academic performance, with poorer performance noted for lower income students

Young, Deindra (1999) revealed that SES had certainly some impact on the overall performance of students. They found the effect of other variables like self concept, class – room environment also, when they conducted a survey on 3397 also, covering 28 rural and urban schools in Australia.

Saxena (2001) revealed that the students who secured first division in high school examination, belong to the middle socio-economic status, indicating that the SES had only a little effect on the academic achievement.

Karla, R and Pyari, A (2004), investigated into the relationship between family climate and income and academic achievement. Their findings are :

1. The achievement of the students having favourable family climate
2. The study finds in congruence with many research findings (Hari Krishnan 1992, Garg, V.P. 1992) that student achievement is found to be affected by the income status of the family.

Achievement and 14 Personality Factors (HSPQ)

Personality of a student plays an important role in his/her scholastic achievement. Some Indian researchers have attempted to isolate the personality structure of good and poor students. A few studies are comprehensive, while a few others, have concentrated on specific aspects and dimensions of personality assessment. Some of the studies showing the relationship between personality and scholastic achievement are given below :

Cattell, *et al.*, (1966) claimed that high school. Personality questionnaire (HSPQ) was predicting the school achievement of the students.

Vyas (1982) observed that personality adjustment was significantly related to university practical marks.

Joshi, Anuradha (1990) reported that the personality of class IX students, effected the academic achievement. The extroverts were found to benefit significantly more through the developed instructional strategy, as compared to the intraverts

Sethi, Vijaya Kumar (1990) studied the personality patterns of high achieving and low achieving students in professional courses (Engineering, Medicine and Teaching)

The major findings are:

1. High and low achieving students taken together differed significantly from each other on personality factors of Lower-higher scholastic mental capacity (Factor-B); emotional instability (Factor-C); experience conscientiouness (factor G); shyness – venture some ness (H); placidity apprehensiveness (factor O) and Low-High ergictension (Factor-Q_1).
2. High achieving students were found to differ significantly from each other, on personality factors of Lower-higher scholastic mental capacity (Factor-B); desurgency-surgancy (Factor-F) and tough mindedness-tender mindedness (Factor-I).
3. Low achieving students were found to differ significantly from each-other on factors of reservedness-out goingness (Factor-A), Low-Higher scholastic mental capacity (Factor-B), tough mindedness-tendermindedness (Factor-I); trust placement suspiciousness (Factor-L) and Lower-higher ergictension (factor Q_4).

Mavi and Iswarpatel (1997) explored the relationship between academic achievement and selected personality variables of 9th grade students. The personality variables are Personality adjustment, intelligence, self-concept and level of aspirtation. It was found that there was a weak relationship between the personality variable and academic achievement, in the case of tribal students. The non-tribal students, scored higher than the tribal, overall.

Koteswara and Ramachandra Reddy (1998) reported that :

1. All the 14 factors of HSPQ have significant influence on reading achievement in Telugu language high school students.
2. Students whose personality characteristics for outgoing, more intelligent, emotionally stable, excitable, assertive happy-go lucky, superego strength, venturesome, tense minded, doubting, apprehensive, self-sufficiency, controlled and tense, performed significantly better on reading achievement in Telugu language, than the students, whose personality characteristics were observed as less intelligent emotionally less stable, phlegmatic, obedient, sober, moral standards, shy tough minded, vigourous, placid, group dependent, undisplined and relaxed.

Panchanadhan (1999) found that maintaining emotional balance, among students, through a psychologist by using auto counselling increased their academic performance.

Nateson and Susila (2000) indicated that the choosen personality factors (cattell's children personality questionnaire) are not significantly influencing the achievement of 5th standard boys (N = 300) and girls (N =300) in the age group of 9 to 10 years studying in the schools.

Reddy, Govinda (2002) investigated that, factors B, E, F, M, Q_2 and Q_4 of 16 PF have significant influence on the total scholastic achievement of DIET students

Kagade (2002) observed that :

1. There was no significant relationship between educational adjustment, home adjustment, and educational achievement of pupils (N=1941) studying classes VIII and IX.
2. There was a significant relationship between social adjustment and educational achievement.

Ayodya (2007), while studying the emotional problems of school children and their relation to life events and school achievement found that :

1. Secondary school children had high rate of emotional problems.

2. Boys had high life event scores and more number of events.
3. Boys out numbered girls in decreased scholastic achievement.
4. The emotional problems found were of minor nature
5. Emotional problems did not have influence on scholastic achievement in the present study.
6. Life events too did not have influence on scholastic achievement.
7. No difference was found with regard to socio-demographic factors and emotional disorders, scholastic achievement.
8. No association was found between scholastic achievement and intelligence.

It is observed that few studies are found establishing the relationship between, scholastic achievement and personality of 10th class students. Hence, personality is taken as one of the variables in the present study.

Subramanyam K. and K. Sreenivasa Rao (2008) while studying to assess the impact of gender on emotional intelligence and academic achievement of secondary school pupils, concluded that :

1. There is significant difference between boys and girls with regard to their emotional intelligence.
2. There is no significant difference between boys and girls with regard to their academic achievement.
3. There is no relation between academic achievement and emotional intelligence.

Achievement and Study Habits

Individual study habits play an import role in determining the academic achievement of pupils in different subjects. The students performance in the class room depends upon several factors namely, the interest in the subject, study facilities, own study habits etc.

Most of the previous investigators pointed out that there is much impact of study habits on the academic achievements.

In this connection, it is worth mentioning the former president A.P.J. Abdul Kalam's views, on inculcating good reading habits in children and youth of the country.

He inaugurated a book fair held in Delhi and told the people to encourage their children and students with the advice that if they give one hour a day exclusively to book reading, they will become a knowledge centre in a few years. To acquire the habit of reading is to construct for yourself a refuge from almost all of the miseries of life. Reading is certainly one of the best experiences, a child can have and habits developed at a young age stay with a person for the rest of his life. What a gift for a child! There is more treasure in books than in all the pirated loot of Treasure Island. The more that you read, the more things you will know. The more that you learn, the more places you'll go. Students who score higher on "tests, tend to come from schools which have more library resources, staff and more books, periodicals and videos, and where the instructional role of the teacher librarian involvement in co-operative programme planning and teaching is more prominent"

A wonderful thing about a book, in contrast to a computer screen, is that you can take it to bed withy you. Reading is to the mind, what exercise is to the body. The brains of the next generation need to be sharpened so that we can make our dream to be one of the best in world come true.

Some of the studies already made previously on the relation between the academic achievement and study habits of the individuals are presented here under.

Woodruff (1940) found that study habits failed to show some definite relationship with academic achievement.

Gordon (1941) found that the coefficient of correlation between scores on study habits and course grades was higher when students were tested late in the semester than when tested at its beginning.

Wrenn and Humber (1941) found that there existed relationship between the study habits and academic achievement in general.

Esther, Mary (1945) found that there existed statistically significant differences in the achievement of most successful students with good study habits and least successful students with poor study habits.

Burnett (1951) reported that the student who has taken the course "How to study" increased their scores, as compared with those who had not taken the course.

Corter (1955) found a moderate positive linear relationship between the study habits and academic achievement.

Brown and Holtman (1955), Patel (1981), and Chauhan and Singh (1982) found that there exists significant relationship between study habits and academic scores among school going children

Noltan (1959) conducted an investigation into the relationship between study habits and achievement in general science and found that there existed no relationship between them.

Diener (1960) obtained the similarities and differences between over achieving and underachieving students and observed that the two groups differed significantly in their study habits, indicating a positive relationship between them.

Richard and verginia (1967) found a positive relationship between good study habits and achievement.

Brown and Dubois (1964) revealed that there existed a moderate positive relation ship between the study habits and academic scores.

Samuel and Rao (1967) conducted a study on a sample of 500 pre-university course (P.U.C.) students and showed that there is a significant positive relationship between the study habits and academic achievement.

Agarwal and Saini (1969) found that the coefficient of

correlation between the study habits score and scores on achievement in mathematics of class VIII and IX students came to be + 0.014. Although this index seems to be quite poor, it was found significant at 0.05 level of confidence.

Murthy, Krishna and Rao (1969) conducted a study on 300 students. They observed that there existed significant correlation between study habits and academic achievement of urban students.

Sinha (1960 and 1972) found that there is significant relationship between study habits and scholastic achievement.

Marentic-Pozaranik (1974) found positive relationship between study habits and scholastic achievement of Class IX pupils.

Girija, *et al.*, (1975) made a study on the relationship between the study habits and academic achievement of first and final year students of under-graduates of University of Agricultural Sciences, Bangalore. They found the two groups differed significantly with regard to their study skills and achievement.

Bhatnagar, Asha (1980) made a study on 600 students of Xth class of Delhi and found that there existed a positive relationship between the study habits and academic achievement.

Tuli (1980), Patel (1981), Chopra (1982) found that there was a positive relationship between study habits and academic achievement.

Sharma, Premalath (1986) reported that the underachieving rural girls significantly differ in their study habits from high achieving rural girls of IXth and Xth class students.

Singh, Harbans (1989) showed no significant differences in the study habits at different levels of achievement of Xth class scheduled caste pupils (N = 300). But boys were found to have significantly better study habits than girls.

Deb and Gravel (1990) reported that the study habits and the academic achievement of BSc final year students are positively related.

Lee Ruth (1992) revealed that the development of study skills in IXth and Xth class students resulted in improvement of grades.

Stella and Purushothaman (1993) showed that there is no significant difference between study habits of under achieving boys and Girls.

Chitra, *et al.*, (1993) found that the academic habits and achievement were positively related to intelligence of higher secondary students.

Ramamurthi (1993) found that despite the students possessing good intelligence, their academic achievement hampers due to the absence of good study skills.

Aruna (1994) found that study habits of Xth class pupils have significant influence on their scholastic achievement in all the subjects.

On Tsk Ka and Wat Kins (1994) found that the study habits are significantly correlated with school grades of first year school students in Hong Kong.

Rawat and Leela (1995) found that there was no significant difference between the study habits of boys and girls and their academic achievement.

Patel, M.R. (1996), revealed that :

1. The achievement scores of the pupils having high and low general ability were significantly different.
2. Those pupils who had good study habits did get significantly more achievement scores than those who had poor study habits.
3. It was found that sex and study habits interacted significantly in explaining achievement scores.

Varma (1996) found that the academic achievement in mathematics and general science is more or less same in the case of students with good study habits and students with poor study habits.

Kumar (1998) reported that there existed a significant positive correlation between academic achievement and study habits.

Darlene, Gordan (1998) found that the students having good study habits possessed good achievement. Hurl Venden *et al.*, (1998) showed that the study habits of medical students were correlated with their academic achievement.

Verma, S and Kumar, R. (1999): found that

1. The achievement in mathematics was positively and significantly correlated with the study habits of the Students.
2. Overall achievements were significantly and positively related to the study habits of students.

Raj, Sam Sanada and Sreethi (2000) found that study habits and academic achievement of students are positively and significantly related.

Nagaraju (2001) concluded that the academic achievement in all the school subjects has positive significant influence at 0.01 levels on the study habits of the pupils (N=1800).

Reddy, Govinda (2002) found that study habits of a DIET student have significant influence on achievement.

Vamadevappa (2002) found that there existed positive and significant relationship between study habits and achievement of pre-university students in Biology subject.

Archana and Mona Sharma (2002) conducted a study on 26 Grade-1 children in Indoor. The results found that the instructional material could positively influence the achievement of students.

Reddy, Naveen Kumar (2003) reported that study habits and academic achievement are positively and significantly related.

Guravaiah (2004) investigated into the academic achievement of Xth class students in all the school subjects and found that study habits of pupils do not have any significant influence on the scoring.

Rajani (2004) observed that the academic achievement of Intermediate students (N=1200) in all the subjects including group subjects is positively related to their study habits.

Lakshmi (2004) identified positive relationship between study habits and achievements of a DIET student.

Rao, Bhaskara *et al.*, (2004) have identified a positive relationship between study habits and academic achievement.

Sood, Ramana and Dal Vinder Kumar (2007) found that learners having good study habits have better academic achievement.

Manchala (2007) showed that all the ten areas of study habits inventory have significant influence on scholastic achievement of B.Ed students. Better study habits is associated with better scholastic achievement.

Achievement and Self-concepts

Self-concepts play an important role in the life of pupils. Muktha Rani Rasthogi's (1974) self-concept scale is adopted in this study to examine the impact of self-concepts on the achievement of 10th class students in mathematics. Some of the earlier studies showing the relationship between scholastic achievement and self-concepts are presented hereunder.

MacAculay (1990) reported that there is a positive significant relation between academic achievement and home environment.

McRobbie and Fraser (1993) found that there existed a positive relation between academic achievement and home environment.

Martin (1995) concluded that there was a significant relationship between academic achievement and home environment.

Richard, Walf (1996), Marjoribanks (1996), Walberg and Paik (1997) reported that there existed positive significant relationship between academic achievement and home environment.

Basantia and Mukhopadhyaya (2001) indicated that the achievement of secondary school rural students was significantly related to their home environment. Both home environment and school environment were significantly related to each other.

Miscellaneous Studies on Achievement

Misra *et al.*, (1960) found that children coming from high home environment achieve better in schools than their counter parts coming from low family environment.

Morrow and Willianson (1961) while analyzing the back ground of the family factors responsible for higher achievement of physically challenged group children, concluded that more congenial home environment, less parent domination and sympathetic parental encouragement, have been found to be responsible for achievement of children.

Husen (1967) in his study "International Study of Achievement in Mathematics : A Comparison of Twelve Countries" found that boys were on the whole superior to girls in mathematics.

Husten (1967), Dave and Dave (1971) found that poor academic achievement was due the low educational standards of their parents.

Lalithamma, K. N. (1975) conducted a study on "Some Factors Affecting Achievement of Secondary School Pupils in Mathematics". It revealed that :

1. The average performance of pupils in mathematics was 23.14 with S.D of 8.20 and the distribution was negatively skewed
2. There was significant difference in the performance of boys and girls in mathematics, the difference being in favour of boys.

3. The urban pupils were superior to rural pupils in mathematics.
4. Intelligence and interest in mathematics were higher in boys and urban pupils than in their respective counter parts.
5. The achievement in mathematics is positively related to intelligence, interest in mathematics, study habits and socio-economic status.
6. Studying lessons daily, studying mathematics by writing, repetition in learning spaced learning, over learning etc. influenced the achievement in mathematics positively.
7. Private tuition, electric light facilities, radio equipment for study etc influenced the achievement in mathematics.
8. Achievement of the first born was better than that of the last born, and
9. Achievement of the students of scheduled castes and tribals was lower than that of the total sample.

Long and Resh (1976) could not find significant differences between father's income and child's level of abstract achievement.

Sharma (1977) made an attempt to examine the achievement of children in relation to the school system. He found that children of the recognized private schools achieved higher scores in Arithmetic than those of the corporation schools.

Brand, Hilde and Patricia (1978) have shown positive relationship between educational environment and child's performance in mathematics.

Desai (1979) found that low achievers of high school had high ability in mathematics and less favourable attitude to the subject ; they came from families with very strict standards or discipline, they were kept very busy in domestic work and did not receive any out side help for the study.

As no reliable and valid scale to measure the attitude towards mathematics was available, Rajendra Mishra (1980) developed a Likert-type attitude scale in his study. "A Study of Attitudes Towards Mathematics of Secondary School Students". Of all the variables studied it has been found that parent's qualifications influence boys but not girls in their attitude towards mathematics. No strong evidence has been found to prove the influence of parent's profession, family size, parent's income and study room facility in this regard.

Sinha, Sudha R. (1980) in the study "Effect of School System on the Competence of Secondary School Students", investigated into the difference between the system of private and government schools and how it influenced the competence of its students. Three aspects of the system were, examined- the material, organizational and human relations. The findings revealed that despite less physical facilities and higher workload, the private schools had better organizational structure and more competent students than the government schools.

Head (1981) found that extraverted boys and introverted girls did well within their own sex group, when they were given mathematics activities.

Gakhar, Dr. S.C (1982) in his article "A Study of Acquisition of Mathematical Concepts Among 8th Graders of Different Types of Schools", clearly demonstrates the differential effects of the type of the school on the acquisition of the mathematical concepts by the students on the whole. Students studying in private schools had better achievement than those studying in government schools.

This achievement was due to the strict supervision by the principal and managements of private schools, better teacher-pupil interaction, good educational environment, teachers special care of the weak students, teachers interest in the study of the children and sense of security and guidance and counseling in private schools.

Chopra (1982) found that students achievement was not

significantly different in different organizational climate of schools even at 0.05 level. There was no significant relationship between students' achievement and teachers' job satisfaction.

Vyas (1982) reported that age, academic achievement, verbal intelligence, non-verbal intelligence and SES contributed to the supervisors rating in case of a total of 300 male samples of BEd Students.

Lalthanhawla (1983) studied the causes of failures in science and mathematics among high school students of the Mizoram State and found that general standard of achievement in science was 33.24 per cent as compared to 27.86 per cent in mathematics. Students from urban areas and from privately managed schools and older schools did better than those in rural areas and government schools and newly established schools. The provision of good library, laboratory and special coaching classes are not related to the students achievement in these subjects.

Pattison and Grive (1984) studied whether sex differences contribute to special skills to tackle different types of mathematical problems. They found that boys excelled in problems related to measurement and proportion and in special problems, where as girls performed better in more abstract and deductive problems.

Davidson (1985) reviewed studies that compared students achievement in small group settings with traditional whole class instruction. He found that using small groups of students to work on activities, problems and assignments can increase student's mathematics achievement.

Chada and Sunanda Chandna (1990) observed that there is a positive and significant correlation at 0.01 level between creativity and intelligence of XIth grade students', when the effect of scholastic achievement is partialed out.

There is a positive and significant correlation at 0.01 level between intelligence and scholastic achievement when the effect of creativity is partialed out.

There is negative and significant correlation at 0.01 between creativity and scholastic achievement when intelligence is partialed out.

Venkataiah and Jayachandrarama Naidu (1990) reported that there is significant difference between academic achievement of dropouts N=(39) and Non-Starters (N=261) at Non-Formal Education Centres (NFE). The dropouts from formal primary schools are superior to non starters in their academic achievement as NFE centres.

MacAculay (1990) reported that there is a positive significant relation between academic achievement and home environment.

Yeh-Hsiang-Yeng (1991) reported that weak but positive correlation existed between achievement motivation and academic achievement.

Sundararajan, Dr. S. and B. Dhandapani (1991) conducted a study on the achievement in mathematics of higher secondary students of Pondicherry. The important findings of the study reveal the following:

- There is no significant difference in the achievement of boys and girls in the case of government and private schools.
- Urban students are better than rural students in respect of their achievement in mathematics.

Cobb (1991) and his colleagues found that students number sense was improved by a problem centred curriculum that emphasized students interaction and self generated solution methods. Students also demonstrated increased persistence in solving problems.

Swamy, Kumar (1992) investigated that variations in the amount of General Ability possessed by the adult learners significantly effects their achievement.

Vyas (1993) found that academic failure was associated with lower affiliation, teacher control, rule clarity and teacher support variables.

Newankwo and Kemjika (2003) found that the relationship between test anxiety and academic achievement were inversely proportional at secondary levels.

Varghese (1995) found that the achievement scores showed a systematic improvement with improvement in facilities of school and that the difference in the mean achievement scores between the learners in the last facility schools and the best facility schools was very large in both in Hindi and Mathematics.

Martin (1995) concluded that there was a significant relationship between academic achievement and home environment.

Shui Feng (1997) conducted a study on the influence of family factors on the academic achievement and concluded that children's academic achievement has been shown to be influenced by many family factors. It indicated that authoritative parenting and children's academic achievement were significantly correlated.

Slemmer (1997) found that required tutoring seemed to be an effective way of improving the academic achievement of marginal students of 10th, 11th and 12th grades.

Walberg and Paik (1997), Marjoribanks (1996), Walf Richard (1996), Martins (1995), McRobbie and Fraser (1993) and MacAculay (1990) reported that there is a positive significant relation between academic achievement of students and their home environment.

Khalid (1997) focused his research on factors affecting mathematics achievement and found that confidence, socio-economic status, gender, location of the school and school environment contributed significantly for the achievement in mathematics.

Vasanthi, Dr. R. and Bhama Lalithmbika (1997) in their article "interest of high school students in Mathematics" concluded that there is significant difference in the interest between the students of :

1. Private schools and government schools
2. Private schools and government aided schools
3. Private schools and cooperation schools, and

There is no significant difference between the students of :

1. Government schools and government aided schools
2. Government schools and corporation schools
3. Government aided schools and corporation schools

It also shows that educational qualifications of parents has a powerful bearing on the interest of the students in mathematics.

Kumar (1998) in his study concluded that there existed a significant positive correlation between academic performance and study habits.

Sumangala, Dr. V. (1998) in her article "Effect of Tutoring on Achievement in Mathematics of Secondary School Pupils", found that home-tutoring in Mathematics, whether by parents or by sibling has significant positive but low effect on achievement in mathematics.

Ediger, Marlow (1999) in his article "parents the teacher and mathematics" suggested the following for the good of the child, in the achievement of mathematics :

1. Having parent-teacher conferences
2. Meeting Parents at PTO meetings
3. Using educational psychology for providing a model to parents in assisting their off spring in home work.
4. Integrating human relations and curricular improvement in Teaching- Leaning situations.

Wood (1999) found that whole-class discussion works best, when discussion following individual and group work improves students achievement.

Molia, M.S. (1999) showed that the use of inductive thinking models improved the achievement of the students in mathematics.

Panda (2000) found that :

1. Rural students exhibited better performance in all the school subjects as compared to their urban and tribal class mates
2. Boys and girls studying in different areas did not differ in their performance in all the school subjects.
3. Non-SC/ST students performed better in mathematics as compared to their counter parts in rural areas
4. Children of college educated father had shown better achievement in mathematics, general science and language subjects in rural areas, where as children of middle income group had shown better performance in science achievement in urban areas.
5. Father's occupation and tuition did not have any significant impact on the learning achievement in all the three areas.
6. Students studying in urban schools had shown better performance in mathematics where P.G. trained mathematics teachers taught the subject.
7. Rural students performed better in all the school subjects where infrastructure facilities were available in the schools compared to the schools with less facility.

Dhall, *et al.*, (2000) revealed that the teaching of students with low achievement with remedial materials prepared after diagnostic test increased their achievement. Alam AM (2001) showed that :

1. The academic achievement of normal children was found to be significantly higher than that of learning impaired children in both boys and girls when taken together and when taken separately
2. The normal students were found to be higher in academic achievement.

Basantia and Mukhopadyaya (2001) indicated that academic achievement of secondary school rural students

(N=320) was significantly related to their home environment, but the school environment was not significantly related to academic achievement, where as both school environment and home environment were significantly correlated to each other.

Christman *et al.* (2001) reported that a cost effective analysis was performed to determine the relationship between district expenditure and 11th grade mathematics and reading achievement during 4-year period from 1995 to 1999. The study indicates that the increases on expenditures were accompanied by decreases in academic achievement.

Elegbelye and Akoda (2001) investigated that there existed a significant difference between the academic performance of pupils (N=150) of secondary schools from single and double parenting background.

A significant difference was observed between the performances of father present, absent children in mathematics.

Academic performance of children of mother present was significantly better than children of mother absent.

Rose and Elizebath (2001) examined the patterns of academic progress and outcome in different inner city school settings for African American and white, lower, middle and upper socio-economic strata students. They revealed that the overall academic out comes were higher for gifted students enrolled in the programme sometime during their school career than for general education students.

Soundaravalli (2001) found that the academic achievement of standard 12th students (N=300) had significant relationship with physical problems and family problems scores.

Anuradha and Bharati (2002) found that a trend of negative association was observed between classes III, IV and V children (N=300) academic achievement and their amount of TV watching. Watching only a selected programmes improved children's academic achievement significantly rather than watching all the programmes.

Basantia, *et al.* (2002) revealed that psycho-social constraints and academic achievement of high school students are negatively correlated with each other.

Hamingthanzuala (2002) found that students of Xth standard who had higher interest in business were found good at English, Social Science and in overall academic performance.

Panda (2002a) observed that V class pupils (N=882), who were taking midday meal, free Uniform, Scholarships and free textbooks as incentives performed well when compared to that of not receiving any incentives.

Chakraborthi, Bhupal Prasad (2002) found that the urban and semi-urban students performed better when they were provided with multiple choice items and that the urban students performed better both in multiple choice items and non multiple choice items than semi urban students in mathematics.

Agrawal, Archana (2002) found that :

1. Significant positive relationship was found between academic achievement and intelligence.
2. Academic achievement was found to be positively related with their socio-economic status.
3. There was significant negative relationship between the academic achievement and size of the family.
4. Significant negative relationship was found between academic achievement and birth order. The study has no reference.

Arya, Kalpana, and Kistwaria (2002) found that :

1. The involvement of adolescent daughters in the household activities of employed home makers was more than corresponding non-employed home-makers.

2. A majority of the adolescent daughters of non-employed mother's devote more time for their studies in comparison with the corresponding employed mother's.
3. A higher percentage of the adolescent daughters of employed mother's were not participating in co-curricular activities than that of the other respondents. The study cites 6 references.

Goel, Swami Pyari (2002) in their study on the relationship of achievement and feeling of security, family attachment found that :

1. Low achievement had a positive relationship with the feelings of security, where as the average and high achievement had a negative relationship with the feeling of security.
2. Family attachment and achievement scores were negatively related. A related factor responsible for higher educational achievement was parental attitude.
3. Feelings of security- insecurity were significantly and positively related to the family attachment.
4. Theoretical, aesthetic and religious values were positively related with achievement score, but economic and political values were negatively related with achievement score. Social value had a positive relationship with the average achievements but the low and high achievements were negatively correlated.
5. There was no difference in value pattern of low and average achievers where as high achievers gave the first preference to theoretical, value, than to social, political, economic, aesthetic and religious value. The study has eight references

Sharma, J. S. Nidhi (2002) in their study examined the effect of parental involvement and aspirations on academic achievement of +2 students found that.

1. Parents of high and low achieving students exhibited differentiated behavioral profiles with regard to some dimensions of parental involvement. Parents of high achieving students often provided academic guidance to their and also planned various cultural activities such as arranging picnics, dance show and other festivals.
2. Achievement scores of children belonging to high, average and low groups of parental educational aspirations were not equal.
3. The academic achievement scores were different for children belonging to different parental involvement groups.
4. High parental involvement group, scores higher on educational aspirations as compared to their counter parts in the low parental involvement group.
5. Higher parental involvement resulted in higher occupational aspirations of students.
6. High, average and low parental occupational aspirations groups yielded unequal levels of learning styles.

Mohanty, A.K. (2002) conducted a survey to see whether components of family environment bear any relationship with academic achievement of gifted, underachievers and his findings were:

1. The mean score of boys was higher than that of girls
2. The boys scored higher on cohesion, intellectual cultural organization, Moral and Religious emphasis, while the girls scored higher on conflict, achievement orientation and organization of components of family environment scale (FES).
3. Inutility the underachievers' academic achievement was significantly related with all components of FES except active Recreational organization.

For underachieving boys no correlation between a component of FES and academic achievement was found to be significant. However in the case of underachieving girl's cohesion, independence and control components of FES were found to be correlated significantly with academic achievement.

Upadhyaya (2003) found that constructivism was found to be a better technique of teaching mathematics.

Ravindra, *et al.* (2003) showed that :

1. Boys were found good in abstract thinking and symbolizing concepts in mathematics, where girls were good in logical thinking and mathematical modelling
2. Both males and females have the same level of liking for mathematics
3. Both males and females have the same level perception of mathematics
4. Males and females gave the same reason for liking and disliking the individual branches of mathematics like arithmetic, algebra and geometry.
5. Males stated that "social factors do not favor girls to go for higher studies in mathematics" as the main reason for not having top level women mathematicians. But females stated that " Vocational interests of women are different" as the main reason.

George (2003) concluded that mathematical backwardness was due to neglect of mathematical basis during early years. Positive attitude should be developed towards mathematics, he suggested teachers should present mathematics in an interesting manner.

Devi and Mayuri (2003) revealed that

1. Family factors were not found to be critically important for the achievement of residential school children.
2. School factors like, qualified teachers good physical facilities and classroom organization, checking of the curriculum and subject matter, time maintenance

impressive method of teaching and teacher student interaction contributed significantly to the academic achievement.

Rahman, M.H. (2003) in his comparison of achievement in mathematics of eighth grade students of different ethnic groups of Nepal found that

1. There was significant difference among the four ethnic groups with regard to the over all achievement in mathematics.
2. Tamang students were found to be the best among the four groups in over all achievement in mathematics
3. The four ethnic groups differed significantly from each other with respect to the achievement, on knowledge in arithmetic
4. Ethnic groups significantly differed from each other with respect to the achievement on knowledge, skill, comprehension and application levels.
5. No significant difference was found between Tamang and Magar groups in knowledge
6. Sarkari children were found to be the lowest achievers on knowledge among all ethnic groups. The study cited two hundred nineteen references

Prakash (2003) found that

1. The ascendance, vigorous and persistent temperaments were significantly related with mathematics achievement in girls and total sample
2. Among boys, the ascendance, accepting, vigorous, cooperative and tough-minded temperaments were significantly and positively correlated with mathematics achievement.
3. The memory of the subjects was significantly and positively correlated to their mathematics achievement.

4. Girls with low sociability appeared significantly higher in mathematics achievement than girls with higher sociability at high memory level only.

Singh, Suneel Kumar *et al.* (2003) in the article "Achievement difference of Class II Students in Mathematics with Regard to the Area, Gender and Social Groups", reveal that locality affects the Achievement in mathematics.

Urban students were found better than rural students where as sex would not affect the achievement in mathematics.

Shukla (1981), Rao (1983), Chitkara (1985), Bhattacharya (1986), Patadia (1987), Bharadwaj (1987), Deshmukh (1988), Doshi (1989), Dutta (1990), Mishra (1991), Vasanthi (1991), Bhatia (1992), Dandapani (1992), Prabha (1992), Rosali (1992), Srivatsava (1992), Hazelaker and Deforah Jean (1997), Jackson and Jeanetha Williams (1997), and Sumangala (1998) conducted research on the improvement of learning and teaching of school mathematics and found that :

1. It is generally seen that less importance has been paid to students attitude by the classroom teachers or researchers in comparison with considerable amount of attention, given to the cognitive achievement.
2. Mathematics, specially, can be quoted as an example in which very few attempts at measuring attitudes towards it's study have been made.
3. Mathematics is generally regarded as a difficult subject for study.
4. It is not so popular even at the college level where less number of students offer it for their studies. Even now models of teaching, innovations and modern techniques of teaching the subject, have not changed the situation.

Nagappa, Dr. Shahpur and Panchalingappa (2004) while investigating the influence of the study habits, family climate adjustment and academic achievement of *devadasi*, children of Karnataka State, found that

1. There is no significant difference between boys and girls children of *devadasi* with respect to family climate.
2. There is no significant difference between boys and girls children of *devadasi* in respect of their academic achievement.
3. There is no significant difference between rural and urban children of *devadasi* in respect of their academic achievement.
4. There is no significant difference in interaction effects of sex and location in terms of academic achievement of *devadasi* children.
5. There is no significant difference between boys and girls children of *devadasi* in respect of academic achievement.
6. There is no significant difference between boys and girls children of *devadasi* in respect of their study habits.

Mehera (2004) found that :

1. Achievement in mathematics was significantly related to major learning environment, attitude towards the subject, mathematics.
2. Urban students showed significantly higher achievement in mathematics, better learning environment and better attitude towards mathema-tics than their rural counter parts
3. No sex-wise difference was found in achievement of students in mathematics.

Sensarma (2004) while attempting to determine the relationship between class-room interaction variables of different branches of mathematics and mathematics achievement and attempting to predict the achievement from interaction variables concluded that :

1. Higher values of praise, acceptance of pupil's ideas, asking questions by teacher, pupil's response and the rate of class-room transaction are associated with higher pupil's achievements in mathematics.
2. Higher values of lecturing, criticizing and justifying authority and silence and confusion are instrumental in lowering pupil's achievement in mathematics.
3. Teacher's tendency to react to the ideas and feelings of pupil's is positively and significantly related to the better achievements in algebra, arithmetic, and geometry.
4. Velocity of class-room transition is positively and significantly related to the achievement in algebra, arithmetic and geometry separately.
5. The pupil's initiation is negatively associated with mathematics achievement in all the branches, algebra, arithmetic and geometry.

Sirohi (2004) investigated that :

1. All under-achievers indicated deficiency in study habits
2. 98.7 per cent of the under achievers tend to possess unfavourable attitude towards teachers and needed guidance.
3. 97.50 per cent of the students had poor concentration
4. 92.50 per cent of students indicated deficiency in school and home environment.
5. 72.80 per cent of them faced mental conflicts
6. 72.80 per cent of underachievers were low in self confidence
7. 24.60 per cent of them indicated deficiency in attitude towards education

Uma, S. (2004) on studying the role of computers in the performance found that :

1. The achievement scores improved in the test conducted after the revision of the lesson by 'teacher'.

2. Thoroughly revising the lesson through computers has increased their performance, the best scores are when the revision is by the Teacher and when computers are not used.
3. Some of the interesting points observed by her are
   (*i*) Learning through computers was high with below average students than with good students.
   (*ii*) The attention span and interest duration of the slow learners is comparatively, less than that of very good students.
   (*iii*) Very good and good students have better reading and comprehension skills. Thus they were fast on the computers. The below average students took time to read and comprehend. Thus they usually took more time to complete the work on computers.

Kumar, S. and Anita (2004) from their findings revealed that :

1. Both the variables self-learning module and classroom environment can not be ignored in respect of their effect on achievement.
2. There was no interaction between mode of teaching and classroom environment.

Bose, S and Joshi, V (2004) studied the effect of parents involvement in the achievement of students and found that

1. Children whose parents were involved in their education led a disciplined life at home and had better academic achievement at school.
2. Involvement of parents was also reflected in the activities that a child pursued in his leisure time.
3. It was found that parents could not reinforce the things, the children learnt at school and some children attended tutorials.

4. Tutorials did not help the children in performing better, rather the children who attended school regularly and received proper care at home, fare better.
5. The study also found that home environment that indoctrinates children into a disciplined life and healthy life style ensures better academic achievement.

Rao, Bhaskar *et al.* (2004) have identified a positive relationship between study habits and academic achievement.

Madankar (2004) observed that : Residence, Peer group, Curriculum, Classroom teaching and Evaluations have negative and significant relationship with academic achievement, where as 'food' and 'co-curricular activities' have negative and not significant relationship with academic achievement of school subjects.

Swamy, Peria (2005) showed that the teaching and learning of addition and subtraction through activity based learning materials (TLM) improves academic achievement of IVth standard pupils (N=30).

Sindhu, I.S. (2005) revealed that better liking of teachers contributed to better achievement of boys.

Vamadevappa, H.V. (2005) conducted a study to find out the relationship between parental involvement and academic achievement. His findings were

1. There was positive and significant relationship between parental involvement and academic achievement.
2. There was a significant difference in the achievement scores of boys and girls of high parental involvement group.
3. There was no significant difference in the achievements of boys and girls of high parental involvement group.

4. There was significant difference between high achievers and low achievers with respect to the parental involvement.
5. There was no significant difference between boys and girls in their academic achievement.

Prakash, Satya and Patnaik SP (2005) made a study to find out the effect of cooperative learning and found the following:

1. There was positive effect of cooperative learning on achievement motivation.
2. Cooperative learning has a positive effect on achievement in biology in terms of understanding, knowledge and application of objectives as well as total achievement.

Dwivedi, R.D. (2005) conducted a study to compare the educational achievements of students belonging to different categories of schools, according to their environment and found the following:

1. The students from schools with enriched environment had significantly better academic achievement than students from poor school environment.
2. The students who were high approval seekers had significantly greater achievement than the students who were low approval seekers.
3. Academic achievement of students of the urban schools was significantly higher than that of the schools of the rural schools.

GEORGE, NEETHA ANITHA RAVINDAN 2005) revealed that there is a linear relationship among accuracy in time perception, coping styles and level of academic achievement In other words time consciousness or punctuality is a quality that would enhance the academic achievement. They suggested that these results can be considered in helping low achievers.

Panigrahi, Manas Ranjan (2005) while studying the influence of intelligence and socio-economic status on academic achievement of high school students concluded that :

1. There exists a significant and positive correlation between academic achievement and intelligence. It is also found that high intelligence leads to better academic success.
2. There exists a low positive correlation between academic achievement and socio-economic status. It is observed that high socio-economic back- ground might not always facilitate high academic success.
3. It is found that there is no significant difference between boys and girls with respect to academic achievement.
4. The students having higher intelligence are high achievers in academic performance than students having low intelligence.
5. High socio-economic status has effected the girls greatly to be very conducive to high achievement and vice-versa is the case with boys.
6. The girls of high socio-economic status are high achievers in academic performance than boys of high socio-economic status, boys of low socio-economic status and girls of low economic status.

Panda, Manoranjan (2005), in his study on correlation between academic achievement and intelligence of class IX students Dhenkanal district of Orissa State concluded that :

1. There is significant difference in academic achievement of students studying in different categories of schools.
2. There is no significant difference in intelligence of students studying in different categories of schools.
3. There is low relationship between academic achievement and intelligence in different categories of schools.

Avinashilingam N.A.V. and Sharma, G. (2005) made a study to find out the factors influencing the student's academic achievement.

Gurubasappa (2005) while studying the effects of adjustment and mental ability on scholastic of secondary school children, concluded that : (*i*) The well adjusted children's achievement in school is high, (*ii*) The children with better mental ability will definitely achieve high and (*iii*) The product of learning academic achievement of students is certainly influenced by some psychological factors like adjustment and mental ability.

Arockiadoss (2005) studied the correlation between study habits and academic performance of college students (N=025) He reported that the academic performance of college students in influenced by study habits.

Ahuja, Malvinder (2006) studied the impact of parental involvement and socio-economic status of the family on academic achievement of IXth class students. Their findings indicated that (1) socio-economic status of the family and parental involvement were associated with each other (2) socio-economic status and academic achievement of students were independent of each other (3) academic achievement of high and low parental involvement group were not significantly different. (4) There was an interaction effect of socio-economic status and parental involvement on academic achievement of IXth class students.

Ayodya, P. (2007) revealed that : (*i*) Emotional problems did not have any influence on the scholastic achievement in the present day. (*ii*) Life events did not have any influence on the scholastic achievement. (*iii*) No difference was found with regard to socio demographic factors and emotional disorders, scholastic achievement and life events. (*iv*) No association was found between scholastic achievement and intelligence.

Manchala (2007) showed that all the ten areas of study habits inventory have significant influence on scholastic achievement of BEd students. Better study habits is associated with better scholastic achievement.

Subramanyam, K. and K. Sreenivasa Rao (2008) established that there is no significant difference in the achievement of boys and girls with regard to their emotional intelligence.

Pandey and S.N. Md Faiz Ahmed (2008) conducted a study on a sample of 621 students of XIth standard Male Adolescents (417) and Female Adolescents (204) and found that there is no significant difference between male and female adolescents on measures of achievement motiveation.

Annakkodi (2008), in her study entitled "Study of Scientific Attitude of Pupils of Class Xth and their Achievement in Science, concluded that : (*i*) There was positive significant difference in the scientific attitude of students in relation to their achievement in Science. (*ii*) It was found that there was a high significant difference in the scientific attitude of students based on their type of school, the corporation school students show high mean value of scientific attitude when compared to Government aided schools. (*iii*) It was found that there was high positive significant difference in the scientific attitude of rural and urban students. (*iv*) It was found that there was a significant difference in the scientific attitude of students based on their Gender.

The N.C.E.R.T. (2008): conducted a mid-term national survey to gauge the learning achievement of class V children. The survey covered 8,43,22 students, 14,810 teachers and 6828 schools, across. Two hundred and sixty-six districts, in the country. The survey tested the learning achievement of class V level students in mathematical, environmental studies and languages. It concluded that : (1) Mother's education is important than father's education. (2) The schools that enjoyed better infrastructure and facilities like TV, computer, more number of teachers and community participation contributed ten per cent more in (EVS) Environmental studies, 8.4 per cent better in mathematics and 19.6 per cent better in languages.

APPRAISAL

From the brief review presented in the foregoing pages it may be seen that a few studies have been carried on, in the area of academic achievement at secondary level and more particularly the achievement in mathematics. A gain by and large, except on a few variables the results obtained are not coinciding, which necessitates, further exploration in this area. Further, studies on the relative impact of each of the several independent variables that effect academic achievement are rare to find.

Selection of some important demographic variables, sociological and psychological variables are supported by many other studies, even though, they are not exhaustive for obvious reasons.

It is an attempt to see the relationship between the academic achievement and various psycho-sociological variables. The area under investigation is novel and unexplored with respect to the 10th class students and their achievement levels in mathematics.

Further the study aims at providing some mathematical models with which it can be possible to prove the academic achievement of 10th class students in mathematics. The need for research on the area of scholastic achievement in mathematics of 10th class students, is rather warranting.

The above crucial conditions lead the investigator to make an attempt in this area of scholastic achievement of 10th class students in mathematics in relation to certain psycho-sociological factors. Keeping all these observations in view the problem is stated clearly with it's objectives and suitable hypotheses are formulated in the succeeding chapters.

The Present Study

This chapter deals with the statement of the problem, title of the problem, need for the present study, purpose of the study, scope of the study, definitions of various terms, objectives of the study, hypotheses formulated, variables included and limitations of the present study.

INTRODUCTION

Education plays a very import role in the life of human beings. The development of a country is primarily determined by the quality of it's human resources. India today needs effective and productive citizens with scientific and constructive thinking and positive attitudes. This need can be met by well-planned educational curricula, including a systematic mathematics programme at the school level.

At present in our country, there are five levels of education. Pre-Primary, Primary, Secondary, Intermediate and Higher education levels. Primary and secondary levels are considered very important, as they lay proper foundation in the life of the students.

Mathematics is one of the subjects of study both at primary and secondary levels of education. Different education commissions set up by the Government of India have stressed the need for strengthening the teaching of mathematics at school level. National Policy of Education 1986, made a mention about mathematics education as "Mathematics should be visualized as the vehicle to train a child to think, reason, analyse and articulate logically. Apart from being a specific subject, it should be treated as a concomitant to any subject, involving analysis and reasoning".

The achievement in mathematics of Xth class students is the primary concern of the investigator, in the present study. Mathematics has been considered a difficult subject by majority of students at secondary level. Is it due to lack of proper teaching of the subject? or due to lack of proper attitude towards the subject - lack of proper encouragement - lack of proper study habits - one should ponder. But research in psychology has shown that "almost every subject can be taught in some intellectually honest form to any child at any stage of development, if it is properly taught". No system of education, no methodology and no textbook, can rise above the level of it's teachers. If a country wants to have quality of education, it must have quality teachers. Hence, the mathematics teacher plays a pivotal role in making the students to develop positive attitude towards the subject and to remove the fear of the subject.

At present, the state of teaching mathematics, in the majority of our schools is far from satisfactory. The rate of failures is considerably high when compared with other subjects. The mathematics teachers have to think over this problem of failures in mathematics or under achievement in mathematics and try to change the situation, by suitably finding ways and means of improving the achievement in mathematics. The author wants to find out the effect of various psycho-sociological and demographical variables on the achievement in mathematics at secondary level. It is against this backdrop that a comprehensive and constructive research work is felt necessary, relating to the achievements in mathematics, to suggest various ways and means of improving the achievement in mathematics of Xth class students.

After reviewing the related literature in the area of academic achievement particularly the scholastic achievement in mathematics, the investigator observed that there were no studies on the effect of variables like 'number of study hours', 'time spent daily for mathematics working', 'help from family members for mathematics' and 'separate study room' etc. on the scholastic achievement. Hence, the author has shown some interest to know the effect of these variables on the achievement of 10th class students in mathematics.

STATEMENT OF THE PROBLEM

The present study is concerned with the finding out the effect of various psycho-sociological and demographic variables on the achievement in mathematics of Xth class students of chittoor district, belonging to the different regions; i.e the four revenue divisions of Chittoor district. It examines the achievement in mathematics of Xth class students of the schools belonging to the above regions. It establishes the relationship between the various psycho-sociological and demo-graphical variables and other variables namely study habits, personality factors, self-concepts and socio-economic conditions of the students and achievement in mathematics of Xth class students of chittoor district. It also predicts scholastic achievement with the help of different sets of psycho-sociological variables/independent variables.

TITLE OF THE PROBLEM

The title of the present study is stated as Performance in Mathematics.

NEED FOR THE PRESENT STUDY

In olden days, the system of education was totally different from that of the present-day system. The teacher and the students lived together and they had devoted their entire time for studies exclusively. Now things have changed, as civilization improved and with the explosion of knowledge, the life style of people is changed beyond imagination.

The societies have come under the impact of science and technology and as a result of which, there are many means and sources of learning. Various psychological theories came into existence, which have their impact on methods of teaching. Both the teachers and students have to adopt new methods of teaching and efficient procedures of learning.

Everybody needs some knowledge of mathematics in one way or other. It is felt that for an ordinary man, the knowledge acquired during primary and upper primary level is sufficient. Consequently, there is a great controversy over making it an optional or compulsory subject of study at the secondary level. It is believed that mathematics is exceptionally a difficult subject. Its study requires some special ability and intelligence and hence everybody should not be burdened with the study of this subject. But the other view is that mathematics does not require special ability for its successful performance but it needs general intelligence. A dedicated and honest teacher of mathematics can make the learning very interesting and exciting, thus changing the attitude and outlook of mathematics. However, it has been widely accepted for its inclusion in the school curriculum as a compulsory subject up to 10th class level on the recommendations of various Education Commissions appointed by Government of India. It is clear that at the secondary level mathematics functions as a strong foundation for those who want to pursue mathematics at higher level. At the same time it functions as a tool to provide necessary mathematical skills for those who want to opt for arts, commerce, or humanities at higher level. Hence the role of mathematics at the secondary level is very significant as it safeguards the interests of both types of students. Accordingly mathematics teachers at secondary level have to realize the role of mathematics and teach the fundamental concepts in the subject, thus creating interest for the subject among the pupils.

Syllabus in various subjects has been constantly under revision and so also in mathematics. Various factors will have their effect on the achievement in various subjects and so in mathematics. Having accepted the influence of various factors on achievement in mathematics, the investigator desires to establish a relationship between achievement in mathematics and various psycho-sociological factors and demographic variables. Scholastic achievement continues to be one of the most important variables held in high esteem in all cultures, countries and times. Hence the research related to the area of academic achievement is an ever growing concern of the researchers, educationists and administrators.

Academic achievement is of paramount importance, particularly in the present socio-economic and cultural contexts. There is a need to identify the psycho-sociological factors, which influence the scholastic achievement in mathematics of 10th class students, in order to draw conclusions and suggest, remedial measures, if any. It is rather interesting to know which of the variables of personality, study habits, socio-economic status, socio-demographic etc contribute to the scholastic achievement in mathematics. There is a need to develop mathematical models to explain the relationship between scholastic achievements in mathematics of 10th class students and psycho-sociological variables.

Though there are considerable studies on the scholastic achievement in relation to sociological and psychological factors at primary and secondary level school subjects, very few studies are found particularly in mathematics of 10th class students. The present investigation is to find the relationship between achievement in mathematics and socio-psychological, and demographical factors and also to predict the achievements in mathematics with the help of various independent variables. Further, there is no much research study showing the relationship of scholastic achievement of 10th class students in mathematics with sociological variables like caste, birth order, age, sex, and personal factors like time spent for mathematics daily, help from family members, total number of hours of study and separate room for study. Hence there is a need of research study to know the influence of the above factors on the achievement in mathematics. The main aim of present study is to predict the multiple effects of independent variables on the scholastic achievement and further to suggest suitable regression equations in the prediction of scholastic achievement of 10th class students in mathematics.

The above crucial conditions lead the investigator to make an attempt in this area of scholastic achievement of 10th class students in mathematics in relation to various psycho-sociological factors.

PURPOSE OF PRESENT STUDY

In view of the important role of mathematics in the modern world, it has been imperative for any nation or the world to promote mathematics education in their respective countries. But mathematics has been considered by majority of students as a difficult subject. Hence, it is necessary for a mathematics teacher, to know the factors influencing achievement in mathematics. Learners motives, emotions, needs, attitudes, outlook and interests play a very important role in learning the subject. Certain factors like, parents' educational background, home environment, study habits, type of the managements, environment in the school, abilities, self-confidence, general habits, social environment and emotional feelings etc. may have some impact in the achievement of mathematics. Hence, every mathematics teacher has to evince a keen interest in knowing the effect of these factors and act accordingly so as to make the students learn the subject effectively.

Mathematics education provides a good mathematical background with the knowledge of concepts and theories. It also provides ability to apply mathematical concepts and knowledge of theorems to new situations. Sufficient mathematical skills are needed to meet the demands of the daily life. The fundamentals in mathematics have got an immense practical value in life. The knowledge and skills in these processes can be provided in an effective and systematic manner, only by teaching mathematics in schools.

The teachers of mathematics are now required to up-date their knowledge in the subject. The mathematics teacher will have to be essentially a learner. He must also have the knowledge of the factors which influence the achievement in mathematics. Sound knowledge of the effect of these factors enable the mathematics teachers to discharge their duties effectively. The variations in the performance of the pupil in mathematics may probably be due to some personal, socio-demographic, psychological factors, which the mathematics teachers are expected to know and hence the present study.

If mathematics teachers are aware of factors influencing the achievement in the subject, they can accordingly choose the methods of teaching, use of teaching-learning materials and there by creating interest in mathematics among the students.

In general, the public examination results of 10th class (SSC) reveal that more percentage of students fail in mathematics, as compared with other school subjects. Hence, it is necessary for mathematics teachers to know which of the personal, socio-demographic, psychological etc variables influence the learning and achievement of mathematics. Hence the present investigation is taken up for the purpose of knowing the influence of various variables on the achievement of 10th class students in mathematics.

The present study aims at establishing a relationship between the achievements in mathematics of 10th class students and various psycho-sociological factors and demographic factors. It attempts to answer the following questions:

1. Whether there is any significant influence of demographic factors on the achievement in mathematics of 10th class students?
2. Whether there is any significant influence of study habits of 10th class students on their academic achievement in mathematics?
3. Whether there is any significant influence of self-concepts of the students on the achievement of 10th class students in mathematics?

4. Whether there is any influence of 14 P.F personality factors on the achievement in mathematics of 10th class students?
5. Whether there is any impact of socio-economic factors on the achievement in mathematics of 10th class students?
6. Whether there is any influence of personal factors like sex, religion, caste, birth order, number of members in the family, time spent for mathematics study and separate room for study, etc on the achievement in mathematics?
7. Whether it is possible to predict the achievement in mathematics with the help of various psycho-socio-logical factors?

SCOPE OF THE STUDY

The main intention of the present study is to find out the relationship between achievement in mathematics of 10th class students and psycho-sociological factors, and demographic variables. The personality factors, the study habits and self concepts are measured by using relevant tools. An achievement test is constructed with the help of senior mathematics teachers and experts in the subject and standardized by the investigator, following the procedure described by H.E. Garrett in the textbook *"Statistics Psychology and Education."* The score obtained in the test is taken as achievement in mathematics (Dependent Variable).

Academic achievement depends on a number of factors. It is not possible to include each and every factor in this study. Only a few variables like, management, sex, locality, caste, educational and occupational level of parents, religion, economic status of the family, size of the family, help from family members for mathematics etc have been included in this study. Attitude of pupils towards mathematics, intelligence of pupils, teachers' commitment and so many other variables having impact on achievement are beyond the scope of this study.

The study attempts to identify the type of relationship between dependent variable and independent variables (psycho-sociological variables).

The study also attempts to predict the achievement in mathematics with the help of different sets of independent variables.

The study also attempts to suggest suitable regression equations in the prediction of scholastic achievement of 10th class students in mathematics.

OPERATIONAL DEFINITIONS OF THE TERMS

The definitions of some of the important terms used in this study are given below:

Academic Achievement

(*i*) Knowledge attained or skills developed in the school subjects, usually designated by test scores or by marks assigned by teachers or by both **(Good 1973)**

(*ii*) Accomplishment or proficiency, performance in a given skill or body of knowledge, progress in school theoretically different from intelligence but overlaps with it to a great degree. **(Good 1973)**

Measured ability and achievement level of a learner in school subjects or particular skills. **(Derek Rowntree 1981)**

Refers to performance in school or college in a standard series of educational testing. **(Teneja 1991)**

Accomplishment of specified objectives, past performance and what an individual or organization has accomplished in the past, in contrast with ability which refers to what an individual or organization can do now (in the present) or in future (Madhu Raj 1996 & S.K. Sing 2002).

Successful accomplishment or performance in particular subjects, areas, or courses, usually by reasons of skills, hard work and interest.

Typically summarized in various types of grades, marks, scores or descriptive commentary (Bellingham, 2004).

A measure of knowledge gained in formal education usually indicated by test scores, grade points, averages, and degrees (Raj, 1996; Bellingham, 2004).

Scholastic

Used to denote relationship with school, for example, scholastic average. Relating to school or school men, pendantic (*Webster's New Dictionary and Tresaurus*, 1975). Of or concerning Universities, schools, education, teachers etc. (Della Thompson, 1996).

Pertaining to or characteristic of scholar's education or schools (*Britannica Word Language Dictionary* 1961)

Achievement

(*i*) Accomplishment or proficiency of performance in a given skill or body of knowledge.

(*ii*) Progress in school, theoretically different from intelligence but overlaps with it to a great degree (Good 1973)

Refers to the performance in school or college in a standardized series of educational tests (Taneja, 1991)

Academic

Pertaining to the fields of English, Foreign language, History, Economics, Mathematics and Science. (Good 1973).

(*i*) A scholarly teacher and/or researcher in higher education.

(*ii*) Relating to the school activities especially when concerning a discipline or a subject, not necessarily at higher educational level (Derek Rowntree, 1981)

Achievement Test

A test designed to measure a person's knowledge, skills, understandings etc. in a given field, taught in school, for example a mathematics test or an English test etc (Good 1973).

Refers to a test designed to measure the effects of specific teaching or training in an area of the curriculum. (Taneja 1991).

A standardized test designed to measure and compare levels of knowledge and understanding, in a given subject already learned (Bellingham 2004)

In the present contest, achievement test means, an objective achievement test (OAT) constructed and standardized by the investigator.

Objective Test

Any examining device, whose scoring is not dependent upon the discretion of the examiners. In a psychological testing, any test for which the use of subjective judgment, by test scores is virtually eliminated, so that, qualified educators, scoring the test independently, would derive essentially the same scores (Bellingham 2004).

Personality

A psychological term that refers to the predictable and unique indicators of the way, an individual might respond to the environment. A personal reference that usually connections acceptability and likeability. (Raj 1996: Bellingham 2004).

Personality is that which permits a prediction of what a person will do in a given situation. **(Cattell 1970)**

The total psychological and social reactions of an individual, the synthesis of his subjective, emotional and mental life, his behaviour, and his reactions to the environment; the unique or individual traits of a person are connoted to a seller degree by "personality" than by the term "character". **(Good. C.V. 1973)**

For individual all the aspects of behaviour, thought and feeling that make the person unique. For psychologists a major area of theory and research.

(Derek Rowntree. 1981)

Personality Trait

A general aspect of a person that may pre-dispose how he or she reacts to particular situations (Madhu Raj, 1996 Bellingham 2004).

Socio-Economic-Status

The background or standing of one or more persons in the society on the basis of both social class and financial situation. (John Bellingham 2004).

The level indicative of both economic positions of an individual or group (Good 1973).

A person's status or position within the society (or any smaller social group) as determined by social class and wealth or income (Rowntree, 1981).

Refers to a person's position in any given group society or culture (Jajena, 1996; and a group of Experts, 2003).

An indicator of an individual or family's social ranking, based on such factors as level of education, income, neighbourhood of residence or type of occupation (Raj 1996 and 2002).

The background or standing of one or more persons in the society on the basis of both of social class and financial situation (Bellingham 2004).

Factor

(*i*) An element in the composition of any thing or in bringing about a certain result.

(*ii*) A fact, which has to be taken into account or which affects the course of events. (Davidson *et al.* 1998)

Teacher

A person employed in an official capacity for the purpose of guiding and directing the learning experiences of pupils or students in an educational situation, whether public or private (Good 1973).

Study Habits

(*i*) The basic features involved in the application of mind to a problem or subject.

(*ii*) The academic pattern which an individual follows in learning about things and people (Good 1973).

The evaluation of pupils behaviour in terms of attitudes, appreciation and habits of work is fundamental to a well-rounded study of out comes of the teaching (NSSE 1935).

Study habits include student's habits of concentration, note taking, time budgeting and study methods (Smith, 1961).

The complex of reading behaviour of a person, resulting from the varying degrees of interaction of a number of variable factors. Study habits are regular reading hours and routine characteristics of most of the general features. In preparing for examinations, greater reliance is placed on text books and self prepared text (Kunchu, 1989).

The techniques, a student employs to go about his or her studies which are consistent and have become stereotyped, as a result of long application or practice (Onubugwv, 1990).

Self-concept

An individuals perception of himself, as a person, which includes his abilities, appearance, performance in his job, and phases of daily living (Good 1973).

How a person sees himself (e.g competent, amusing, homely etc.). This may differ from other people's views of him, though they will have influenced it. (Derek Rowntree 1981).

Self-concept refers to the picture or image, a person has of himself (Taneja 1991 and A group of Experts 2003).

(*i*) An individual's perception of self.

(*ii*) A psychological contact that is more complex, than implied or assumed by most educators. (Raj, 1996).

Class

A group of pupils or students scheduled to report regularly at a particular time to a particular teacher. (Good 1973).

(*i*) A group students assigned to one or more teachers or other staff members for a given period of time for instruction other activity in a situation where the teacher(s) and students are in presence of each other.

(*ii*) All students in the same grade level such as fifth grade class or tenth grade class.

(*iii*) The group of students who graduate at the same time such as the class X of 1989. (Madhu Raj 1996 & S.K. Sing 2002).

Secondary School

Schools with classes VI to X are called high schools or secondary schools in the State of Andhra Pradesh in India. There will be a public examination at the end of classes VII and X in these schools in Andhra Pradesh.

Mathematics

One of the compulsory subjects of study from I class to X class in schools of Andhra Pradesh.

Mathematics is the science of numbers and space. Mathematics is the science, which draws necessary conclusions.

Mathematics is a way to settle in the mind a habit of reasoning.

Management

For the present study, management means the authority under which the schools function. In this study schools under the authority of Zilla Parishad, Government, municipalities, Andhra Pradesh Social Welfare Department and unaided private, have been considered for present investigation.

Locality

The scholastic achievements of students coming from rural areas, villages) semi urban areas (small towns) and urban areas (municipal areas) may differ. Hence students are divided into three groups namely rural, semi urban and urban students and scholastic achievements have been studied. In this investigation locality means rural, semi-urban and urban.

Caste

In the present educational system, which is in vogue, in Andhra Pradesh, students are categorized into scheduled castes and scheduled tribes, back ward castes and other castes not covered under the above two types. In the present investigation the students are divided into three categories basing on their caste, namely SC/ST, BC classes and OBC students.

Sex

Male and female students (boys) and (girls) are considered as sub samples to carry the differential analysis.

Age

The chronological age of the students as reported by them through the personal data sheet, is considered to divide the sample into three sub groups to study the variations in their achievements.

Size of the Family

It refers to the number of total living members of the family as on the date of collecting the data for the present study.

Sample

(*i*) A sample possessing the same characteristics as the population with reference to some variables other than, but thought of to be related to, the one under investigation.

(*ii*) Some times used to refer to a stratified sample, in which the sub sample numbers are proportional to the size of the strata (Good 1973).

A sample drawn from a population in such a way that it should (or does) contain members of various categories and classification in the same proportions as they appear in the population. (Rowntree 1981)

Sample refers to a group that is selected from a large group or population for examination with a view to making generalizations about the population, as a whole (Taneja, 1991).

Sample that corresponds to or matches the population of which it is a part with respect to characteristics important for the purpose under investigation. (Raj 1996, Sing 2002 and Bellingham 2004).

Variable

Any trait that changes from one case or condition to another, more strictly, the representation of the trait, usually in quantitative form, such as a measurement or an enumeration (Good 1973).

Refers to a factor in educational research that influences the observation or management of an educational phenomenon (Taneja, 1991 and a group of experts, 2003).

In educational research, an entity that can vary.

Independent Variable

(*i*) A variable to which values may be assigned at will.

(*ii*) The variable on which an estimation or prediction is based in a regression problem.

(*iii*) In the plural, often used to refer to variables that are unconnected, when presented graphically, the x-axis or horizontal axis is conveniently used for the independent variable. (Good 1973).

In a statistical study, the variable whose values are deliberately changed (or natural difference observed) in order to see how this influences the values of another variable (the dependent variable) (Rowntree 1981).

Refers to variable whose changes are considered as not dependent upon transformations in other specific variables (R.P. Taneja 1991).

In experimental research, the aspects of the study that the investigator manipulates or controls in order to observe the effect on the dependent variable (Raj 1996).

An independent variable is one that the researcher manipulates; e.g, a type of instructional programme (Bellingham 2004).

Dependent Variable

A dependent variable is one that changes in consequence with changes in the independent variable (Bellingham 2004).

A variable whose magnitude depends on or is a function of, the value of the another variable (or other variables); a variable whose value is being estimated (for example by regression techniques) from that of one or more independent variables to which it is related; when represented graphically, the y-axis or vertical line is conveniently used or the dependent variable (Good 1973).

In a statistical study, the variable in whose values, we are expecting to see changes as a result of changes, we have made or observed in the values of some other variable (the independent variable) (Rowntree, 1981).

Refers to a variable that is the presumed effect of a presumed cause of an event (Taneja 1991 and A Group of Experts 2003).

A factor in an experimental relationship which has or shows variation that is hypothesized to be caused by another independent factor or variable (Raj, 1996 and S.K. Singh 2002).

Demographics

(*i*) Statistics showing an area's population characteristics such as age, race, income and education.

(*ii*) Basic information about an individual including such characteristics as age, place of residence and marital status. (Singh 2002, Bellingham 2004)

Regression

(*i*) The tendency for observations that show a high deviation from the mean and a low degree of variability among themselves in regard to one trait to display wider variability and markedly less deviation (on the average) from the mean in a second trait;

(*ii*) The psychological mechanism of retreat from difficulties of adult world of reality to an imaginary world patterned on an earlier, more comfortable mode of life, as in childhood; normally seen in adults as play and make believe;

(*iii*) A movement of the eyes, backward from right to left along the line of type being read;

(*iv*) An error in silent or oral reading in which the reader retracts or goes back over what he has seen reading– Good, 1973).

The term relates to the techniques of analyzing relationships between two or more variables with a view to prediction (or estimating) values of one from values of other(s). (Derek Rowntree 1981).

(*i*) In the context of child development, the temporary lapses or set backs that occur in the other wise smooth course of normal development.

(*ii*) In the context of learned behaviour or skills, the loss or forgetting of previously learned skills in the absence of opportunities for continued practice.

(*iii*) A psychological withdrawal to an earlier period of life, which may be manifested by infinite or immature behaviour (Raj 1996 and Singh; 2002).

In the context of child development, the temporary lapses or set backs that occur in the otherwise smooth course of normal development (Bellingham 2004).

A method which makes use of a correlation in order to predict probable relationships. (Taneja 1991 and A group of Experts, 2003).

A method for describing the nature of relationship between two variables, so that the value of one can be predicted if the value of the other is known. Multiple regression analysis involves more than two variables.

(Raj, 1996 and D.R. Singh 2002)

OBJECTIVES OF THE STUDY

1. To understand the present status of Xth class students with regard to their achievement in mathematics.
2. To study the influence of the variables management, sex and their interaction on the scholastic achievement.

3. To study the influence of locality, caste and their interaction on scholastic achievement in mathematics.
4. To establish a relationship of scholastic achievement with personal variables like age, birth order, education of mother, education of father, occupation of mother, Occupation of father, Income, Religion, Economic status, Size of the family, Work at home, Study hours at home, Separate room for study, and number of hours spent daily for mathematics.
5. To study the impact of personality factors on the scholastic achievement in mathematics of Xth class students.
6. To study the influence of study habits on the scholastic achievement of Xth class students in mathematics.
7. To study the impact of self-concepts on the scholastic achievement of Xth class students in mathematics.
8. To predict the scholastic achievement of Xth class students in mathematics with the help of socio-demographic variables, personality factors, study habits and self-concepts, etc.
9. To predict the scholastic achievement of Xth class students in mathematics with the help of all independent variables in the investigation.
10. To develop mathematical equations for predicting the scholastic achievement of Xth class students in mathematics.
11. To summarize the findings of present investigation
12. To make appropriate recommendations on the basis of present findings.
13. To provide suggestions for further investigation.

HYPOTHESES FORMULATED

On the basis of the above objectives the following major hypotheses, in the null form are formulated for testing in the present study:

1. All the Xth class students would not have the same scholastic achievement abilities in mathematics.
2. Management, sex and their interaction would not have any significant influence on the scholastic achievement in mathematics of 10th class students.
3. Locality, caste and their interaction would not have any significant influence on the scholastic achievement of Xth class students in mathematics.
4. Socio-demographic variables would not have any significant impact on the scholastic achievement of Xth class students in mathematics.
5. Personality factors would not have any significant influence on the scholastic achievement of Xth class students in mathematics
6. Study habits would not have any significant impact on the scholastic achievement of Xth class students
7. Self- concepts would not have any significant impact on the scholastic achievement of Xth class students in mathematics
8. It would not be possible to predict the scholastic achievement with the help of socio-demographic variables, personality factors, study habits and self-concepts.
9. It would not be possible to predict the scholastic achievement with the help of all independent variables.
10. It would not be possible to develop mathematical equations with the help of different sets of independent variables
12. None of the 52 independent variables in this study turns out to be a significant predictor of achievement in mathematics of Xth class students

VARIABLES INCLUDED IN THE PRESENT STUDY

On basis of study of related literature, it has been found that the achievement in mathematics of the students of all classes in general and Xth class in particular depends on several factors. The investigator has selected the following psycho-sociological variables for the present study.

Dependent Variables

The scores obtained by all the subjects (all the students of the sample) in the achievement test, constructed and standardized by the investigator has been taken as dependent variable.

Independent Variables

The independent variables studied in this investigation are given below.

1. **Personal and socio-demographic variables :** The personal and socio-demographic variables included in the present investigation are:

   Gender, Caste, Age, Locality, Type of Management, Size of the Family, Birth order, Mothers Education, Fathers Education, Occupation of Father and Mother, Religion, Income of the family, Economic status, Separate room for study, Study hours at home, Help from the family members, Works at home, and Time spent for mathematics in a day.
2. **Psychological Variables :** The following psychological variables are included in the present study: HSPQ consisting of 14 Personality Factors, Study Habits questionnaire consisting of seven areas, and Self-Concept questionnaire consisting of 10 areas.

METHOD OF STUDY

The author following the scientific principles and procedures of test construction, developed a preliminary objective test with 150 multiple choice questions with the help of senior mathematics teachers for the use of pilot study. The preliminary form is standardized following the method described by Garrette (1973) and after deleting 50 questions, a final objective achievement test (OAT) paper is prepared with one hundred multiple choice questions carrying one mark each. A questionnaire is prepared to collect the necessary information about the pupils regarding their personal characteristics, home background and socio-economic conditions of the family. Cattel's *High School Personality Questionnaire* (HSPQ) is used to collect the information regarding the personality characteristics of the students of the sample. Study Habits Inventory of Dr. B.V. Patel is adopted to measure the study habits of pupils regarding mathematics. Dr (Miss) Rani Rasthogi's Self-Concept Scale is adopted to measure the self-concepts of pupils.

A sample of 1444 students representing all categories of pupils is selected by following the standardized procedures. The necessary data are collected in a planned way and are analized using appropriate statistical techniques and the results are interpreted accordingly.

LIMITATIONS OF PRESENT STUDY

The following are the limitations of the present study:

1. The study is confined to only Chittoor district of Andhra Pradesh
2. The study is confined to a few schools i.e. 22 schools in the four revenue divisions of Chittoor district only.
3. The study is confined only to the Xth class students of the above-mentioned schools of Chittoor District.
4. The present study concerns itself for the subject of mathematics of Xth class students only.
5. The effect of only a few independent variables on the achievement in mathematics of Xth class students has been studied.
6. The achievement scores are taken only from the achievement test constructed and standardized by the author.
7. The study is based on survey research, where in the techniques of analyzing the data, are based on the questionnaires only.

8. The scholastic achievement of Xth class pupils depends on a number of psychological, sociological, demographic and environmental factors. It is not possible to include each and every factor in this investigation.
9. It is only a presage product study in the area of scholastic achievement.

Chapter 4: Methods of Investigation

This chapter deals with various procedures followed in the construction and standardization of data gathering instruments to measure the different variables, included in the present investigation. A brief description of methods adopted in the selection of the sample, collection of data, scoring, analysis and statistical techniques employed, are presented here under.

The flow chart showing the procedure followed in the present investigation is given in Fig-1.

Tools used in the Present study

The following tools used in the present study are shown here:

1. Objective Achievement Test (OAT)
2. Cattell's High School Students Personality Questionnaire (HSPQ).
3. Dr. B.V. Patels' Study Habits Inventory.
4. Dr. (Miss) Muktha Rani Rastogis' Self-concept Scale.
5. Personal Data sheet Prepared by the Investigator.

Construction of Objective Achievement Test (OAT)

An achievement test is essentially a tool or a device of measurement that helps in ascertaining quantity and quality of learning at the end, in a subject of study or group of subjects, after a period of instruction; *Dictionary of Education* (1998) refers it, to the performance in a school or a college in a standardized series of educational testing. Longman Active

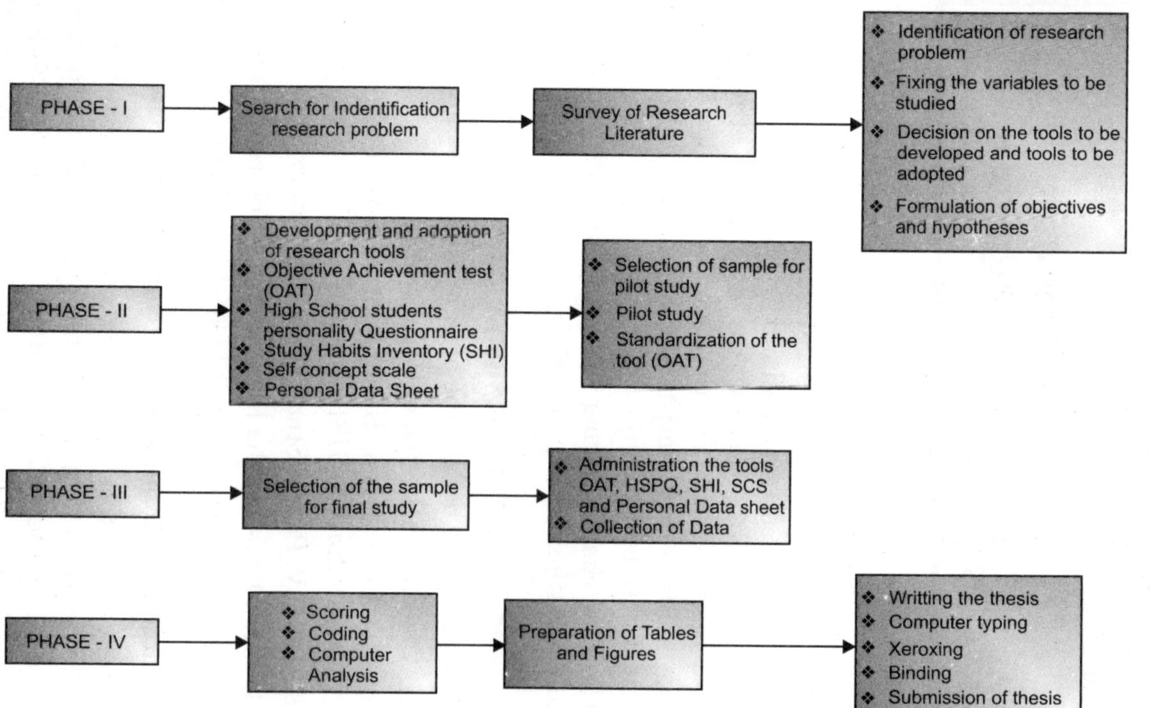

Fig. 1 Flowchart showing the procedures follwed in the present study

study *Dictionary of English* (1998) and *Cambridge International Dictionary* (1996), regarded it a success in reaching an aim, especially after a lot of hard work. It is also defined as the specified level of attainment or proficiency in academic work, designed by test scores.

In the present study "Achievement" refers to the attainment of marks in an objective achievement test constructed and standarised by the investigator in the subject, mathematics for 10th class pupils.

The Board of Secondary Education of Andhra Pradesh conducts a public examination at the end of each academic year, for 10th class, in which mathematics is one of the compulsory subjects. The mathematics subject consists of two papers – Paper-I and Paper-II. Paper-I consists of the following chapters:

(1) Statements and sets (2) Functions (3) Polynomials over integers (4) Progressions (5) Linear Programming (6) Real numbers. Paper II consists of the chapters, namely (1) Analytical Geometry (2) Trigonometry (3) Matrices (4) Statistics (5) Computing.

In each paper there are two parts – Part A and Part B. Part A in each paper consists of all subjective questions where as Part B in each paper consists of objective type questions. In objective type questions there are ten multiple choice questions, ten fill in the blank questions and ten matching type questions. Total number of objective questions are 30, each question carrying half a mark. The subjective questions in Part A in each paper again consists of short answer questions and long answer questions carrying two, four and five marks each. If two different persons evaluate the subjective questions, there is likely to be a variation in their evaluation. In view of this, the investigator constructed an objective achievement test (OAT) in mathematics for Xth Class pupils, taking the total syllabus, with one hundred and fifty questions, each question carrying one mark each.

Construction of the Preliminary Form

Before constructing the OAT, the investigator referred the Xth class mathematics textbook, the syllabus and previous public examination question papers. The investigator consulted the senior teachers, teaching the subject, for Xth class, the subject experts and experts in the construction of objective questions. After the setting of questions by the investigator, it was thoroughly reviewed with the help of senior mathematics teachers and subject experts. Some questions are deleted and some others are added on their advice and finally the OAT is constructed, with 150 questions, each question carrying one mark.

All the questions are multiple choice questions, with four alternatives for each question. Only one alternative is the correct answer out of the four alternatives. The pupils are asked to chose the correct alternative for each question.

Pilot Study

The Telugu version of the preliminary form of OAT, is administered on 436 students of different schools. The schools are selected at random. The sample design for pilot study is shown in the Table 4.1. The schools selected are four ZP high Schools and one A.P. Social Welfare Residential high school, one private high school and one Municipal High School.

Administration of the Pilot Study

The investigator obtained the prior permission from the heads of the institutions, selected for pilot study, to conduct the test, after explaining them the purpose of the study and convincing them. The investigator explained the purpose of the test to the students and asked them to prepare well on the total syllabus. The test is conducted, after giving sufficient time for preparation. The test is conducted with the help of the teachers and all the answer sheets are collected. The investigator visited the different schools on different dates and conducted the test according to the schedule, given earlier.

Table 4.1 : Sample Design for Pilot Study

Sl. No.	Name of the school	Management	Boys	Girls	Total
1.	Z.P. High School, Madanapally	ZP	39	23	62
2.	Z.P. High School, Angallu	ZP	26	16	42
3.	Z.P. High School, Kurabala Kota	ZP	40	32	72
4.	Z.P. High School, C.T.M	ZP	38	27	65
5.	Hope Municipal High School, Madanapally Municipality	39	26	65	
6.	APSWR School, B.Kotha Kota	Social Welfare Department	63	-	63
7.	Gnanodaya High School, Madanapally	Private	42	25	67
	Total		**287**	**149**	**436**

Scoring Procedure

One mark is awarded for each correct answer and the total marks obtained by each student is marked on the right top corner of the sheet.

Item Analysis

This procedure of item analysis is adopted from the prescribed standardized procedure, for construction and use of tests for class room examinations. For the present study, the difficulty index and validity index of each item are computed, by following the procedure in the text book *"Statistics in Psychology and Education"* by Garrett (1973).

On the basis of total marks obtained in the OAT, the answer sheets are arranged in descending order. The upper 27 per cent of papers and lower 27 per cent of the papers are separated and are named as High group and Low group. These two groups of papers are taken for analysis and the rest are excluded from analysis. Papers of High group are then computed to find out how often, the correct answer to each question, has been chosen by the pupils in the group. The numbers thus obtained are recorded. Papers of low group are also corrected in the same procedure. Percentages of correct responses are also recorded.

If the validity index approaches to 1.00, the question tends to discriminate perfectly between high and low achievers. As the validity index approaches to zero (0), the question does not discriminate between high and low achievers.

After ascertaining the difficulty Index and validity index for each item in the preliminary test as per the guidelines given by Garrett (1973) 50 questions whose validities are less than 0.37 are deleted and a final test is constructed. The difficulty index and validity index (Discriminating power) of OAT are given in the Table 4.2.

The questions deleted from the preliminary OAT are also shown in the Table 4.2.

Table 4.2: Difficulty index and validity Index of the items of Pilot form of objective Achievement Test

Item No.	Percentage of correct Responses		Difficulty Index (Difficulty value)	Validity Index (Discriminating pwer)	Remarks
	High Group	Low Group			
1	2	3	4	5	6
1	96	80	0.88	0.29	Deleted
2	91	37	0.64	0.58	Retained
3	81	22	0.52	0.59	Retained
4	96	65	0.81	0.44	Retained
5	58	25	0.42	0.32	Deleted
6	78	37	0.58	0.44	Retained
7	81	32	0.57	0.48	Retained
8	70	06	0.38	0.68	Retained
9	84	67	0.76	0.21	Deleted
10	85	55	0.70	0.34	Deleted
11	54	15	0.35	0.44	Retained
12	72	44	0.58	0.29	Deleted
13	78	31	0.55	0.49	Retained
14	64	28	0.46	0.37	Retained
15	14	19	0.17	-VE	Deleted
16	70	13	0.42	0.62	Retained
17	60	36	0.48	0.25	Deleted
18	53	33	0.43	0.22	Deleted
19	47	24	0.36	0.26	Deleted
20	70	24	0.47	0.47	Retained
21	78	35	0.57	0.43	Retained
22	50	29	0.40	0.22	Deleted
23	56	16	0.36	0.45	Retained
24	72	20	0.46	0.53	Retained
25	68	17	0.43	0.53	Retained
26	92	44	0.68	0.55	Retained

...(*Contd.*)

1	2	3	4	5	6
27	83	20	0.52	0.63	Retained
28	73	23	0.48	0.50	Retained
29	81	30	0.56	0.52	Retained
30	76	19	0.48	0.57	Retained
31	70	29	0.50	0.41	Retained
32	92	21	0.57	0.72	Retained
33	86	55	0.71	0.37	Retained
34	25	14	0.20	0.17	Deleted
35	42	19	0.31	0.26	Deleted
36	35	10	0.23	0.34	Deleted
37	18	21	0.20	-VE	Deleted
38	63	33	0.48	0.33	Deleted
39	66	26	0.46	0.41	Retained
40	89	35	0.62	0.55	Retained
41	92	39	0.66	0.58	Retained
42	86	29	0.58	0.58	Retained
43	78	37	0.58	0.43	Retained
44	59	23	0.41	0.38	Retained
45	57	19	0.38	0.40	Retained
46	66	27	0.47	0.40	Retained
47	64	18	0.41	0.48	Retained
48	89	42	0.66	0.51	Retained
49	57	24	0.41	0.35	Deleted
50	96	29	0.63	0.72	Retained
51	98	64	0.81	0.60	Retained
52	93	18	0.56	0.68	Retained
53	88	29	0.59	0.60	Retained
54	91	50	0.72	0.50	Retained
55	76	29	0.53	0.48	Retained
56	54	22	0.38	0.34	Deleted
57	80	18	0.49	0.62	Retained
58	47	17	0.32	0.36	Deleted

...(*Contd.*)

1	2	3	4	5	6
59	96	51	0.74	0.56	Retained
60	92	75	0.84	0.28	Deleted
61	98	81	0.90	0.44	Retained
62	52	23	0.38	0.31	Deleted
63	72	23	0.48	0.40	Retained
64	72	16	0.44	0.57	Retained
65	69	42	0.56	0.28	Deleted
66	64	25	0.45	0.41	Retained
67	91	41	0.66	0.57	Retained
68	84	34	0.59	0.52	Retained
69	56	21	0.39	0.38	Retained
70	55	25	0.40	0.33	Deleted
71	86	43	0.65	0.47	Retained
72	63	21	0.42	0.45	Retained
73	63	25	0.44	0.41	Retained
74	80	47	0.64	0.35	Deleted
75	91	19	0.55	0.71	Retained
76	85	20	0.53	0.64	Retained
77	89	33	0.61	0.68	Retained
78	92	39	0.66	0.58	Retained
79	70	22	0.46	0.49	Retained
80	94	47	0.74	0.58	Retained
81	79	31	0.55	0.49	Retained
82	86	28	0.57	0.59	Retained
83	37	6	0.22	0.46	Retained
84	68	14	0.41	0.56	Retained
85	97	64	0.82	0.48	Retained
86	87	45	0.66	0.48	Retained
87	59	14	0.37	0.50	Retained
88	81	25	0.53	0.56	Retained
89	21	7	0.14	0.27	Deleted
90	81	16	0.49	0.64	Retained

...(*Contd.*)

1	2	3	4	5	6
91	39	23	0.31	0.19	Deleted
92	17	31	0.24	-VE	Deleted
93	19	9	0.14	0.23	Deleted
94	47	20	0.34	0.31	Deleted
95	86	79	0.73	0.11	Deleted
96	91	46	0.69	0.53	Retained
97	90	25	0.58	0.66	Retained
98	36	22	0.29	0.17	Deleted
99	69	23	0.46	0.47	Retained
100	58	47	0.53	0.11	Deleted
101	69	19	0.44	0.50	Retained
102	83	33	0.58	0.52	Retained
103	69	42	0.56	0.28	Deleted
104	78	22	0.50	0.56	Retained
105	31	21	0.26	0.15	Deleted
106	37	23	0.30	0.16	Deleted
107	54	38	0.46	0.16	Deleted
108	56	28	0.42	0.30	Deleted
109	78	31	0.55	0.49	Deleted
110	33	15	0.24	0.23	Deleted
111	81	53	0.67	0.31	Deleted
112	77	22	0.50	0.55	Retained
113	87	25	0.51	0.62	Retained
114	36	19	0.28	0.21	Deleted
115	44	20	0.32	0.28	Deleted
116	73	26	0.50	0.47	Retained
117	50	26	0.38	0.26	Deleted
118	89	19	0.54	0.68	Retained
119	80	16	0.48	0.63	Retained
120	47	21	0.34	0.36	Deleted
121	33	12	0.23	0.30	Deleted
122	83	19	0.51	0.63	Retained

...(*Contd.*)

1	2	3	4	5	6
123	62	18	0.40	0.47	Retained
124	97	22	0.60	0.78	Retained
125	93	52	0.73	0.45	Retained
126	93	84	0.89	0.17	Deleted
127	97	57	0.77	0.53	Retained
128	91	38	0.65	0.59	Retained
129	95	45	0.70	0.63	Retained
130	66	25	0.46	0.42	Retained
131	51	12	0.32	0.47	Retained
132	40	19	0.30	0.25	Deleted
133	78	24	0.51	0.54	Retained
134	64	33	0.49	0.35	Deleted
135	67	29	0.48	0.43	Retained
136	83	14	0.49	0.68	Retained
137	33	30	0.32	0.03	Deleted
138	92	24	0.58	0.69	Retained
139	84	13	0.49	0.70	Retained
140	79	35	0.57	0.44	Retained
141	33	38	0.36	-VE	Deleted
142	70	25	0.48	0.45	Retained
143	67	31	0.49	0.40	Retained
144	78	33	0.56	0.46	Retained
145	44	14	0.29	0.36	Deleted
146	82	39	0.61	0.46	Retained
147	91	47	0.69	0.51	Retained
148	66	25	0.46	0.42	Retained
149	47	19	0.33	0.32	Deleted
150	90	55	0.73	0.44	Retained

Validity

The validity of a test is concerned with, what is measured. It refers to the degree to which extent, the test scores predict some practical criterion measures. There are various methods of estimating the validity of a measuring instrument.

Table 4.2 shows the difficulty index and validity index of each item of the OAT. The following validities are established for the OAT:

1. **Content validity :** This form of validity is estimated by evaluating the relevance of the test items, individually and as a whole. Validity of content should not depend upon the subjective judgement of only one specialist. In the present case, the previous question papers were thouroulv reviewed, views of specialists in the subject were taken, the investigator thoroughly referred the total syllabus, the items in the test were thoroughly scrutinized with respect to the subject matter and hence it is assumed that the OAT has content validity.
2. **Item validity :** The validity index calculated for each of the items is a measure of the extent, to which a given item differentiates the low groups and high groups. Thus the items in the inventory with validity index, equal to or greater than 0.37 ensure the item validity of the OAT. Hence, the OAT has item validity.
3. **Intrinsic Validity :** Guilford (1954) defined intrinsic validity as, "The degree to which a test measures what it purports to measure". This can also be stated in terms of how well, the obtained scores measure the test's true score component. This validity is given by the square root of its reliability. Hence the intrinsic validity of the OAT is 0.97.
4. **Face validity :** If a common thread of achievement runs through all the items of the test, then the test is said to have face validity. All items in the OAT have a common thread for measuring the achievement of Xth Class pupils in mathematics. Hence, the OAT has face validity.
5. **Construct Validity :** Construct validity of a test measures particular characteristics of the individual taking the test. A test is valid from the construct point of view, if it can indicate the individual's actual achievement of instructional objectives. All the

questions in the objective achievement Test (OAT) are based on the objectives of instruction. Hence, there is construct validity for the OAT.

6. Concurrent validity and predictive validity:

   In a situation of some observable criterion, the scale's validity can be investigated by seeing how good an indicator it is. This approach leads to two categories of validity (i.e) 'Predictive Validity' and 'concurrent validity'.

   Predictive validity is concerned with how the scale can fore cast a future criterion and concurrent validity with how well it can describe a present one. The results in the succeeding chapter show that the OAT has both concurrent and predictive validities.

Final Study

The final OAT paper is prepared after deleting, the invalid 50 items whose validity index is less than 0.37, from the preliminary inventory. Garrettee (1973), suggested that the items with validity index less than 0.20 are invalid. In the present investigation, the investigator wants to retain one hundred items for the final study. Hence the items with validity index more than 0.36 are retained for final study. The final version of the OAT paper is translated into English. The translation is observed by three experts in English and they confirmed that there is no any ambiguity in the translation.

Reliability

Next to validity, reliability is the most indispensable characteristic of any measuring instrument. It refers to the consistency of scores obtained by the same individuals at different occasions or with different sets of equivalent items.

A tool is said to be reliable, if it reveals similar results in various situations. The test-retest and parallel form methods of estimating reliability may be common and legitimate for both power and speed tests. In the power test each student has enough time to write what he knows. The Split-half technique is not proper for speed test, in which he does not have time to respond to some questions, for which he knows the correct answer. Speed test usually yields spuriously high reliability co-efficient, when split-half and internal consistency methods are employed. (Stanley *et al.* 1978).

Split-Half reliability is some times called as co-efficient of equivalence. The test is split into two equivalent halves, usually by pooling the odd numbered items for one half where as, the even numbered items forming the second half of the test. This usually makes the two scores obtained from a single test reasonably equivalent.

The reliability of the OAT is tested by employing (1) Test-Retest method on a sample of 250 with a gap of 15 days for retest, (2) Split-Half Technique and (3) K.R. Formula-20. The Reliability coefficients of the OAT are presented in Table 4.3.

Table 4.3. The Reliability Co-efficients of the Objective Achievement Test

Sl. No.	Type of the Reliability	Mangnitude of Reliability
1.	Test-Retest method	0.90
2.	Split-Half Technique	0.88
3.	K.R. formula-20	0.94

The magnitude of the coefficient of correlation in all the above three methods is more than 0.85. Hence the reliability of the OAT is very high.

PERSONALITY QUESTIONNAIRE

Personality of an individual plays an important role in his/her scholastic achievement. The review of related literatures showed that there are a number of studies showing the relationship between personality and scholastic achievement at school level. Hence the investigator felt a need to investigate the relationship between personality of the child and its scholastic achievement particularly, the achievement in mathematics of Xth class students. This motivated the author to search for a suitable personality questionnaire.

The author studied all the personality theories and searched for a suitable means of measuring the total behaviour of an individual and is convinced that Cattell's theory, of all the various theories, is the only theory based on the principle of totality of behaviour of an individual.

Selection of the Tool (HSPQ)

Different psychologists have given different definitions for the term "personality".

Personality is a dynamic organization within the individual of those psycho-physical systems that determine his unique adjustment to his environment (Allport 1949).

According to Cattell (1950), 'personality is that which permits a prediction of what a person will do in a given situation'. One can not pass a judgement over one's personality, by just looking through one's physique or sociability. One has to go carefully into all the aspects, biological and social and then only one can asses the personality of an individual. Sometimes some researchers and even psychologists fall easily into the mistake of settling, on a single test, dealing with any one dimension of personality, for example extroversion, self-realization etc. and from that they try to asses all kinds of behaviour, which is not advisable.

For the individual all aspects of behaviour, thought and feeling that make the person unique. For psychologists a major area of theory and research (Rowntree 1981).

Keeping this in view, the personality of the students in the present study is assessed using Cattell's Junior-Senior High School personality questionnaire (HSPQ). It is applicable to the age group of students 12 to 18 years. It is a culture free test. It helps to obtain scores on 14 dimensions of the personality. They represent basic concepts, which are understood by psychologists, so that insightful under-standings of the individual and his development as well as statistical predictions are possible. The above point weighted in favour of selecting the HSPQ for assessing the personality traits of the students. Cattell's 14 personality factors are given here under.

A brief description of Cattell's fourteen HSPQ personality factors is given below:

Description of the HSPQ Factors

Factor A: Reserved vs. Outgoing

The person, who scored low on Factor-A tends to be stiff, cool and alone. He likes things rather than people, working alone and avoiding class of view points. He is likely to be precise and rigid in his way of doing things and personal standards.

The person who scores high on Factor-A, tends to be more matured, easy going, emotionally expressive, ready to co-operate, attentive to the people, soft hearted, kindly adaptable. He readily forms active groups. He is generous in personal relations, less afraid of criticism and better able to remember the names of the people.

Factor B: Less Intelligent vs. More Intelligent

Less intelligent, concrete thinking vs. more intelligent, abstract thinking.

The person scoring low on Factor-B tends to be a slow learner, dull and sluggish. He tends to have little capacity for higher forms of knowledge.

The person who scores high on Factor -B tends to be more intelligent, quick in grasping, and a fast learner. Low score, in contrast indicate deterioration of mental functions in pathological conditions.

Factor C: Emotionally Less Stable vs. Emotionally Stable

The person who scores low on Factor-C tends to be low in frustration, tolerance for un-satisfactory conditions and neurotically fatigued.

The person who scores more on Factor-C tends to be emotionally mature, more stable, calm, and be able to maintain high group morale.

Factor 'D': Phlegmatic vs. Excitable

Phlegmatic, Deliberate, Inactive vs. excitable, Impatient, Demanding, Overactive.

The person scoring low on Factor-D is thought of same as 'C' with which it has some behaviour in common. However, it is distinguishable by more immediate, "temperate mental" quality of excitability and by an irresponsible, positive, assertive emphasis in the emotionality.

The person who scores high on 'D' tends to be a restless sleeper, easily distracted from work by noise. He is hurt and angry, if he is not given important positions.

Facror 'E' Obedient, Mild, Conforming, submissive vs. Assertive, Independent, Aggressive, Stubborn, Dominant.

The person who scores low on Factor-E tends to be dependent, a follower, and takes action which goes along with the group. This, positively, is part of many neurotic syndromes.

The person who scores high on Factor-E tends to be assertive, self assumed, Independent, bold in his approach to the situations. He may at times, be hard, a law to himself, hostile, authoritarian and dis-regards authority.

Factor 'F': Sober Vs. Happy - Go-Lucky, Gay Enthusiastic, Impulsively Lively.

The person who scores low on Factor-F tends to be restrained and introspective. He is some times pessimistic, anxious and considered to be swung- he tends to be a sober, dependable person.

The person who scores high on this factor tends to be cheerful, active, talkative, frank, expressive, quick and un-perturbable. He is frequently chosen as an elected leader. He may be impulsive and mercurial.

Factor 'G' Moral standards Vs. super ego-strength.

Expedient, Evades rules vs. conscientious, preserving and rule bound.

The person who scores low on factor 'G' tends to be unsteady in purpose. He is often casual and lacking in effort for group under takings and cultural demands.

The person who scores high on this factor tends to be strong in character, preserving, responsible, determined, consistent, playful and well organized. He prefers hard working people to witty companions.

Factor 'H': Shy Vs. Venturesome Shy, Restrained, Different, Timid Vs. Venture Some, Socially Bold, Uninhibited, Spontanious.

The person who scored low on 'H' tends to be shy, withdrawing, cautious, retiring, and cooling. He usually has inferiority feelings. He tends to be slow in speech, dislikes occupations with personal contacts and prefers one or two close friends to large groups and is not given to keeping in contact with all that is going on around him.

The person who scores high on this factor tends to be more sociable, bold, ready to try new things, spontaneous and abundant in emotional response. His "thickskinnedness" enables him to face wear and tear in dealing with people. He tends to be pushy and actively interested in the opposite sex.

Factor 'I': Though Minded Vs. Tense Minded. Though Minded, Self-reliant, Realistic Vs. Tender Minded, Dependent, Over Protected and Sensitive.

The person who scores low on Factor-I tends to be practical, realistic, masculine, independent, responsible but skeptical of subjective and "uncultured". He is some times unmoved, hard, cynical, and smug.

The person who scores high on this factor tends to be tender-minded, day dreaming, artistically fastidious. He is sometimes demanding of attention and help, impatient, dependent and impractical. He dislikes crude people and rough occupations. He tends to be slow in group performance.

Factor 'J': Vigorous Vs Doubting

Vigorous, justify to action Vs Doubting, Obstructive, Individualistic, Reflective and Unwilling etc.

The person who scores low on Factor-J has 'no' for a difficult pattern to interpret. It has been called variously the Hamlet factor neurasthenia, etc.

The person who scores high on this trait prefers to do things on his own in physically and intellectually fastidious, thinks over his mistakes and how to avoid them, tends not to forget if he is unfairly treated, has private views differing from the groups, but prefers to keep himself in the back ground and avoid argument, knows he has fewer friends.

Factor 'O': Placid Vs Apprehensive

Placid, confident, serene, untroubled vs Apprehensive, worrying, depressive, troubled, Guilt proneness.

The person who scores low on Factor-O tends to be placid, calm, with unshakable nerve. He has a mature, unanxious, confidence in himself and has capacity to deal with things. He is resilient and secure.

The person who scores high on Factor-O tends to be depressed, moody, worried, suspicious, brooding and avoiding people. He has a child like tendency to anxiety in difficulties. He does not feel accepted in groups or free to participate.

Factor 'Q_2': Group Dependent Vs Self-sufficient

The person who scores low on Factor-Q_2 prefers to work and make decisions with other people and depends on social approval and administration. He tends to go alone with the group and may be lacking individual resolution. He needs group support.

The person who scores high on this trait, is temperamentally independent, accustomed to go in his own way, making decisions and taking action on his own. He discounts public opinion, but is not necessarily dominant in his relation with others. He does not dislike people but simply does not mind their agreement or support.

Factor Q_3: Undisciplined Vs Controlled

Undisciplined, self-conflict, careless of protocol follows own urges, low integration vs controlled, socially precise, self-disciplined, compulsive, high self concept, control.

The person who scores low on Factor-Q_3 will not be bothered with will-control and regard for social demands. He is not over considerable, careful or painstaking. He may feel, maladjusted.

The person who scores high on Factor- Q_3 tends to have strong control of his emotions and general behaviour, inclined to be socially aware and careful and regards for social reputations. Effective leaders and some paranoids are high on Q_3.

Factor Q_4: Relaxed Vs Tensed

Relaxed, tranquil, torpid, unfrustrated Vs Tense, driven over, wrought, Frustrated.

The person who scores low on factor Q_4 tends to be sedate, relaxed, composed, and satisfied. In some situations, his over satisfaction may lead to laziness and low performances in the sense that low motivation produces little trail and error.

The person who scores high on this trait, tends to be tense, excitable, restless, fruitful, and impatient. He is often fatigued, but unable to remain inactive. In groups, he likes a poor view of the degree or unity, orderliness and leadership.

One of the Unique features of HSPQ and other personality scales developed by cattell, is that each of the items in any factor is selected on the basis of their own correlation with pure factors. In other words the HSPQ of cattell has factorial validity. The research carried out over years with these factors, has produced constant and substantial correlation of these primary factor scales, to a wide arrary of criteria in educational, clinical, occupational and other areas establishing its criterion of validity.

Having decided to make use of HSPQ (cattell), the questionnaire is translated into telugu, the mother tongue and the regional language of the subjects on whom, it has to be applied. Five judges who are well versed with psychological testing, checked the translation. Necessary instructions are given to the students and they were asked to answer the items as per the instructions given to them.

Adoption of the Instrument (HSPQ)

Junior- senior high school personality questionnaire (HSPQ) Form-A, prepared and standardized by cattell (1950) is adopted for the study. Telugu version of HSPQ Form-A is used for the present study.

Validity and Reliability of HSPQ

For calculating Validity and Reliability, the procedure suggested by Garrett (1973) is followed. Reliability of two subjects of each factor as obtained by the split half technique and validity, which is the square root of reliability are presented in Table 4.4. The split half reliability is calculated on a sample of 250 pupils.

Table 4.4. Reliability and validity of HSPQ Form-A, Using Split-Half Method

Factor	A	B	C	D	E	F	G
Reliability	0.592	0.731	0.765	0.658	0.812	0.741	0.725
Validity	0.769	0.855	0.875	0.811	0.901	0.861	0.851
Factor	**H**	**I**	**J**	**O**	**Q2**	**Q3**	**Q4**
Reliability	0.721	0.691	0.712	0.567	0.762	0.646	0.657
Validity	0.849	0.831	0.844	0.753	0.873	0.804	0.811

Re-test was also conducted on a sample of 250 pupils with a gap of 15 days. The test retest Validity and Reliability for each factor is presented in the Table 4.5.

Table 4.5. Reliability and Validity of HSPQ- Form A Using Test- Retest Method

Factor	A	B	C	D	E	F	G
Reliability	0.552	0.741	0.782	0.672	0.852	0.741	0.732
Validity	0.742	0.861	0.884	0.820	0.923	0.861	0.856
Factor	**H**	**I**	**J**	**O**	**Q2**	**Q3**	**Q4**
Reliability	0.798	0.645	0.712	0.704	0.716	0.676	0.721
Validity	0.893	0.803	0.844	0.839	0.846	0.822	0.849

The results of Validity and Reliability of HSPQ Form-A show that all the factors of HSPQ are highly valid and reliable.

Scoring Procedure for HSPQ

There are 142 items in the HSPQ. Three alternatives are given for each item. The student has to choose only one alternative which he feels appropriate for him. The scoring is done for each student and for each factor using the scoring key given by the author.

Administration of HSPQ

The Telugu version of HSPQ is administered on all the pupils (N=1444) with the help of the teachers in the morning session. Through inspection is done whether the students are following the instructions or not. All the answer sheets are collected and evaluated, as per the scoring key.

STUDY HABITS INVENTORY

A few definitions of a study habit are presented hereunder:

The complex of reading behaviour of a person resulting from varying degrees of interaction of a number of variable factors, may be defined as a study habit.

The ability to schedule his aims, the habit of note taking, reviewing, judicious application of the whole and part method etc. form learners study habits.

The words 'study habits' is used to refer students' way of

studying-systematic or unsystematic-efficient or in efficient (Good 1973).

Study habits include students' habit of concentration, note taking, time budgeting and study methods (Smith 1961).

Study habits mainly depend on motivation for reading, interest in the subject, attitude, encouragement by others, personality traits etc. Effective learning takes place only with good study habits.

Factors Affecting the Study Habits

Some of the noteworthy factors affecting the study habits are presented here under

1. **Home:** Parents are the first teachers and home is the first place of learning for every child. Parents and other family members may influence the childrens' learning methods and study habits. The level of education and occupation of the parents may also have some influence on childrens' study habits.
2. **Intelligence :** Intelligent students can more quickly develop good study habits than dull students.
3. **Personality :** Students with better adjustments to the environment, can develop better study habits.
4. **Community :** Community resources like library facilities, meetings with learned people inculcate good study habits among children.
5. **School :** The school atmosphere and teachers play an important role in developing good or bad study habits.
6. **Curriculum :** The curriculum should be suitable for the standard of the child. If the curriculum is above the standard of the children, pupils may be frustrated and may develop bad study habits.
7. **Demographic factors :** Locality, sex, education of parents, income of the family, number of members in the family, social status of the family etc. influence the study habits of the pupils.

Factors Helping for Developing Good Study Habits

"Study is nothing but a passion of Mind"

-Thomous hobbs

1. **Efficient use of time:** The first and most important thing for success in the class room is efficient use of time, outside the class-room. There are 24 hours a day. Two or three hours, each day are to be set aside for studying. It is not the amount of time spent on study that matters much, but it is how effectively time is spent.
2. **The power of co-operation:** Education often looks like competition. Pupils compete for marks or, for grades when they are in school. They compete for jobs, when they leave school. In such a climate, it is easy to overlook the power of co-opeartion that is developed through study groups. Hence pupils are to remember, their friends, classmates and support group, when they study.
3. **Mixing with social activities:** The most successful students balance school activities with good study habits. A diversion from studies will alleviate stress and help prevent from becoming fatigued. Hence, pupils have to take small breaks after some hours of study for sharpening their concentration.
4. **Setting a comfortable pace:** A good grade, in a course is almost neverthe result of luck. The key is to set a comfortable pace of study. Each pupil will have his own pace of learning. Hence, planning a convenient study schedule and adhering to it, will guarantee better grades.
5. **Changing Habits:** Some students may have very poor study habits. Those poor study habits such as not completing assignments, missing classes, not regular at studying, etc. Hence, changing these poor habits will result in better life.
6. **Immediate review of class notes:** Reviewing as soon as possible what they have heard and learnt in

the class, improve their retention of the sub-matter for long. Otherwise 80 per cent of what was learnt, will be forgotten. Hence, the pupils must review the class notes before they go to next chapter.

7. **Time management:** Time management is one of the most important factor in the student life. Research indicates that unless a lesson is reviewed within twenty four hours, 80 per cent of the material can be forgotten. Hence, reviewing information as soon as possible, decrease the hours of study, needed before examinations. Using small amounts of time for reviewing and avoiding marathon study sessions are advisable. Learning to budget the time, will give more time for frequent reviewing, so that less time is spent for cramming. A large part of time spent in study, would, however, need to be spent in repetition and in drill.

   The teachers are to keep the above points in mind and popularize them among the pupils, for their benefit.

8. **Parents involvement to improve study habits:** Parents should try to encourage their children's natural curiosity about the world. Parents can do this by talking to their children, by listening to their children and by answering their questions. Parents should also try to expose their children to as many exciting, stimulating things, as possible. Parents should take an interest in their children's education by joining Parents-Teachers Association (PTA) meetings or by becoming involved in their school activities. This will help to reinforce what they are learning.

EVERY STUDENT CAN LEARN, JUST NOT ON THE SAME DAY OR THE SAME WAY

Construction of the Study Habits Inventory

Study habits of an individual play an important role in his/her scholastic achievement. The review of related literature showed that there were a number of studies which established the relation, between study habits and academic achievement at school level. Very few studies were found which showed the relationship between study habits and achievement in the subject mathematics of 10th class students. Hence, the investigator felt it necessary to find a relationship between study habits of 10th class students and achievement in mathematics.

Though there were many Study Habits Inventories (SHI), constructed by Wrenn in 1933, ST Mary Esther in 1945, Jammur in 1958, on the students concentration, note taking, time budgeting, the investigator felt that the study Habits Inventory (SHI) constructed and standardized by Dr.B.V. Patel (1975), is worth using for the present investigation. The inventory consists of 45 statements which are classified into seven areas. The seven areas are:

1. Home environment and planning of the work
2. Their reading and note taking.
3. Their planning of the subject.
4. Their habits of concentration.
5. Their preparation for examination.
6. Their general habits and attitudes.
7. Their school environment.

Adoption of Study Habits Inventory

On examination of various instruments, developed to measure the study habits of secondary school children, the study habits inventory developed and standardized by Dr. B.V. Patel in 1975, is adopted to measure the study habits of the subjects included in the sample (N=1444), for the present study. The SHI consists of 45 items, out of which 27 items are positive and 18 are negative. The positive items are 1, 2, 3, 4, 8, 9, 10, 11,12, 13, 16, 17, 18, 19, 22, 26, 32, 33, 36, 37, 38, 39, 40, 41, 42, 43 and 44. The negative items are : 5, 6, 7, 14, 15, 20, 21, 23, 24, 25, 27, 28, 29, 30, 31, 34, 35 and 45.

Scoring Procedure

There are five alternatives for each item. The alternatives are Always, often, some times, seldom and never. For 'Positive' items marks 5 to 1 in the descending order are to be awarded and for negative items 1 to 5 in the ascending order are to be awarded. The above method of scoring is followed, while evaluating the SHI answer sheets. The English version of SHI is translated into Telugu, the regional language of the subjects. Five judges who are well versed with psychological testing, cheeked the translation. Terms which are ambiguous, are discussed and resolved.

The numerical values for different alternatives of positive and negative items are presented in Table 4.6.

Table 4.6. Numerical Values for Different Alternatives of Positive and Negative Items of SHI

Item	Alternatives				
	Always	Often	Some-times	Seldom	Never
Positive	5	4	3	2	1
Negative	1	2	3	4	5

At the end of each item five brackets are given and the students are asked to put a tick mark (√) in the appropriate bracket, which they felt is nearer to their study habit.

Administration of SHI

The Telugu version thus prepared is administered on all the subjects of the sample (N=1444) in the forenoon session. Necessary instructions are given to the pupils for answering the items and with the help of teachers the sheets are collected and scoring is done according to the weightage given by the author.

Reliability and Validity

For calculating reliability and validity of SHIs, the procedure suggested by H.E. Garrett (1973) is followed. The reliability of SHI is tested by employing split-half technique on a sample of 250. The reliability coefficient for half test is 0.88 and for the full test is 0.94. Test-retest reliability on a sample of 250 with a gap of 20 days is 0.96. This shows that the reliability of SHI is very high.

The validity of a test is an estimate of the correlations between the raw test scores and true criterion scores. There are various methods of estimating the validity of a measuring instrument. For the present study the following validities are established:

1. **Intrinsic validity:** Guilford (1954) stated that the square root of reliability gives the validity and hence it is 0.98.
2. **Face validity:** If a common thread runs through all the items of an inventory, the resultant test has face validity. All the items in the SHI of Dr. B.V. Patel have a common thread for measuring the study habits. Hence, there is face validity in SHI.

SELECTION OF SELF-CONCEPT SCALE

Self-concept has been variously defined as "The self as known to the self" (Murphy, 1947).

"Those aspects of the individual which seem most vital and important to the person." (Jersield 1960)

An infant does not bring Self-concept with him/her at the time of it's birth. Children acquire it by means of accidental or incidental learning. In the process of learning from interaction with others, the child not only develops self-concept but also develops an ideal towards which, it has to strive. Thus self-concept is a key variable in the behaviour of an individual.

In psychological discussion, the word 'self' has been used in many ways. Two chief meanings emerge - the 'self' as the subject or agent and the 'self' as the individual, who is known to himself/herself.

The term 'self-concept' has come into common use, to refer to the second meaning, which refers to the phenomenological approach. Self-concept refers to "The pictures or images a person has himself" (Taneja, 1991).

Allport (1961) has described self-concept as "Some thing of which we are immediately aware". We think of it as the warm, central, private region of our life. As such it plays a crucial part in our consciousness (a concept broader them self), in our personality (a concept broader than consciousness), and in our organism (a concept broader than personality). Thus it is some kind of core in our being.

Research studies have shown, how self-concept built in early years of life and reinforced in later experience, influence behaviour and characteristic reactions to the people and situations.

Because self-concept is dominant in personality pattern, the measurement of self-concept becomes very essential. If we want to understand the personality of an individual, to understand and predict his life adjustment and his success and failure, we can not proceed further without knowing this "self-concept". Thus, it is some kind of core in our being.

Adoption of the Self-concept Scale

On examination of the various instruments developed to measure self-concept, the investigator felt that the self-concept scale (SCS) developed by Rastogi (1974) is more suitable for the purpose of present study. This scale consists of 51 items, divided into 10 areas. Out of these 51 items, 23 are positive and 28 are negative. It is a five-point attitude scale with alternatives, Strongly Agree (SA), Agree (U), disagree (DA), and Strongly DisAgree (SDA). The ten areas are:

1. Health and sex appropriateness,
2. Abilities,
3. Self-confidence,

4. Self-acceptance,
5. Worthiness,
6. Present, past and future,
7. Beliefs and convictions,
8. Feeling of shame and guilt,
9. Sociability, and
10. Emotional maturity.

Table 4.7. The Item Numbers in Each Area of the Self-concept Scale

Sl. No.	Description	Item Numbers							
1.	Health Sex Appropriateness	6 P	20 P	29 N	22 N	34 P	46 P		
2.	Abilities	4 P	8 P	12 N	23 N	36 P	38 N	39 N	42 P
3.	Self-confidence	7 P	9 P	14 N	15 N	44 P			
4.	Self-acceptance	2 P	10 N	17 N	35 N				
5.	Worthiness	1 P	3 N	19 N	25 P	27 P	41 N	48 P	
6.	Present, Past & future	18 P	22 P	26 N	31 N	40 P			
7.	Beliefs and Convictions	24 N	47 P	49 P					
8.	Feeling of Shame and guilt	5 N	13 N	28 N	30 N	50 N			
9.	Sociability	33 N	37 P	43 P	45 N				
10.	Emotional Maturity	11 N	15 N	21 N	51 N				

Note: The letters P or N Shown below indicate positiveness or negativeness.

This scale is translated into Telugu version with experts in psychological tests and is used for the present investigation. The item numbers of each area of self-concept scale are presented in the Table 4.7.

The self-concept inventory consists of 51 items of which 23 are positive and 28 are negative.

Scoring Procedure

The adapted SCS is a five-point scale with alternatives, Strongly Agree, Agree, Undecided, Disagree and Strongly Disagree. For the purpose of scoring, numerical values were assigned for each of the above shown alternatives, which are shown in The Table 4.8.

Table 4.8. Numerical Values for Different Alternatives of the Positive and Negative Items of the SCS

Item	Alternatives				
	Strongly Agree (SA)	Agree (A)	Undecided (U)	Disagree (DA)	Strongly Disagree SDA
Positive	5	4	3	2	1
Negative	1	2	3	4	5

Validity of the Scale

The validity of the scale or tool refers to its "accuracy", how closely it measures, what it actually intends to measure. For this self-concept scale, the author Rastogi (1974) reported the following validies (*i*) Content validity (*ii*) Criterion validity and (*iii*) Construct validity.

Reliability

Reliability can be defined as the degree of consistency between two measures of the same thing. Several methods are used to estimate the reliability. The more common ones reported in the text manuals are:

1. Measures of stability (test-retest)
2. Measures of equivalence
3. Measures of internal consistency
4. Split-Half method
5. Kurder-Richardson's estimates.

Split-Half Reliability : In this study internal consistency is measured thorough Split-Half method by the investigator. The procedure described by Garrett (1973) is employed. The correlation coefficient for half test, with a sample of 250, is 0.8432. The correlation coefficient for full test

$$\left(r = \frac{2r_h}{1 + r_h} \right)$$

is also calculated which is equal to 0.9149. It shows the reliability of the instrument is very high.

Administration of Self-concept Scale (SCS)

The Telugu Version of SCS is administered on all the subjects (N=1444) of the sample, in the forenoon session of the school. Necessary instructions for answering the items, are given to the students. Teacher's help is taken in conducting the test and collecting all the data sheets. Scoring is done according to the weightage, given by the author.

PERSONAL DATA SHEET

The personal data sheet prepared by the investigator with the help of experts in the field of education consists of the following particulars, with regard to the pupil's personal, socio-demographic variables.

1. Name of the pupil
2. Name of the school
3. Gender (sex)
4. Locality

5. Age
6. Caste
7. Birth order
8. Number of members in the family
9. Mother's education
10. Father's education
11. Mother's occupation
12. Father's occupation
13. Religion
14. Income of the family
15. Economic status
16. Separate Room for study
17. study hours at home
18. Help from family members
19. works at home
20. Time spent for mathematics daily

FINAL STUDY

The final study is conducted after the construction and standardization of all the tools and adoption of the tools as described in the preceding pages.

Selection of Sample for Final Study

After the construction, standardization and adoption of all the test tools, the investigator has planned for the selection of the sample for the final study. Geographically the district is divided into four revenue divisions namely, Tirupati, Madanapally, Palamaner and Chittoor. The investigator selected 22 schools, in the four revenue divisions, following the stratified random sampling method. The total sample consists of 1444 students of 10th class. The sample design for the final study is shown in the Table 4.9.

Table 4.9 : Sample Design for Final Study

Sl. No.	Name of the School	Management	Total No. of students	Remarks
1.	Z.P.Girls High School, Vayalpad	Zilla Parishad	56	Only Girls
2.	Z.P. High School, Tariganda	Zilla Parishad	96	Co-education
3.	Z.P. High School, Rompicherla	Zilla Parishad	71	Co-education
4.	Z.P. High School, Kurabala Kota	Zilla Parishad	82	Co-education
5.	Z.P. High School, Bandapalli	Zilla Parishad	49	Co-education
6.	Z.P. High School, Angallu	Zilla Parishad	43	Co-education
7.	Z.P. High School, Chintaparthi.	Zilla Parishad	102	Co-education
8.	Z.P. High School Pachikapallam	Zilla Parishad	101	Co-education
9.	Z.P. High School, Papanaidu Pet	Zilla Parishad	92	Co-education
10.	Z.P. High School, Naraharipet	Zilla Parishad	49	Co-education
11.	P.C.R. Govt. High School, Chittoor.	Government	47	Co-education
12.	Govt. High School, Madanapalli	Government	78	Girls
13.	Govt. High School, Piler	Government	79	Co-education
14.	Hope Municipal High School, Madanapally	Municipality	88	Co-education
15.	T.P.P.M School, Tirupati	Municipality	53	Co-education

Sl. No.	Name of the School	Management	Total No. of students	Remarks
16.	Municipal High School, Kongareddy pally, Chittoor	Municipality	51	Co-education
17.	A.P.S.W.R. Junior College Burakayala Kota	Social Welfare Dept	62	Girls
18.	A.P.S.W.R School, Palamaneru	Social Welfare Dept	50	Girls
19.	A.P.S.W.R School, Rama Kuppam	Social Welfare Dept	51	Boys
20.	Vidyavihar E.M. School, Chittoor	Private Un aided	37	Co-education
21.	Rayalaseema High School, Tirupati	Private Un aided	42	Co-education
22.	Gnanodaya High School, Madanapally	Private Un aided	65	Co-education
	Total		1,444	

Revenue Division-wise Schools

Eight schools from Madanapally Revenue Division, six schools from Chittoor Revenue Division and four Schools each, from Tirupati and Palamaner Revenue Divisions are selected for final study.

Management-wise Schools

Ten schools, under the management of Zilla Parishad, three schools under the management of government, three schools under the management of Social Welfare Department, Government of Andhra Pradesh, and three schools under private management unaided schools are selected for final study. The criterion of selection of the number of schools from different managements, is the total number of schools, under these managements in the entire district. The sample design for Management vs sex is presented in Table 4.10.

Table 4.10. The Sample Design for Management Vs Sex

Management	Z.P.	Govt.	Municipal	A.P.S.	Private	Total
Female	388	128	114	112	52	794
Male	353	76	78	51	92	650
Total	**741**	**204**	**192**	**163**	**144**	**1444**

The sample design for Locality Vs Caste is shown in the Table 4.11.

Table 4.11. The Sample Design for Locality Vs Caste

Locality Caste	Village	Small Town	Municipal Town	Total
SC/ST	77	171	145	393
BC	237	198	193	628
OC	116	122	185	423
Total	**430**	**491**	**523**	**1444**

The Geographical map showing Chittoor District in Andhra Pradesh is presented in Fig. 4.2.

Administration of Tools

Having selected the schools, following stratified random sampling method, the investigator consulted the heads of Institutions selected, personally and explained them, the purpose of the test and took their permission for holding the test. The test dates for different schools were intimated sufficiently in advance. The students were thoroughly motivated for the tests and they were given proper instructions for answering the different sets of test tools. The investigator visited all the schools personally, as decided and intimated earlier. In the morning session, the sets of HSPQ, self concept scale and study habits inventories are given to the students and with the help of teachers of concerned schools, the tests are administrated. In the afternoon session, the OAT paper and personal data sheets are given to the students. Through inspection is made with the help of

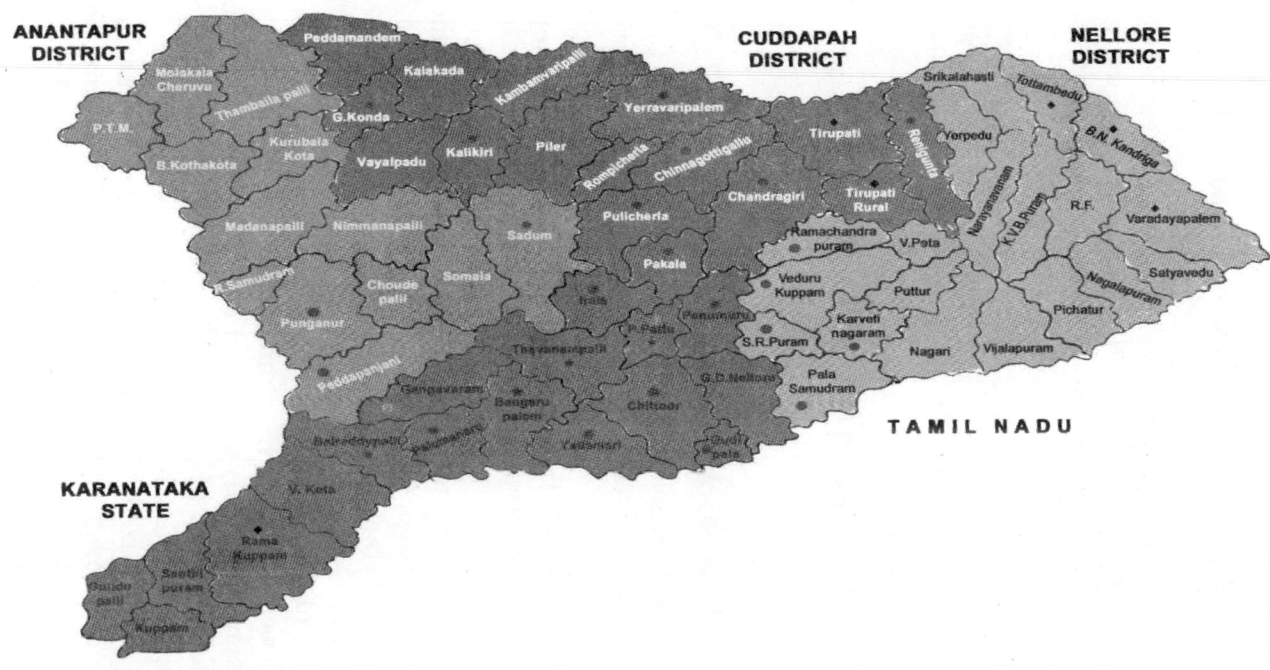

Fig. 2: The Geographical map showing Chittoor District in Andhra Pradesh

concerned school teachers, when the students are answering the different test tools. The students who attended the school on the day of collection of data are considered for the purpose of investigation. All the data gathering instruments are collected from the students and they are evaluated following the weightages given by the test constructing authorities concerned. All the collected data are given for statistical analysis.

SCORING

Scoring is done as already explained in the preceding pages, under each tool

CODING OF THE DATA

The data on each variable is properly coded to suit for computer analysis.

STATISTICAL ANALYSIS

On the basis of the objectives of the investigation, statistical analysis is carried out by employing appropriate statistical techniques.

Frequency distribution tables, on the scholastic achievement are prepared for the total sample, for different managements, for male students, female students, for different localities and castes. Measures of central tendency, measures of dispersion, skewness, kurtosis, co-efficient of variation and standard error of mean are computed and used wherever necessary. The inferential statistical techniques like 't' test and 'F' tests are employed to test the different Hypotheses. Multiple "R" is computed by carrying out, step wise regression analysis to find out, whether it would be possible to predict scholastic achievements in mathematics of X class students. The services of S.V. University computer centre are utilized. The obtained numerical values are adumberated by graphical representations. For dividing the groups, quartile values and Sten values are used wherever necessary. Sufficient number of tables are prepared.

For Statistical Formulae, the following text books were consulted:

1. "Fundamental Statistics in Psychology and Education" by Guilford (1950).
2. "Statistics in Psychology and Education" by Henry. E. Garrette, (1973).
3. "Psychometric Methods" by Guilford (1954).
4. "Statistical Principles in Experimental Design" by Winner (1971).
5. "Non-Parametric Statistics for the Behavioural Science" by Sidney Siegel (1956).
6. "Statistics in Psychology" by YATE (1965).
7. "Statistics in Psychology and Education" by S.K. Mangal (2002).
8. "Applied Regression Analysis" by Dr. Apper and Smith (1981).
9. "Statistical Methods" by Gupta (1974).
10. "Statistical Methods for research workers" by Fresher (1950).
11. Techniques of Attitude scale construction by ED Wards (1969).

The significant levels employed with respective symbols are given here under:

1. ** Indicates significant at 0.01 level.
2. * Indicates Significant at 0.05 level.
3. @ Indicates insignificant at 0.05 level.

Analysis and Interpretation of the Data

This chapter deals with analysis and interpretation of the data. The analysis is presented in the following form:

1. Frequency Distribution Tables.
2. Factorial Designs
3. 't' values and 'F' Ratios with respect to the influence of the independent variables on the dependent variable, and
4. Regression Analysis.

FREQUENCY DISTRIBUTION TABLES

The frequency distribution tables for the scholastic achievement scores of 10th class students in mathematics are presented in the following pages.

Frequency Distribution of Scholastic Achievement Scores for the Whole Group

The scholastic achievement test in mathematics is conducted for 100 marks. The test consists of 100 multiple choice questions. The data are collected on 1444 students studying under different managements. It is clear from Table 5.1 that the mean value is 44.97. The median and mode values are 41.00 and 33.06 respectively. The values of skewness is 0.82 and Kurtosis is 3.39. For normal distribution the value of skewness is 0.00 and Kurtosis is 3.00. Hence, the frequency distribution is positively skewed and leptokurtic. (The values skewness and Kurtosis are computed based on moments; Aggarwal, 1990). It implies that the scores are massed at the low/left end of the scale, and are spread out gradually towards high right end of the scale. The distribution is more peaked than the normal distribution. On the whole the performance of the 10th class students in mathematics is poor, because mean achievement is less than 50.

Table 5.1. Frequency Distribution of Scholastic Achievement Scores of 10th Class Students in Mathematics for the Total Sample

Sl.No.	CI	Limits	Midpoint	f	cf	cpf
1.	11-20	10.5-20.5	15.5	29	29	2.01
2.	21-30	20.5-30.5	25.5	231	260	18.01
3.	31-40	30.5-40.5	35.5	446	706	48.89
4.	41-50	40.5-50.5	45.5	302	1008	69.81
5.	51-60	50.5-60.5	55.5	181	1189	82.34
6.	61-70	60.5-70.5	65.5	124	1313	90.93
7.	71-80	70.5-80.5	75.5	72	1385	95.91
8.	81-90	80.5-90.5	85.5	37	1422	98.48
9.	91-100	90.5-100.5	95.5	22	1444	100

N = 1444, M = 44.97, Md = 41.00, Mo = 33.06, R = 85.00
QD = 10.50, SD = 16.50, S_k = 0.82, K_u = 3.39, CV = 36.69, SE_M = 0.43

The histogram for the distribution of scholastic achievement scores in mathematics for the whole group is presented in Fig. 5.1.

The frequency polygon for the distribution of scholastic achievement scores in mathematics is shown in Fig. 5.2.

The Ogive for the distribution of scholastic achievement scores in mathematics is presented in Fig. 5.3.

The Distribution characteristics namely Mean, (M), Median (Md), Mode (MO), Range (R), Quartile Deviation (QD), Standard Deviation (SD), Skewness (Sk), Kurtosis (KU), Coefficient of variation (CV) and standard error of Mean (SE_M) are also presented in Table 5.1.

Frequency Distribution of Scholastic Achievement Scores for the Variable Management

There are five divisions in the variable 'management' namely 1. Zilla Parishad Schools, 2. Government Schools, 3.

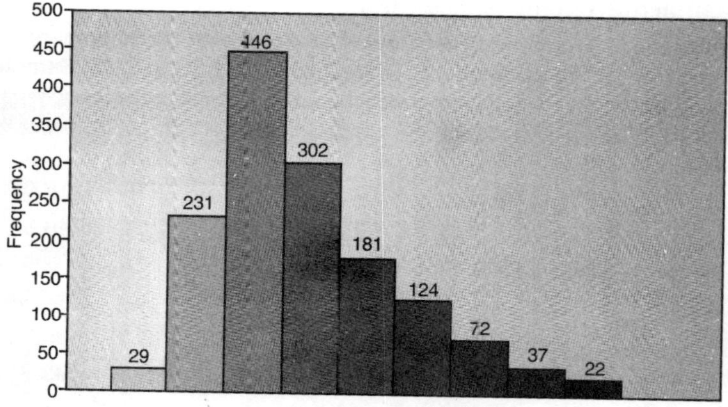

Fig. 5.1. The Historgram for the distrubutionof scholastic achievement scores in mathematics for the whole group

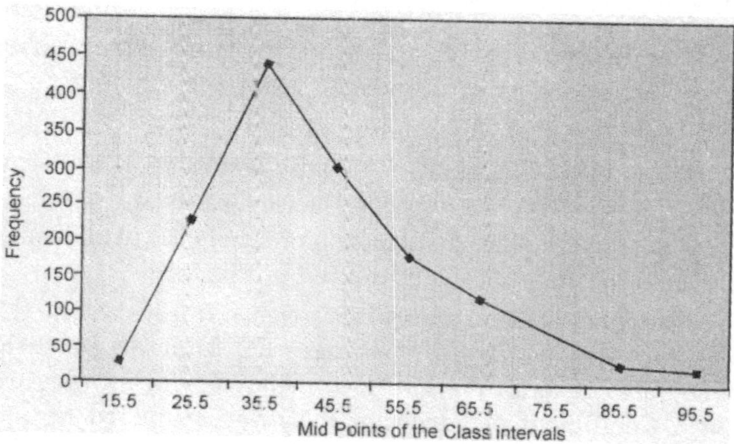

Fig. 5.2. Frequency Polygon for the distribution of scholastic achievement scroes for the whole group

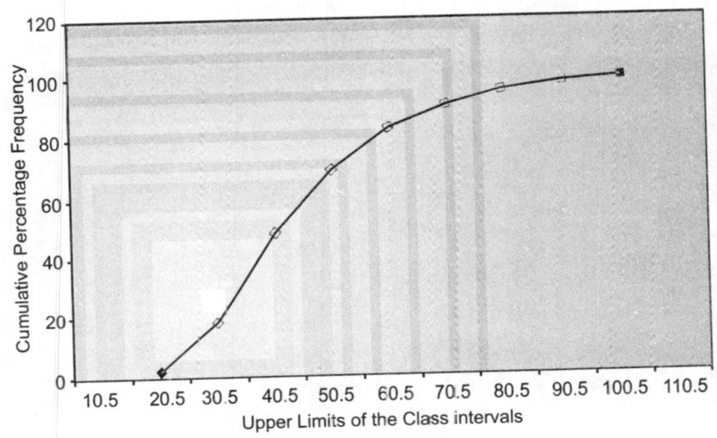

Fig. 5.3. The Ogive for the distribution of schloastic achievement scroes for the whole group

Table 5.2: Frequency Distribution of Scholastic Achievement Scores in Mathematics of 10th Class Pupils for Zilla Parishad Students

Sl.No.	CI	Limits	Midpoint	f	cf	cpf
1.	11-20	10.5-20.5	15.5	8	8	1.08
2.	21-30	20.5-30.5	25.5	108	116	15.65
3.	31-40	30.5-40.5	35.5	239	355	47.91
4.	41-50	40.5-50.5	45.5	266	521	70.31
5.	51-60	50.5-60.5	55.5	96	617	83.27
6.	61-70	60.5-70.5	65.5	66	683	92.17
7.	71-80	70.5-80.5	75.5	32	715	96.49
8.	81-90	80.5-90.5	85.5	15	730	98.52

N = 741, M = 45.05, Md = 41 00, Mo = 32.09, R = 81.00
QD = 10.00, SD = 15.76, S_k = 0.89, K_u = 3.58, CV = 35.00, SE_M = 0.58

It is observed from Table 5.2 to 5.6 that the students studying in private schools have better achievement than the students in other types of schools. The achievement of the students studying in government schools is the lowest as compared to the achievement of the students studying in other types of schools.

Table 5.3. Frequency Distribution Table of Scholastic Achievement Scores in Mathematics of 10th Class Students for Govt. Schools

Sl.No.	CI	Limits	Midpoint	f	cf	cpf
1.	11-20	10.5-20.5	15.5	4	4	5.85
2.	21-30	20.5-30.5	25.5	54	58	31.71
3.	31-40	30.5-40.5	35.5	78	136	61.46
4.	41-50	40.5-50.5	45.5	41	177	82.93
5.	51-60	50.5-60.5	55.5	15	192	94.15
6.	61-70	60.5-70.5	65.5	6	198	97.05
7.	71-80	70.5-80.5	75.5	3	201	98.53
8.	81-90	80.5-90.5	85.5	2	203	99.51

N = 204, M = 38.09, Md = 35.00, Mo = 28.81, R = 68.00
QD = 7.00, SD = 12.05, S_k = 1.71, Ku = 5.35, CV = 31.64, SE_M = 0.84

Table 5.4. Frequency Distribution Table of Scholastic Achievement Scores in Mathematics of 10th Class Students for Municipal School Students.

Sl.No.	CI	Limits	Midpoint	f	cf	cpf
1.	11-20	10.5-20.5	15.5	15	15	3.65
2.	21-30	20.5-30.5	25.5	54	69	35.94
3.	31-40	30.5-40.5	35.5	55	124	64.58
4.	41-50	40.5-50.5	45.5	30	154	80.21
5.	51-60	50.5-60.5	55.5	19	173	90.10
6.	61-70	60.5-70.5	65.5	10	183	95.31
7.	71-80	70.5-80.5	75.5	4	187	97.40
8.	81-90	80.5-90.5	85.5	4	191	99.48

N = 192, M = 38.93, Md = 36.00, Mo = 30.15, R = 79.00
QD = 10.00, SD = 15.43, S_k = 1.09, K_u = 3.99, CV = 39.64, SE_M = 1.11

The Standard Deviation of the achievement scores in private schools is more than all others. The standard Deviation of the achievement scores in government schools is the least. The value of skewness is positive for all the distributions. It implies that the scores are massed at low/left end of the scale and are spread out gradually towards the high/right end of the scale. The distributions of achievement scores are leptokurtic for the students studying in Zilla Parishad, government and municipal schools where as the distribution of achievement scores are platykurtic for the students studying in A.P. Social Welfare Residential and private schools.

Table 5.5. Frequency Distribution Table of Scholastic Achievement Scores in Mathematics of 10th class students for A.P. Social Welfare Residential Schools.

Sl.No.	CI	Limits	Midpoint	f	cf	cpf
1.	21-30	20.5-30.5	25.5	8	8	3.42
2.	31-40	30.5-40.5	35.5	42	50	32.48
3.	41-50	40.5-50.5	45.5	35	85	52.99
4.	51-60	50.5-60.5	55.5	28	113	68.38
5.	61-70	60.5-70.5	65.5	21	134	80.34
6.	71-80	70.5-80.5	75.5	19	153	92.31
7.	81-900	80.5-90.5	85.5	4	157	94.87

N = 163, M = 52.51, Md = 49.00, Mo = 41.96, R = 73.00
QD = 12.00, SD = 16.99, S_k = 0.40, K_u = 2.58, CV = 32.35, SE_M = 1.33

Table 5.6. Frequency Distribution Table of Scholastic Achievement Scores in Mathematics of 10th Class Students for Private Schools

Sl.No.	CI	Limits	Midpoint	f	cf	cpf
1.	11-20	10.5-20.5	15.5	2	2	1.39
2.	21-30	20.5-30.5	25.5	7	9	6.25
3.	31-40	30.5-40.5	35.5	32	41	28.47
4.	41-50	40.5-50.5	45.5	30	71	49.31
5.	51-60	50.5-60.5	55.5	23	94	65.28
6.	61-70	60.5-70.5	65.5	20	114	79.17
7.	71-80	70.5-80.5	75.5	14	128	88.89
8.	81-90	80.5-90.5	85.5	12	140	97.22
9.	91-100	90.5-100.5	95.5	4	144	100.00

N = 144, M = 53.78, Md = 51.00, Mo = 45.44, R = 78.00
QD = 14.50, SD = 18.52, S_k = 0.18, K_u = 2.30, CV = 34.43, SE_M = 1.54

The bar diagram for the mean achievement scores for the different groups of the variable 'management' is shown in Fig. 5.4.

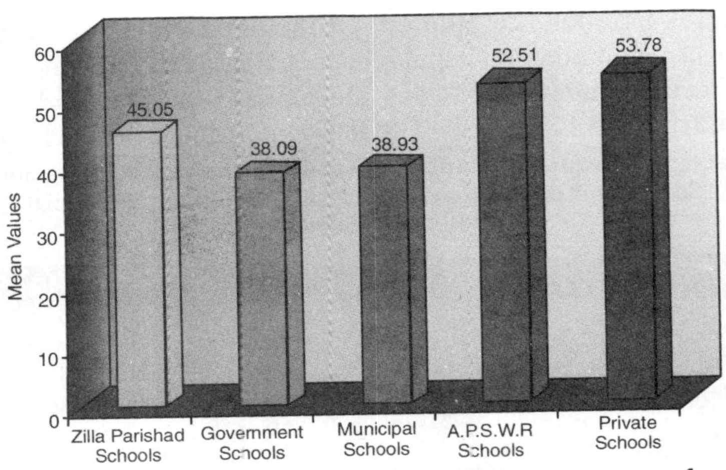

Fig. 5.4. The Bar Diagram for the achievement scroes for different groups of Management

Frequency Distribution Table for the Scholastic Achievement Scores for the Variable 'Sex'

There are two divisions in the variable 'sex' namely 1. Females and 2. Males. The frequency distributions and distribution characteristics on achievement scores for both the groups are presented from Tables 5.7 to 5.8.

Table 5.7: Frequency Distribution Table for Scholastic Achievement Scores in Mathematics of 10th Class Students for Female Students.

Sl.No.	CI	Limits	Midpoint	f	cf	cpf
1.	11-20	10.5-20.5	15.5	21	21	2.64
2.	21-30	20.5-30.5	25.5	132	153	19.27
3.	31-40	30.5-40.5	35.5	260	413	52.02
4.	41-50	40.5-50.5	45.5	164	577	72.67
5.	51-60	50.5-60.5	55.5	85	662	83.38
6.	61-70	60.5-70.5	65.5	64	726	91.44
7.	71-80	70.5-80.5	75.5	40	766	96.47
8.	81-90	80.5-90.5	85.5	18	784	98.74
9.	91-100	90.5-100.5	95.5	10	794	100.00

N = 794, M = 43.86, Md = 40.00, Mo = 32.27, R = 85.00
QD = 9.50, SD = 16.34 S_k = 0.96, K_u = 3.61, CV = 37.26, SE_M = 0.58

Table 5.8: Frequency Distribution Table for Scholastic Achievement Scores in Mathematics of 10th Class Students for Male Students

Sl.No.	CI	Limits	Midpoint	f	cf	cpf
1.	11-20	10.5-20.5	15.5	8	8	1.23
2.	21-30	20.5-30.5	25.5	99	107	16.46
3.	31-40	30.5-40.5	35.5	186	293	45.08
4.	41-50	40.5-50.5	45.5	138	431	66.31
5.	51-60	50.5-60.5	55.5	96	527	81.08
6.	61-70	60.5-70.5	65.5	60	587	90.31
7.	71-80	70.5-80.5	75.5	32	619	95.23
8.	81-90	80.5-90.5	85.5	19	638	98.15
9.	91-100	90.5-100.5	95.5	12	650	100.00

N = 650, M = 46.32, Md = 43.00, Mo = 36.36, R = 81.00
QD = 11.50, SD = 16.59, S_k = 0.69, K_u = 3.18, CV = 35.82, SE_M = 0.65

It is observed from the above tables that there are 650 male students and 794 female students. (Some of the schools selected at random, keeping in view the management and locality, are girls high schools (04). Further in almost all co-education schools the number of female students and male students are nearly equal. Hence, there is a little increase in the number of female students). The mean of female students is 43.86 and that of male students is 46.32. Hence, the male student's performance is slightly better than female students. The standard deviations of achievement scores of both female and male students are almost equal (16.34 and 16.59 respectively). The values of skewness are positive for both the distributions. It implies that the scores are massed at low/ left end of the scale and are spread out gradually towards the high/ right end of the scale for both the groups.

The values of Kurtosis for female and male students are 3.61 and 3.18 respectively. Hence the distributions of achievement scores are slightly lefto-kurtic for both the groups.

The bar diagram for the mean achievement scores for females and males is given in Fig. 5.5.

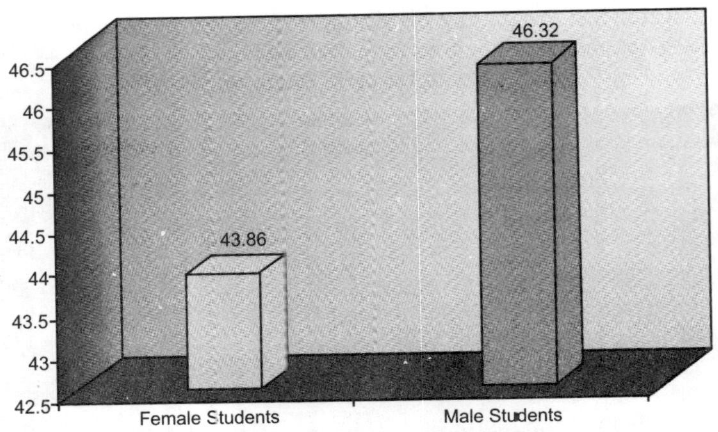

Fig. 5.5. The Bar Diagram for the mean achievements scores for Female and Male students

Frequency Distribution Tables for the Scholastic Achievement Scores for the Variable 'Locality'

There are three divisions in the variable 'locality' namely, 1. students belonging to rural areas (villages). 2. Students belonging to semi-urban areas (small towns) and 3. Students belonging to municipal towns (urban). The frequency

Table 5.9. Frequency Distribution Table for Scholastic Achievement Scores in Mathematics of 10th Class Students for Rural areas

Sl.No.	CI	Limits	Midpoint	f	cf	cpf
1.	11-20	10.5-20.5	15.5	6	6	1.40
2.	21-30	20.5-30.5	25.5	48	54	12.56
3.	31-40	30.5-40.5	35.5	125	179	41.63
4.	41-50	40.5-50.5	45.5	97	276	61.19
5.	51-60	50.5-60.5	55.5	64	340	79.07
6.	61-70	60.5-70.5	65.5	50	390	90.70
7.	71-80	70.5-80.5	75.5	20	410	95.35
8.	81-90	80.5-90.5	85.5	11	421	97.91
9.	91-100	90.5-100.5	95.5	9	430	100.00

N = 430, M = 47.26, Md = 44.00, Mo = 37.48, R = 79.00
QD = 11.50, SD = 16.41, S_k = 0.59, K_u=3.21, CV = 34.73, SE_M = 0.79

distributions and distribution characteristics on achievement scores for the students of three types of localities are presented from the Tables 5.9 to 5.11.

Table 5.10. Frequency Distribution Table for Scholastic Achievement Scores in Mathematics of 10th Class Students for Semi- Urban Areas.

Sl.No.	CI	Limits	Midpoint	f	cf	cpf
1.	11-20	10.5-20.5	15.5	3	3	0.61
2.	21-30	20.5-30.5	25.5	78	81	16.50
3.	31-40	30.5-40.5	35.5	169	250	50.92
4.	41-50	40.5-50.5	45.5	111	361	73.52
5.	51-60	50.5-60.5	55.5	56	417	84.93
6.	61-70	60.5-70.5	65.5	31	448	91.24
7.	71-80	70.5-80.5	75.5	26	474	96.54
8.	81-90	80.5-90.5	85.5	9	483	98.37

N = 491, M = 44.39, Md = 40.00, Mo = 31.23, R = 80.00
QD = 10.00, SD = 15.75, S_k = 1.26, K_U = 3.92, CV = 35.48, SE_M = 0.71

Table 5.11. Frequency Distribution Table for Scholastic Achievement Scores of 10th Class Students in Mathematics for Urban Areas

Sl.No.	CI	Limits	Midpoint	f	cf	cpf
1.	11-20	10.5-20.5	15.5	20	20	3.82
2.	21-30	20.5-30.5	25.5	105	125	23.90
3.	31-40	30.5-40.5	35.5	152	277	52.96
4.	41-50	40.5-50.5	45.5	94	371	70.94
5.	51-60	50.5-60.5	55.5	61	432	82.60
6.	61-70	60.5-70.5	75.5	26	501	95.79
7.	71-80	70.5-80.5	85.5	17	518	99.04
8.	81-90	80.5-90.5	95.5	5	523	100.0

N = 523, M = 43.63, Md = 39.00, Mo = 29.71, R = 84.00
QD = 11.00, SD = 17.06, S_k = 0.77, K_U = 3.75, CV = 39.10, SE_M = 0.75

From the Table 5.9 to 5.11 it is observed that there are 430 rural students, 491 semi urban students and 523 urban students. The means for rural, semi urban and urban pupils are 47.26, 44.39 and 43.63 respectively. These values show that the performance of rural pupils is better than semi urban and urban students. The achievement of semi-urban pupils is better than urban pupils.

The values of skewness is positive for all the distributions. It implies that the scores are massed at low/ left end of the scale and are spread out gradually towards the right end of the scale.

The values of kurtosis for rural, semi urban and urban students are 3.21, 3.92 and 3.75 respectively. Hence, the distributions of achievement scores for all the groups are slightly lepto-kurtic.

The bar diagram showing the mean achievement of rural, semi urban and urban pupils is presented in Fig. 5.8.

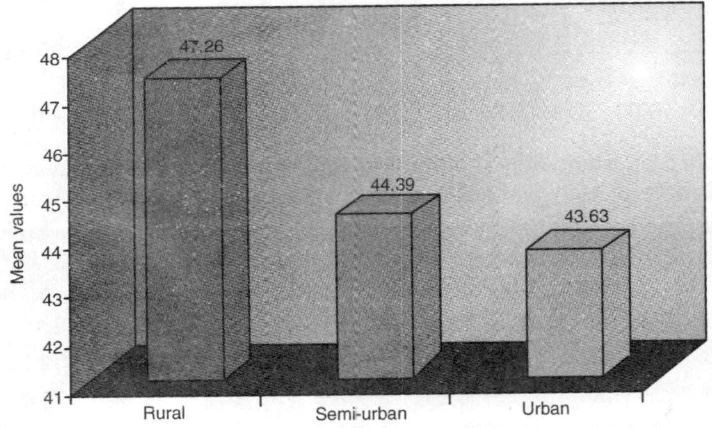

Fig. 6. The Bar Diagram for the mean achievemetn scroes of Rural, Semi-urban and Urban Pupils

Frequency Distribution Tables for the Scholastic Achievement Scores for the Variable 'caste'

There are three divisions in the variable 'caste' namely 1. Scheduled Caste/ Tribes (SC/ST), 2 Backward Caste (BC), 3. Other Castes (OC). The frequency distributions and distribution characteristics on achievement scores for the students of the above three types, are presented from Tables 5.12 to 5.14.

Table 5.12: Frequency Distribution Table for Scholastic Achievement Scores of 10th Class Students in Mathematics for SC/ST Students

S.No.	CI	Limits	Midpoint	f	cf	cpf
1.	11-20	10.5-20.5	15.5	8	8	2.04
2.	21-30	20.5-30.5	25.5	58	66	16.79
3.	31-40	30.5-40.5	35.5	134	200	50.89
4.	41-50	40.5-50.5	45.5	79	279	70.99
5.	51-60	50.5-60.5	55.5	50	329	83.72
6.	61-70	60.5-70.5	65.5	29	358	91.09
7.	71-80	70.5-80.5	75.5	21	379	96.44
8.	81-90	80.5-90.5	85.5	6	385	97.96
9.	91-100	90.5-100.5	95.5	8	393	100.00

N = 393, M = 44.54, Md = 40.00, Mo = 30.93, R = 80.00

QD = 10.00, SD = 16.06, S_k = 1.07, K_U = 3.75, CV = 36.06, SE_M = 0.81

Table 5.13: Frequency Distribution Table for Scholastic Achievement Scores of 10th Class Students in Mathematics for BC Students

S.No.	CI	Limits	Midpoint	f	cf	cpf
1.	11-20	10.5-20.5	15.5	14	14	2.23
2.	21-30	20.5-30.5	25.5	121	135	21.50
3.	31-40	30.5-40.5	35.5	82	317	50.48
4.	41-50	40.5-50.5	45.5	131	448	71.34
5.	51-60	50.5-60.5	55.5	75	523	83.28
6.	61-70	60.5-70.5	65.5	55	578	92.04
7.	71-80	70.5-80.5	75.5	26	604	96.18
8.	81-90	80.5-90.5	85.5	14	618	98.41

N = 628, M = 44.00, Md = 40.00, Mo = 32.01, R = 85.00

QD = 11.00, SD = 16.58, S_k = 0.88, K_U = 3.51, CV = 37.68, SE_M = 0.66

From the Tables 5.12, 5.13 and 5.14, it is observed that there are 393 SC/ST students, (as the number of ST students are very less, SC and ST are clubbed), 628 BC students and 423 OC students (Total sample N=1444). It is observed from the above tables that the mean performance of SC/ST (44.54) and BC (44.00) students is almost equal where as the performance of OC (46.8) students is better than SC/ST and BC students. The standard deviations of the achievement scores of OC students is more than all others. The value of skewness is positive for all the distributions. It implies that the scores are massed at low/ left end of the scale and are spread out gradually towards the high/ right.

Table 5.14: Frequency Distribution Table for Scholastic Achievement Scores in Mathematics of 10th Class Students for OC Students

S.No.	CI	Limits	Midpoint	f	cf	cpf
1.	11-20	10.5-20.5	15.5	7	7	1.65
2.	21-30	20.5-30.5	25.5	52	59	13.95
3.	31-40	30.5-40.5	35.5	130	189	44.68
4.	41-50	40.5-50.5	45.5	92	281	66.43
5.	51-60	50.5-60.5	55.5	56	337	79.67
6.	61-70	60.5-70.5	65.5	40	377	89.13
7.	71-80	70.5-80.5	75.5	25	402	95.04
8.	81-90	80.5-90.5	85.5	17	419	99.05
9.	91-100	90.5-100.5	95.5	4	423	100.00

N=423, M=46.81, Md=43.00, Mo=35.37, R=80.00

QD=10.50, SD=16.64, S_k=0.59 K_U=3.00, CV=35.54, SE_M = 0.81

The values of kurtosis for SC/ST, BC and OC students are 3.75, 3.51 and 3.00 respectively. Hence, the distributions of achievement scores for SC/ST and BC students are slightly leptokurtic whereas the distribution of achievement scores for OC students is meso kurtic (Normal).

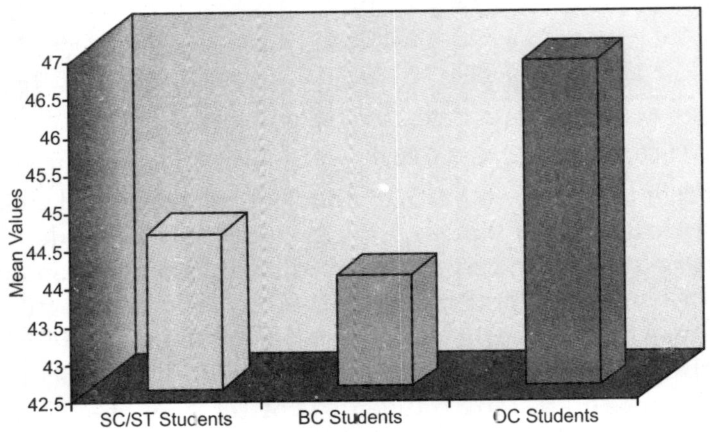

Fig. 5.7. The Bar Diagram for the Mean achievement scross of SC/ST, BC, OC Students

The bar diagram for the mean achievement scores of SC/ST, BC and OC students is presented in Fig. 5.7.

The values of N, M, SD, S_k, K_u, R and SE_M for the distribution of scholastic achievement scores.

The values of N, M, S.D, S_k, K_u, R and SE_M for the distribution of scholastic achievement scores in mathematics of 10th class students for the different groups of the sample are presented in Table 5.15.

Table 5.15: The values of N, M, S.D, S_k, K_u, R and SE_M for the Distribution of Scholastic Achievement Scores in Mathematics of 10th Class Students for the Different Groups of Sample

Sl. No.	Group	N	M	SD	S_k	K_u	R	SE_M
1.	Whole group	1444	44.97	16.50	0.82	3.39	85	0.43
2.	Zilla Parishad Schools	741	45.05	15.77	0.89	3.58	81	0.58
3.	Government Schools	204	38.10	12.05	1.71	5.35	68	0.84
4.	Municipal Schools	192	38.93	15.43	1.10	3.99	79	1.11
5.	A.P. Social Welfare Residential Schools	163	52.52	16.99	0.40	2.58	73	1.33
6.	Private Schools	144	53.78	18.51	0.18	2.30	78	1.54
7.	Males	650	46.31	16.60	0.69	3.18	81	0.65
8.	Females	794	43.86	16.34	0.96	3.61	85	0.58
9.	Rural	430	47.26	16.41	0.59	3.21	79	0.79
10.	Semi-urban	491	44.39	15.75	1.26	3.92	80	0.71
11.	Urban	523	43.63	17.06	0.77	3.23	84	0.75
12.	SC/ST	393	44.54	16.06	1.07	3.75	80	0.81
13.	BC	628	44.00	16.58	0.88	3.51	85	0.66
14.	OC	423	46.81	16.64	0.59	3.00	80	0.81

It is clear from the Table 5.15 that the mean scholastic achievement for the students of private schools is the highest (53.78) among all the groups and the lowest (38.10) for the students of Government schools. The standard deviation of achievement scores for the students of private schools is the highest (18.51) among all the groups and the lowest (12.05) for the students of government schools.

The values of skewness for all the groups is positive. It implies that the scores are massed at low/left end of the scale and slowly spread over towards the high/right end of the scale. The value of kurtosis for the OC students is normal. The values of kurtosis for the students of private schools (2.30) and A.P. Social Welfare Residential Schools (2.58) are less than the normal value (3.00) and hence the distributions are platy curtic. The value of kurtosis for the students of government schools (5.35) is the highest among all the groups and the distribution is highly leptokurtic. For all the remaining groups, the values of kurtosis are slightly greater than the normal value (3.00) and hence the distributions are slightly leftokurtic.

FACTORIAL DESIGNS

The influence of the variables management, sex, locality and caste and their interactions on the scholastic achievement of 10th class students in mathematics is studied with the help of factorial designs.

Factorial Design for Management and sex

The influence of management and sex on scholastic achievement of 10th class students in mathematics is investigated by employing 5×2 Factorial Design.

The following hypotheses are formulated :

Hypothesis 1

There would be no significant influence of main effects namely management and sex on the scholastic achievement of students in mathematics.

Hypothesis 2

There would be no significant impact of interaction effect of management and sex on the scholastic achievement.

The above hypotheses are tested through 5×2 factorial design. The results of Analysis of variance (ANOVA) of 5×2 factorial design for scholastic achievement scores are presented in Table 5.16.

Table 5.16: Results of ANOVA of 5 × 2 Factorial Design for Scholastic Achievement Scores of 10th Class Students in Mathematics :

Factor A: Management (5 levels)

Factor B: Sex (2 levels)

Sl. No.	Source of Variance	Sum of Squares	df	Mean Squares	F-value	Level of Significance
1.	A	39526.2700	4	9881.5680	40.7040	**
2.	B	16.8547	1	16.8547	0.0694	@
3.	AB	7038.4840	4	1759.6210	7.2482	**
4.	Error	348127.0000	1434	242.7664		

It is observed from Table 5.16 that the computed value of 'F' for the main effect 'Management' is 40.70. The table/critical value of 'F' for 4 and 1434 degrees of freedom (df) at 0.05 level is 2.38 and at 0.01 level is 3.34. The computed value is far greater than the critical value at 0.01 level of significance. Hence, the hypothesis 1 is rejected for the main effect Management. Hence it is concluded that the management has significant influence on the achievement of 10th class students in mathematics

Similar results were reported by Jagannadhan (1983), Rathore (2000), Panda (2000), Doss and Muthaiah (2002), Behera and Roul (2004) and Srinivas and Arivudayappan (2004) and Manchala (2006).

Contradictory results were reported by Manjuvani and Mohan (2002) and James and Marice (2004).

The computed value of 'F' for the main effect 'sex' is 0.07. It is far less than the table/critical value of 'F' (3.85) for 1 and 1434 df at 0.05 level of significance. Therefore, hypothesis 1 for the main effect sex is accepted at 0.05 level of significance. Hence, it is concluded that sex does not have significant influence on the scholastic achievement of 10th class students in mathematics.

Similar results were reported by Farquhar (1963), Gupta (1968), Rangaswamy and Visveswaran (1977), Dalkia (1980), Asudullakhan et al. (1982), Jagannadhan (1983),

Rangaswamy (1990), Reddy, (2002), Panda (2002), Gakhar and Aseema (2004), Ponday Ahmad (2008), Sapiyonja (2008).

Contradictory results were reported by Padmanabhan Nayar and Visveswaran (1966), (1968), Kumar (1969), Roach (1979), Gupta (1983), Watkins, and (1984), Suneetha and Mayuri (2002), Khayyer and Lacey (2005).

The computed value of 'F' for the two factor interaction effect namely management and sex on the achievement of the students in mathematics is 7.25. It is far greater than table/critical value of 'F' (3.34) for 4 and 1434 df at 0.01 level of significance. Therefore, hypothesis 2 is rejected at 0.01 level of significance. Hence it is concluded that there is significant interaction effect of management and sex on the scholastic achievement of students of 10th class in mathematics.

Factorial Design for Locality and Caste

The impact of locality and caste on the scholastic achievement of 10th class students in mathematics is studied by using 3 × 3 factorial design. The following hypotheses are formulated.

Hypothesis 3

There would be no significant influence of main effects namely locality and caste on the scholastic achievement of 10th class students in mathematics.

Hypothesis 4

There would be no significant influence of interaction effect of locality and caste on the achievement.

The above hypotheses are tested through 3 × 3 factorial design. The results of Analysis of variance (ANOVA) of 3×3 factorial design for scholastic achievement scores are presented in the Table 5.17.

From Table 5.17 it is observed that the computed value of 'F' for the main effect 'Locality' is 4.10. The table/critical value of 'F' for 2 and 1435 df at 0.05 level, is 3.00 and at 0.01 level is 4.63. The computed value is greater than the critical value at 0.05 level of significance. Therefore, Hypothesis 3 is rejected for the main effect 'Locality'. Hence it is concluded that locality has significant influence on the achievement of 10th class students in mathematics.

Table 5.17: Results of ANOVA of 3x3 Factorial Design for Scholastic Achievement Scores of 10th Class Students in Mathematics :

Factor A: Locality (3 levels)

Factor B: Caste (3 levels)

Sl. No.	Source of Variance	Sum of Squares	df	Mean Squares	F-value	Level of Significance
1.	A	2174.8160	2	1087.4080	4.1039	*
2.	B	2035.6690	2	1017.8340	3.8413	*
3.	AB	6364.1750	4	1591.0440	6.0046	**
4.	Error	380234.3000	1435	264.9717		

Similar results were reported by Jagannadhan (1983), Koteswara et al. Kumar (1998), Prakash (2000), Gupta (2002), Panda (2002a), Malik and Singh (2003), Singh et al. (2004), Dwivedi (2005).

Contradictory results were reported by Moorthy (1999), James and Marice (2004) and Panchalingappa (2004).

The computed value of 'F' for the main effect 'Caste' is 3.84. The table/critical value of 'F' for 2 and 1435 df at 0.05 level is 3.00 and at 0.01 level is 4.63. Hence Hypothesis 3 is rejected for the main effect 'Caste' at 0.05 level of significance. It is concluded that the variable 'Caste' has significant influence on the scholastic achievement of 10th class students in mathematics.

Similar results are reported by Dubey and Mishra (1977), Jagannadhan (1983), Gopalacharyulu (1984); Singh (1993), Mehta (1992) and Dash (2002).

Contradictory results were revealed by Kumaraswamy (1992), Naidu (1998) and Reddy (2002). Dubey and Mishra (1999) revealed that there was no consistency in the predictors of academic success across the three groups SC/ST, BC and OC of students.

The computed value of 'F' for the two factor interaction

effect namely locality and caste, on the achievement of students in mathematics is 6.00. It is far greater than the table/critical value of F(3.34) for 4 and 1435 df at 0.01 level of significance. Therefore the hypothesis 4 is rejected at 0.01 level of significance. It is concluded that there is significant interaction effect of locality and caste on the scholastic achievement in mathematics of 10th class students.

THE INFLUENCE OF SOCIO-DEMOGRAPHIC PSYCHOLOGICAL VARIABLES

The influence of socio-demographic variables, psychological variables namely personality factors, study habits and self concepts and personal variables on scholastic achievement of the 10th class students in mathematics is investigated.

The impact of Socio-Demographic Variables on the Scholastic Achievement

The influence of socio-demographic variables on the scholastic achievement of students is studied. The following socio-demographic variables are considered for the analysis.

1. Age
2. Birth order
3. Number of members in the family
4. Mother's Education
5. Father's Education
6. Mother's Occupation
7. Father's Occupation
8. Religion
9. Income of the family
10. Economic status
11. Separate Room for study
12. Study hours at home
13. Help from family members
14. Works at home
14. Time spent daily for mathematics

The following Hypothes is is framed.

Hypothesis 5

There would be no significant influence of socio-demographic variables, on the scholastic achievement of 10th class students in mathematics.

The above Hypothesis is tested for each variable from 1 to 15 shown above by employing one way ANOVA.

Age : The age of 10th class students normally varies from 14 to 18 years. On the basis of age, the students are divided into two groups. The students of age group below 16 years are taken as group I and students of age group 16 years and above are taken as group II. The influence of age on scholastic achievement is investigated by employing 't' technique. The number of students in each age group, the values of mean, standard deviation and 't' values are presented in the Table 5.18.

Table 5.18: Influence of Age on the Scholastic Achievement

Sl. No.	Age	N	M	SD	't'	Level of Significance
1.	Below 16 years	1179	45.29	16.48	1.57	@
2.	16 years and above	265	43.53	16.56		

From the Table 5.18, it is clear that, the computed value of 't' is less than the critical value of 't' (1.96) for 1442 df at 0.05 level of significance. Therefore Hypothesis-5 is accepted at 0.05 level, for the variable 'Age'. Hence it is concluded that 'Age' has no significant influence on the scholastic achievement of 10th class students in mathematics.

Similar reports were given by Gupta (1968), Prakashan et al. (1982) Quraishi and Bhat (1986), Biswas (2001), and Reddy (2002).

Contradictory results were reported by Srivastava (1967), Vyas (1982), Dowson et al. (1999) and Suneetha and Mayuri (2002) and R. Yasoda (2003).

Birth Order : Birth order means order of the child for the parents like first child, second child, third child and so on. In the present investigation there are 555 students with birth order one, 456 students with birth order two and 433 students with birth order three and above Group I is formed with birth order three and above. Group II is formed with birth order two and Group III is formed with birth order one. The number of students in each group, their means, standard deviations and 'F' value are presented in the table.

The impact of the birth order on the scholastic achievement of 10th class students is investigated. The corresponding scholastic achievement of the three groups are analyzed.

The Hypothesis-5 is tested through one way ANOVA technique. The results are shown in the Table 5.19.

Table 5.19: Influence of Birth Order on the Scholastic Achievement

Sl. No.	Age	N	M	SD	't'	Level of Significance
1.	3 and above	433	44.29	16.61	1.24	@
2.	2	456	44.57	16.79		
3.	1	555	45.82	16.19		

It is clear from the Table 5.19 that the computed value of 'F' is less than the critical value of 'F' (3.00) for 2 and 1441 df at 0.05 level of significance. Hence the Hypothesis-5 is accepted at 0.05 level for the variable 'Birth order'. It is concluded that birth order has no significant influence on the scholastic achievement of 10th class students.

Similar results were reported by Jagannadhan (1983), Panda (1991),

Contradictory results were given by Reddy (2002) and Yasosa (2003).

Number of Members in the Family : In the present investigation, there are 462 students with number of members in the family upto four, 482 students with number of members upto five and 500 students with number of members in the family as six and above. The students are divided into three groups; Group I is formed with number of members in the family as Six and above, Group-II is formed with number of members in the family as five and Group-III with number of members upto four. The influence of 'total number of members' in the family on the scholastic achievement of 10th class students is investigated. The corresponding scholastic achievement scores of three groups are analysed accordingly. The Hypothesis-5 is tested for this variable by employing one way ANOVA technique. The results are given in the Table 5.20.

Table 5.20: Influence of No. of Members in the Family on the Scholastic Achievement

Sl. No.	No. of members in the family	N	M	SD	't'	Level of Significance
1.	6 and above (Group-I)	500	44.56	16.61	1.00	@
2.	5 (Group-II)	482	44.54	15.89		
3.	Up to 4 (Group-III)	462	45.86	17.02		

It is observed from the Table 5.20 that the computed value of 't' is much less than the critical value of 't' (3.00) for 2 and df 1441 at 0.05 level of value of significance. Hence Hypothesis-5 is accepted for the variable 'Number of members in the family' at 0.05 level. It is concluded that number of members in the family has no significant influence on the scholastic achievement of 10th class students in mathematics.

This view was contradicted by Panda (1979) by observing that students coming from small families, have better academic achievement than students from big families.

Similar results were reported by Naidu (1998) and Manchala (2007).

Contradictory results were reported by Panda (1991).

Mother's Education : On the basis of mother's education the students are divided into three groups. There are 1037 students in Group I whose mothers have studied upto 5th class or below. There are 364 students in Group III whose mother's education level is between 6th class and 10th class. There are 43 students in Group III whose mothers' education is Intermediate and above.

The influence of 'Mother's Education' on scholastic achievement of 10th class students is investigated. The corresponding scholastic achievement scores of three groups of students are analysied accordingly.

The Hypothesis-5 is tested by using one way ANOVA technique. The results are presented in the Table 5.21.

Table 5.21 : Influence of Mother's Education on the Scholastic Achievement

Sl. No.	Mother's Education	N	M	SD	'F'	Level of Significance
1.	5th class and below (Group-I)	1037	43.28	15.34	19.83	**
2.	6th to 10th class (Group-II)	364	49.16	18.68		
3.	Inter and above (Group-III)	43	50.19	17.10		

It is clear from the Table 5.21 that the computed value of F (19.83) is far greater than the critical value of 'F' (4.63) for 2 and 1441 df at 0.01 level. Hence the Hypothesis-5 is rejected for the variable 'Mother's Education' at 0.01 level of significance. It is concluded that 'Mother's Education' has significant influence on the scholastic achievement of 10th class students. It is inferred that higher the level of mother's education, higher the achievement of students is.

Sarma (1984); Jagannadhan (1986); Vijaya Kumar Sethi (1990); Panda (1991), Moorthy (1999), Reddy (2002), Manchala (2007), NCERT (2008), have found similar results. Gupta (1968), Rangaswamy and Visvesvara (1977) found that there is no significant influence of mother's education on the scholastic achievement of students.

Father's Education : On the basis of 'Father's Education' the students are divided into three groups, with Group I consisting of 1278 students, whose fathers have studied up to 10th class. The Group-II consists of 141 students whose father's level of education is Intermediate and Degree and Group-III consisting of 25 students whose father's level of education is Post-graduation and other professional courses.

The influence of 'Father's Education' on the scholastic achievement of 10th class students is studied. The corresponding achievement scores of all the groups are analyzed accordingly.

The Hypothesis-5 is verified by using one-way ANOVA technique. The results are presented in the Table 5.22.

Table 5.22: Influence of Father's Education on the Scholastic Achievement

Sl. No.	Father's Education	N	M	SD	'F'	Level of Significance
1.	Upto 10th class	1278	44.04	16.02	17.96	**
2.	Inter and degree	141	52.11	18.76		
3.	P.G. and other professions	25	52.08	16.38		

It is found from the Table 5.22 that the computed value of 'F' (17.96) is far greater than the critical value of 'F' (4.63) for 2 and 1441 df at 0.01 level of significance. Hence the Hypothesis-5 is rejected at 0.01 level. Therefore it is concluded that 'Father's Education' has significant influence on the scholastic achievement of 10th class students in mathematics. There is a positive relationship between 'Father's education and scholastic achievement of 10th class students.

Sarma (1984), Jagannadhan (1986), Sethi (1990); Panda (1991), Moorthy (1999), Chakrabarthi and Sarmistha (2002), Reddy and Panda (2002a), Manchala (2007), reported similar results.

Gupta (1968), Rangaswamy and Visveswara (1977), and N.C.E.R.T. report (2008), and Rangaswamy and Visveswara (1977) reported that there is no significant influence of Father's Education on scholastic achievement of students.

Mother's Occupation : On the basis of mother's Occupation, the students are divided into two groups, group-I consisting of 1405 students, whose mother's are house wives and Labourers and group-II consisting of 39 students, whose mother's are Government employees. The influence of 'Mother's occupation' on the scholastic achievement of 10th students is investigated. The corresponding scholastic achievement scores of the two groups of students are analysed accordingly.

The Hypothesis-5 is verified by using 't' technique. The results are presented in the Table 5.23.

Table 5.23: Influence of Mother's Occupation on the Scholastic Achievement

Sl. No.	Mother's Occupation	N	M	SD	'F'	Level of Significance
1.	House wife and Labour (Group-I)	1405	44.72	16.39	3.49	**
2.	Govt. Employee (Group-II)	39	54.03	18.31		

It is clear from the Table 5.23 that the computed value of 't' (3.49) is greater than the critical value of 't' (2.58) at 0.01 level of significance. Hence the Hypothesis-5 is rejected at 0.01 level for the variable 'Mother's occupation'. Hence it is concluded that mother's occupation has significant influence on the scholastic achievement of 10th class students in mathematics. Similar results were found by Pavithran and Feroze (1965), Panda (1991), Goswamy (2002) and Reddy (2002), N.C.E.R.T. Report (2008), Gupta (1968), Dweson (1970), Rangaswamy and Visveswara (1977), Ayishabi and Kuruvilla (1998), Panda (2002a), Manchala (2007) reported contradictory results.

Father's Occupation : On the basis of 'Father's Occupation', the students are divided into three groups. Group-I is formed with the students whose fathers are labourers', agriculturists, and caste occupants. Group-II is formed with the students whose fathers are teachers and business people and Group-III is formed with the students whose fathers are other professionals. There are 1307 students in Group-I, 76 students in Group-II and 61 students in Group-III. The influence of 'Father's occupation' on the scholastic achievement is investigated. The corresponding scholastic achievement scores of the three groups of students are analyzed accordingly.

The Hypothesis-5 is tested for the variable Father's Occupation by employing one way ANOVA. The results are shown in the Table 5.24.

Table 5.24: Influence of Father's Occupation on the Scholastic Achievement

Sl. No.	Father's Occupation	N	M	SD	'F'	Level of Significance
1.	Labour, Agriculture and Cast occupation	1307	44.14	15.95	27.09	**
2.	Teachers & Business People	76	58.17	20.50		
3.	Other professionals	61	46.26	15.96		

From the above Table 5.24 it is seen that the computed value of 'F' (27.09) is far greater than the critical value of 'F' (4.63) for 2 and 1441 df at 0.01 level of significance. Hence Hypothesis-5 is rejected at 0.01 level for the variable 'Father's Occupation'. Hence it is concluded that 'Father's occupation' has significant influence on the scholastic achievement of 10th class students in mathematics. It is inferred that better the cccupation of the fathers and better would be the scholastic achievement of students.

Pavithran and Feroze (1965), Panda (1991), and Govinda Reddy (2002) found similar results. Gupta (1968), Rangaswamy and Visveswara (1977) and Panda (2002a) reported contradictory results.

Religion/Community : The total sample in the present study (N=1444) consists of students belonging to three different Religions. There are 150 Muslim students, 50

Christian students and 1244 Hindu students. Muslim students are taken as Group-I, Christian students as Group-II and Hindu students as Group-III. The influence of community on the scholastic achievement is investigated. The corresponding scholastic achievement scores of the three groups are analysed accordingly.

The Hypothesis-5 is tested for the variable 'Religion' by employing one-way ANOVA. The results are shown in the Table 5.24.

Table 5.24: Influence of Religion/community on the Scholastic Achievement

Sl. No.	Religionn	N	M	SD	'F'	Level of Significance
1.	Muslim (Group-I)	150	42.32	13.56	5.39	**
2.	Christian (Group-II)	50	39.48	16.57		
3.	Hindu (Group-III)	1244	45.51	16.76		

From the Table 36 it is found that the computed value of 'F' (5.39) is greater than the critical value of 'F' (4.63) for 2 and 1441 df at 0.01 level of significance. Hence the Hypothesis-5 is rejected for the variable 'Religion' at 0.01 level. Therefore, it is concluded that Religion has significant influence on the scholastic achievement of 10th class students.

Similar results were reported by Radha Mohan (1998), Kobal – Palcic et al. (1999), Regnerus, and Mark (2000).

Contradictory results were reported by Asudullakhan et al. (1982), Krishna moorthy (1999) and Manchala (2007).

9. Annual income : On the basis of annual income of the family, the students are divided into two groups. Group-I consists of 1326 students whose families' annual income is upto 25000/- and Group-II consists of 118 students whose families' annual income is above 25000/-. The influence of 'Annual Income of the Family' on the scholastic achievement is studied. The corresponding scholastic achievement scores of the two groups are analysed accordingly.

The Hypothesis-5 is tested for the variable 'Annual

Income of the family' by employing 't' techniques. The results of analysis are presented in the Table 5.26.

Table 5.26: Influence of Annual income on the Scholastic Achievement

Sl. No.	Annual income	N	M	SD	'F'	Level of Significance
1.	Upto Rs. 25000/- (Group-I)	1326	44.24	16.04	5.71	**
2.	Above Rs. 25000/- (Group-II)	118	53.19	19.27		

It is seen from the Table 5.26 that the computed value of 't' (5.71) for greater than the critical value of 't' (2.58) for 1442 df at 0.01 level of significance. Therefore Hypothesis-5 is rejected at 0.01 level for the variable 'Annual income of the family'. It is concluded that 'Annual income of the family' has significant influence on the scholastic achievement of 10th class students. It is clear from the Table 5.26 that higher the income, better is the scholastic achievement.

Similar results were revealed by Fraser (1959), Rao (1965), Gupta (1968), Jagannadhan (1986), Sethi (1990), Panda (1991), Reddy (2002), Selvan and Sundaravalli (2002).

Contradictory results were revealed by Wiseman (1964), Naidu (1998) and Krishnamoorthy (1999).

Economic Status : The students are asked to respond, while collecting the data, whether they belong to the category of poor, middle class or rich. On the basis of their responses, it is seen that 1326 pupils stated that they are poor. 107 Pupils stated that they belong to middle class and only 11 students responded to the category of rich. As the number of students belonging to the category of rich is very less, they have been mixed with the category of middle class. Hence the total (1444) students are divided into two groups, namely poor and middle class with 1326 belonging to the poor and 118 belonging to the middle class. The influence of economic status on the scholastic achievement is studied. The corresponding scholastic achievement scores of the two groups are analysed accordingly.

The Hypothesis-5 is tested for the variable 'Economic status' by employing 't' technique. The results of analysis are presented in the Table 5.27.

Table 5.27 : Influence of Economic Status on the Scholastic Achievement

Sl. No.	Economic status	N	M	SD	'F'	Level of Significance
1.	Poor (Group-I)	1326	44.27	16.05	5.40	**
2.	Middle and rich (Group-II)	118	52.76	19.42		

It is seen from the Table 5.27 that the computed value of 't' (5.40) is far greater than the critical value 't' (2.58) for 1442 df at 0.01 level of significance. Therefore, Hypothesis-5 is rejected at 0.01 level for the variable 'Economic status'. Hence it is concluded that "Economic status" of family has significant influence on the scholastic achievement of 10th class students in mathematics.

Gupta (1968), Anand (1973), Menon (1973), Shakiba–Nejad *et al.* (1983), Quaraishi and Bhat (1986), Krishnan and Garg (1992), Vijayalakshmi and Natesan (1992) Deirdra (1999) Karla and Pyari (2004) and Ahuja (2006) have given supporting results.

Pavithran and Feroze (1965), Rao (1965), Srivastava (1967), Bernstein (1968), Sudamma (1973), Sharma and Bhargava (1980), Ramana Sood (1990) and Saxena (2002) and Panigrahi (2005) have revealed contradictory reports.

Separate Room for Study : The students are asked to respond, while collecting the data, whether they have a separate room for study or not. On the basis of their responses, the students are divided into two groups, with Group-I consisting of 1116 students, having separate room for study and with Group-II consisting of 328 students, having no separate room for study. The influence of 'Separate Room for study on the scholastic achievement is studied. The corresponding scholastic achievement scores of the two groups are analysed accordingly.

The Hypothesis-5 is tested for the variable 'Separate Room' by employing 't' technique. The results are shown in the Table 5.28.

Table 5.28 : Influence of Separate room on the Scholastic Achievement

Sl. No.	Separate Room	N	M	SD	'F'	Level of Significance
1.	Yes (Group-I)	1116	44.44	16.15	2.23	*
2.	No (Group-II)	328	46.75	17.57		

It is found from the above Table 5.28 hat the computed value of 't' (2.23) is greater than the critical value of 't' (1.96) for 1442 df at 0.05 level of significance. Hence the Hypothesis-5 is rejected at 0.05 level of significant for the variable 'Separate Room for Study'.

Therefore, separate room for study will have significant influence on the scholastic achievement of 10th class students in mathematics. Hence it is concluded that students having separate study room will have better achievement. Parents should provide a study room for children so as to encourage them for better achievement.

Contradictory results were reported by Mishra (1980).

Study Hours at Home : On the basis of daily study hours at home, the students are divided into three groups. Group-I consists of 134 students who study for one hour and less than one hour daily. Group-II consists of 511 students who study for more than one hour but less than 3 hours. Group-III consists of 799 students whose study hours are three and more than three hours.

The influence of 'Study hours at home' on the scholastic achievement of 10th class students is investigated. The corresponding scholastic achievement scores of three groups of students are analysed accordingly.

The Hypothesis-5 is tested for the variable 'Study Hours at Home' by using one way ANOVA technique. The results are presented in the Table 5.29.

Table 5.29: Influence of Study hours at home on the Scholastic Achievement

Sl. No.	Study Hours at Home	N	M	SD	'F'	Level of Significance
1.	One hour and less than 1 hour(Group-I)	134	39.07	14.52	14.22	**
2.	2 to 3 hour (Group-II)	511	43.85	15.49		
3.	3 and above three hours (Group-III)	799	46.67	17.17		

From the above Table 5.29, it is found that the computed value of 'F' (14.22) is far greater than the critical value of 'F' (4.63) for 2 and 1441 df at 0.01 level of significance. Hence the Hypothesis-5 for the variable 'Study Hours at Home' is rejected at 0.01 level. Hence it is concluded that the number of hours of study at home has significant influence on the scholastic achievement of 10th class students in mathematics. It is clear from the Table 5.29 that more the number of study hours at home, better is the scholastic achievement. Hence, parents must encourage the students for spending as much time as then can, for improvement in the scholastic achievement.

Help from Family Members : On the basis of help from family members towards their studies, the students are formed into three groups. Group-I is formed with the students having no help from the family members. Group-II is formed with the students having help to a little extent and Group-III is formed with the students having help to the full extent. There are 526 students in Group-I, 671 students in Group-II and 247 students in Group-III.

The influence of help from family members on the scholastic achievement of the students is investigated. The corresponding achievement scores of the three groups of students are analyzed accordingly.

The Hypothesis-5 for the variable 'Help from family members' is tested by using one way ANOVA technique. The results of analysis are presented in the Table 5.30.

Table 5.30 : Influence of Help from family members on the Scholastic Achievement

Sl. No.	Study Hours at Home	N	M	SD	'F'	Level of Significance
1.	Nil (Group-I)	526	44.43	16.12	1.64	@
2.	To some extent (Group-II)	671	44.77	16.57		
3.	Full extent (Group-III)	247	46.66	17.11		

From the above Table 5.30 it is seen that the computed value of 'F' (1.66) is less than the critical value of F (3.00) for 2 and 1441 df at 0.05 level of significance. Hence the Hypothesis-5 for the variable 'Help from the family members' is accepted at 0.05 level of significance. Therefore the Help from family members' has no significant influence on the scholastic achievement of 10th class students. Mathematics is a special subject in which interest, concentration and involvement of the individual is required rather than help from others.

Contradictory results were reported by Bose and Joshi (2004) and Vamadevappa (2005).

Works at Home : On the basis of the responses from the students with regard to the works at their homes, the students are divided into two groups. Group-I is formed with students having no other works, except the studies and Group-II is formed with the students having, works other than studies, at home. There are 472 students in Group-I and 1972 students in Group-II.

The influence of 'Works at Home' on the scholastic achievement of students is investigated. The corresponding achievement scores of the two groups of students are analyzed accordingly.

The Hypothesis-5 for the variable 'Works at Home' is tested using 't' technique. The results of analysis are presented in the Table 5.31.

Table 5.31 Influence of Works at Home on the Scholastic Achievement

Sl. No.	Works at Home	N	M	SD	'F'	Level of Significance
1.	No (Group-I)	472	46.51	17.54	2.47	*
2.	Yes (Group-II)	972	44.22	15.94		

It is seen from the Table 5.31 that the computed value of 't' (2.47) is greater than the critical value of 't' (1.96) for 1442 df at 0.05 level of significance. Hence, the Hypothesis-5 for the variable 'Works at home' is rejected at 0.05 level. Therefore it is concluded that the variable "works at home" has significant influence on the scholastic achievement.

Similar results were reported by Desai (1979).

Time Spent Daily for Mathematics : On the basis of responses of the students given during the data collection, the total sample N (1444) of students is formed into three groups. Group-I is formed with students spending 2 hours and less daily for mathematics working. Group-II is formed with students spending between 2 hours and 3 hours daily for mathematics and Group-III is formed with those spending more than 3 hours daily for mathematics. There are 689 students in Group-I, 513 students in Group-II and 242 students in Group-III.

The influence "Time Spent Daily for Mathematics" on the scholastic achievement of students is investigated. The corresponding achievement scores of the three groups of students are analyzed accordingly. The Hypotenses-5 for the variable 'Time spent daily for mathematics' is used is tested using't' technique. The results of analysis are presented in the Table 5.32.

Table 5.32: Influence of Time spent for Mathematics on the Scholastic Achievement

Sl. No.	Time spent for maths	N	M	SD	'F'	Level of Significance
1.	Less than 2 hours (Group-I)	689	45.08	17.00	2.17	@
2.	2 to 3 hours(Group-II)	513	45.71	16.85		
3.	Above 3 hours (Group-III)	242	43.05	14.07		

From the Table 5.32, it is clear that the computed value of 'F' (2.17) is less than the critical value of F (3.00), for 2 and 1441 df at 0.05 level of significance. Hence the Hypothesis-5 for the variable "Time spent daily for mathematics" is accepted at 0.05 level of significance. Hence time spent daily for mathematics has no significant influence on the scholastic achievement of 10th class students in mathematics. Hence, the time spent for mathematics is not the criterion for better achievement. There may be many other factors like intelligence, concentration, positive attitude towards the subject and interest in the subject, besides the time spent for mathematics. Mathematics is a special subject which can not be learnt by simple time spending on it, alone.

The Impact of 14 Personality Factors (HSPQ) on the Scholastic Achievement

The Cattell's Junior-senior High-school personality questionnaire (HSPQ) Form-A is adopted as a tool to asses the personality of 10th class students in the present investigation. The raw scores on each factor are converted into sten values as recommended by Cattell (1970) for the purpose of analysis.

To study the influence of HSPQ on the scholastic achievement of 10th class students, the technique of one way analysis of variance is employed. As recommended by Cattell, the criterion in the divisions of the groups based on the sten values is used. The sten values 1 to 4 are grouped as low scorers (Group-I), 5 and 6 as average scorers (Group-II) and

7 to 10 as high scorers (Group-III). The corresponding scholastic achievement test scores of the three groups are analized. The mean values of scholastic achievement test scores of the three groups are analized. The mean values of scholastic achievement test scores for each personality factor are tested for significance by employing the technique of one-way analysis of variance. The following Hypothesis is formulated.

Hypothesis 6

There would be no significant influence of personality factors on the achievement of 10th class students in mathematics. Employing the technique of one-way Analysis of variance, the above Hypothesis is tested. The results are presented in the Table 5.33.

Table 5.33 shows the impact of 14 personality factors on the scholastic achievement of the students. From the Table 44 it is clear that the computed values of 'F' for the personality factors B, G, H, I, O, Q_3 are far greater than the critical value of 'F' (4.63) for 2 and 1441 df at 0.01 level of significance. The computed value of 'F' for the personality factors 'C' is greater than the critical value of 'F' (4.63) for 2 and 1441 df at 0.01 level. Hence Hypothesis-6 is rejected for these factors namely B, G, H, I, O, Q_3 an at 0.01 level. Further the computed value of 'F' for the personality factor E is greater than the critical value of 'F' for 2 and 1441 df at 0.05 level of significance. Hence Hypothesis-6 is rejected for the factor 'E' at 0.05 level. Hence Hypothesis-6 is rejected for the personality factors-B, C, E, G, H, I, O and Q_3.

The hypothesis-6 is accepted for all the remaining factors namely A, D, F, J, Q_2 and Q_4 at 0.05 level.

From the above results, it is concluded that the students with personality characteristics:

1. More intelligent,
2. Emotionally stable,
3. Obedient,
4. Super-egostrength,
5. Venture some,

Table 5.33: Impact of 14 Personality Factors on the Scholastic Achievement

Sl. No.	Personality factors	No. of Observations			Mean			S.D. Values			F values	Level of Significance
		I	II	III	I	II	III	I	II	III		
1.	FA	547	399	498	44.66	45.07	45.23	16.31	16.13	17.03	0.17	@
2.	FB	470	628	346	39.38	45.49	51.60	13.53	16.29	17.93	59.64	**
3.	FC	384	562	498	45.14	43.43	46.56	16.65	16.18	16.64	4.80	**
4.	FD	415	562	467	45.41	44.47	45.18	17.64	16.29	15.73	0.45	@
5.	FE	477	523	444	46.75	44.41	43.71	16.34	17.34	15.52	4.38	*
6.	FF	438	522	484	45.80	44.23	45.01	16.71	16.16	16.69	1.08	@
7.	FG	370	547	527	41.72	44.14	48.11	15.55	16.14	17.01	17.83	**
8.	FH	511	456	477	42.26	44.51	48.31	15.44	16.31	17.23	17.21	**
9.	FI	356	586	502	42.77	44.41	47.18	15.52	16.26	17.23	8.05	**
10.	FJ	378	627	439	45.73	44.16	45.47	16.43	15.24	18.21	1.37	@
11.	FO	592	438	414	46.72	45.13	42.29	16.53	16.47	16.20	8.88	**
12.	FQ_2	380	679	385	45.09	45.66	43.62	17.01	16.87	15.27	1.89	@
13.	FQ_3	411	546	487	41.47	45.60	47.21	15.75	16.16	17.06	14.36	**
14.	FQ_4	474	589	381	46.03	44.8	44.11	17.41	15.94	16.18	1.59	@

6. Tenseminded,
7. Placid and
8. Controlled

have significantly better scholastic achievement than the students with the personality characteristics:

1. Less intelligent,
2. Emotionally less stable,
3. Assertive,
4. Moral standards,
5. Shy,
6. Though minded,
7. Apprehensive and
8. Undisciplined.

Similar results were found by Cattel, *et al.* (1966), Vyas (1982), Sethi (1990), Rao and Reddy (1998), Panchanadhan (1999), Reddy (2002), Kagade (2002) and Basappa (2005).

Contradictory reports were gien by Joshi (1990), Mavi and Patel (1997), Natesan and Suseela (2000), Ayodya (2007) and Subramanyam and Rao (2008).

The Impact of Study Habits on Scholastic Achievement

Looking into the importance of good study habits, Dr. B.V. Patel's study Habits Inventory is adopted to examine the study habits of Xth class students and to measure the impact of study habits on the scholastic achievement of 10th class students in mathematics. To study the influence of study habits on achievement, the technique of one-way analysis of variance (ANOVA) is employed. The criterion in the division of the groups, based on the Quartile values, is used. Group-I is formed with scores upto Q_1, Group-II is formed with scores above Q_1 and upto Q_3 and Group-III is formed with scores above Q_3. The corresponding scholastic achievement scores of the three groups are analyzed accordingly. The mean values of scholastic achievement scores for the three groups for each area of SHI are tested for significance through one way ANOVA technique. The following hypothesis is formulated.

Table 5.34: Impact of Study Habits on the Scholastic Achievement

Sl. No.	Studty Habits	No. of Observations			Mean			S.D. Values			F values	Level of Significance
		I	II	III	I	II	III	I	II	III		
1.	SH_1	431	655	358	41.19	44.90	49.66	15.30	16.47	16.82	26.30	**
2.	SH_2	393	692	359	41.53	43.71	51.16	15.56	15.44	17.81	37.61	**
3.	SH_3	427	678	339	40.95	44.82	50.24	14.27	16.45	17.80	30.46	**
4.	SH_4	427	762	255	39.92	45.44	51.81	14.21	16.51	17.42	44.01	**
5.	SH_5	414	751	279	38.63	45.23	53.67	12.58	16.56	17.42	76.65	**
6.	SH_6	415	759	270	41.61	45.04	49.91	14.74	16.24	18.49	21.30	**
7.	SH_7	375	717	352	40.86	45.56	48.14	15.23	16.42	17.16	19.03	**
8.	SH_T	378	707	359	39.06	43.31	54.45	13.61	15.26	17.66	98.68	**

Hypothesis-7

There would be no significant influence of different areas of SHI on the scholastic achievement of 10th class students in mathematics.

The above hypothesis is tested by employing one-way ANOVA. The results of Analysis are presented in the Table 3.34.

The impact of study habits on scholastic achievement of 10th class students in mathematics is observed from the Table 45. It is clear from the Table 5.34 that the computed values of 'F' for all the areas of SHI are far greater than the critical value of 'F' (4.63) for 2 and 1441 df at 0.01 level of significance. Hence the Hypothesis-7 is rejected for all the areas of SHI at 0.01 level. The mean values of scholastic achievement of 10th class students in mathematics are in favour of Group-III. It is seen from the Table 5.34, that the mean values of Group-II for all the areas of SHI are greater than Group-I and the mean values of Group-III are greater than Group-II. Hence, it is concluded that students who have better study habits achieved significantly better in mathematics.

Similar results were reported by Bhatnagar (1980), Patel (1981), Chopra (1982), Tiwari (1982) Deb and Gravel (1990), Aruna (1994), Koteswar (1997), Darlene (1998), Rai and Sreethi (2000), Kumaran and Kamala (2001), Nagaraju (2001), Shinde (2001), Reddy (2002), Vamadevappa (2002), Rajani (2004), Arockiadass (2005), Manchala (2007) and Sood and Kumar (2007).

Contradictory results were reported by Woodruff (1940), Nortan (1959), Singh (1989) Ravath and Leela (1995), Verma (1996) and Guravaiah (2004).

The Impact of Self-Concepts on Scholastic Achievement

The self-concept scale (SCS) developed by Rani Rastogi (1974) is adopted to examine the self-concepts of high school students and to find the influence of self-concepts on the scholastic achievement of 10th class students in mathematics. The areas of SCS and the scoring procedure have already been described in Chapter-4. The raw scores on each area of self-concept scale and the total score have been divided into three groups on the basis of quartiles. Group-I is formed with the value upto Q_1, Group-II is formed with values above Q_1, and upto Q_3 and Group-III is formed with the values above Q_3. The corresponding scholastic achievement scores of the three groups are analyzed accordingly. The mean values of scholastic achievement scores for the three groups for each area of self-concept are tested for significance, through the technique of one-way ANOVA. The following hypothesis is formulated.

Hypothesis 8

There would be no significant influence of different areas of Self-concept scale on the scholastic achievement of 10th class students in mathematics.

The above hypothesis is tested by employing one-way ANOVA. The results of Analysis are presented in the Table 5.35.

The impact of self-concept scale on the scholastic achievement of 10th class students is observed from the Table 5.35. It is clear from the Table 5.35 that the computed values of 'F' for the areas of SCS namely SC_2, SC_3, SC_4, SC_5, SC_{10} and SC_T are far greater than the critical value of 'F' (4.63) for 2 and 1441 df at 0.01 level of significance. Hence, the Hypothesis-8 is rejected for the above areas of SCS at 0.01 level. The computed values of 'F' for the areas of SCS namely SC_6, SC_7, and SC_8 are greater than the critical value of F (3.00) for 2 and 1441 df at 0.05 level of significance. Hence the Hypothesis-8 is rejected for SC_6, SC_7 and SC_8 at 0.05 level. It is observed that the computed values, of 'F' for areas SC_1 and SC_9 are less than the critical value of F (3.00) for 2 and 1441 df at 0.05 level of significance. Hence the Hypothesis-8 is accepted for the areas SC_1 and SC_9 at 0.05 level.

Hence it is concluded that Self concepts like,

1. Abilities (SC_2),
2. Self confidence (SC_3),
3. Self Acceptance (SC_4)

Table 5.35: Impact of Self-Concepts on the Scholastic Achievement

Sl. No.	Studty Habits	No. of Observations			Mean			S.D. Values			F values	Level of Significance
		I	II	III	I	II	III	I	II	III		
1.	SC_1	393	773	278	43.98	45.46	45.00	16.04	16.85	16.21	1.05	@
2.	SC_2	409	703	332	41.16	44.32	51.04	15.03	16.11	17.42	35.54	**
3.	SC_3	378	770	296	42.43	45.33	47.27	15.70	16.32	17.60	7.59	**
4.	SC_4	476	666	302	42.48	45.68	47.31	15.83	16.82	16.41	9.19	**
5.	SC_5	466	637	341	43.16	44.70	47.95	15.93	16.73	16.50	8.56	**
6.	SC_6	479	694	271	43.80	44.90	47.32	16.05	16.86	16.33	3.73	*
7.	SC_7	490	618	336	43.43	45.10	46.97	16.34	16.87	15.89	4.62	*
8.	SC_8	395	792	257	43.30	45.39	46.25	15.20	16.90	17.06	3.07	*
9.	SC_9	452	720	272	44.69	44.90	45.62	16.43	16.54	16.60	0.29	@
10.	SC_{10}	390	821	233	42.10	45.45	48.06	14.64	16.96	17.17	10.45	**
11.	SC_T	374	726	344	40.50	44.39	51.03	15.16	16.02	17.16	39.34	**

4. Worthiness (SC_5),
5. Present, Past and Future (SC_6),
6. Biliefs and convictions (SC_7),
7. Feeling of shame and Guilt ($SC\text{-}_8$).

Emotional maturity (SC_{10}) and self-concepts total SC_T have significant influence on the achievement of 10th class students in mathematics.

From the above table, it is clear that the students who scored better in the above self-concepts have also significantly better scholastic achievement in mathematics.

The areas (1) Health and sex appropriateness and (2) Sociability (SC_9) do not have significant influence on the scholastic achievement in mathematics.

STEP-WISE MULTIPLE REGRESSION ANALYSIS

This section deals with the analysis of relative contribution of magnitude of the effect of each of the independent variables on the dependent variable. The scholastic achievement of 10th class students in mathematics is predicted with the help of different sets of independent variables.

In this regard, it is appropriate to know the meaning and nature of regression analysis. Regression means to predict one variable with the help of other variable/variables. The dictionary meaning of the term "regression" is 'act of turning' or 'going back'. In 19th century Francis Galton used the term 'regression' for the first time, while studying the relationship between the height of fathers and their offsprings. Galton found that the children of obnormally tall or short parents tend to 'regress' or 'step back' to the height of overage population. But now, in statistics, the term "regression" is used only as a convenient term without having any reference to the biometry.

In regression analysis, there are two types of variables. The variable whose value is influenced or is to be predicted is called dependent variable and variable which influences values or is used for prediction, is called independent variable. The independent variable is also called the 'regressor' or 'predictor'.

Nowadays regression analysis is used widely in all the scientific disciplines, such as physical and social sciences.

Correlation is a tool of ascertaining the degree of relationship between two variables. The objective of regression analysis is to find the 'nature of relationship' between two variables. The cause and effect of relation is clearly indicated through the regression analysis, rather than by correlation. The stepwise multiple regression analysis is employed in the present study to predict the dependent variable with the help of independent variables.

There are 5.36 valiables in the step-wise multiple regression analysis, in the present investigation. The variable number, description of the variable and symbols used are presented in the Table 5.36.

Table5.36: Variables used for Regression Analysis

Variable Number (VN)	Description of the variable	Symbol used
1.	Management	M
2.	Sex	S
3.	Locality	L
4.	Age	A
5.	Caste	C
6.	Birth order	BO
7.	Number of members in the family	M.F
8.	Mother's education	ME
9.	Father's education	FE
10.	Mother's occupation	MO
11.	Father's occupation	FO
12.	Religion	RN
13.	Income of the family	I
14.	Economic status	ES
15.	Separate Room for study	SR
16.	Study Hours at home	SHH
17.	Help from family members	HF
18.	Works at home	WH
19.	Time spent for mathematics	TSM

Variable Number (VN)	Description of the variable	Symbol used
20.	14PF Factor A	FA
21.	14 PF Factor B	FB
22.	14 PF Factor C	FC
23.	14 PF Factor D	FD
24.	14 PF Factor E	FE
25.	14 PF Factor F	FF
26.	14 PF Factor G	FG
27.	14 PF Factor H	FH
28.	14 PF Factor I	FI
29.	14 PF Factor J	FJ
30.	14 PF Factor O	FO
31.	14 PF Factor Q_2	FQ_2
32.	14 PF Factor Q_3	FQ_3
33.	14 PF Factor Q_4	FQ_4
34.	Home environment and planning	SH_1
35.	Reading and Note taking	SH_2
36.	Planning of the subjects	SH_3
37.	Habits of concentration	SH_4
38.	Preparation for examinations	SH_5
39.	General Habits and Attitudes	SH_6
40.	Social Environment	SH_7
41.	Study Habits total score	SH_T
42.	Health and Sex Appropriateness	SC_1
43.	Abilities	SC_2
44.	Self confidence	SC_3
45.	Self acceptance	SC_4
46.	Worthiness	SC_5
47.	Past, Present and Future	SC_6
48.	Beliefs and convictions	SC_7
49.	Feelings of shame and guilt	SC_8
50.	Sociability	SC_9
51.	Emotional Maturity	SC_{10}
52.	Self-concepts total	SC_T
53.	Achievement Test Score	ATS

Scholastic achievement in Mathematics (ATS) (ie) variable number 53 in the Table 5.36 is the dependent variable in the present investigation. Scholastic achievement of students in mathematics is very important and is related to a number of psycho-sociological and Demographic variables.

Prediction of scholastic achievement in mathematics

The prediction of achievement test scores (ATS) and the relative contribution of various variables namely (1) socio-demographic variables, (2) personality factors (HSPQ), (3) Study Habits (SHI), (4) Self concepts (SCS) and (5) All independent variables on the dependent variable (ATS) is studied, with the help of step-wise multiple regression analysis.

Prediction of Scholastic Achievement with the Help of Socio-demographic Variables (1-19)

The achievement test score (ATS) variable number-53 in the Table 5.37 is predicted with help of socio-demographic variables (1-19) using step-wise multiple regression analysis. The results of the regression analysis are presented in the Table 5.37.

It is seen from the Table 5.37 that the first variable entered into the step-wise regression analysis is Mother's Education (ME). The multiple correlation (R) obtained is 0.158. It implies that the strength of the relationship between the two variables (ATS and ME) is about 15.8 per cent. It could be seen that R is significant (F=37.09) beyond 0.01 level of significance for 1 and 1442 df. The critical value of 'F' is 3.85 at 0.05 level and 6.66 at 0.01 level for 1 and 1442 df. The coefficient of multiple R^2 is 0.025. This shows that 2.50 per cent of the variance in ATS is accounted by ME.

The standard error of Multiple R (SER) is 16.30. From this it may be inferred that nearly 68 per cent of actual ATS value would lie with in M ± 16.30 of ATS value predicted with the help of this variable (ME).

Table 5.32: Prediction of Scholastic Achievement with the help of Socio-demographic Variables (1-19)

Step No.	IV (VN)	R	R^2	SER	F value for R	b (VN)	't' value for b	Constant	B	r	% of variance
1	2	3	4	5	6	7	8	9	10	11	12
1.	ME	0.158	0.025	16.30	37.09**	4.991(8)	6.09**	38.42	0.158	0.108	2.51
	(8)				(1,1442)		(1442)				
2.	SHH	0.205	0.042	16.17	31.42**	4.788 (8)	5.88**		0.152		2.41
	(16)				(2,1441)	3.241 (16)	5.01**	30.71	0.129	0.137	1.77
							(1441)				
3.	M(1)	0.237	0.056	16.05	28.65**	3.841(8)	4.61**		0.122		1.93
					(3,1440)	3.374 (16)	5.21**	28.56	0.134	0.151	1.83
						1.45 (1)	4.71**		0.124		1.87
							(1440)				
4.	L(3)	0.359	0.129	15.43	53.19**	3.555 (8)	4.44**		0.113		1.179
					(4,1439)	3.250 (16)	5.26**		0.130		1.78
						4.662 (1)	11.16**	38.37	0.397	–0.108	5.98
						–7.781 (3)	10.94**		–0.382		3.34
							(1439)				

Continue...

Table 5.37 (continue)

1	2	3	4	5	6	7	8	9	10	11	12
5.	F(11)	0.364	0.133	15.39	44.24**	3.078 (8)	3.76**		0.098		1.55
					(5,1438)	3.168 (16)	5.14**		0.390		1.73
						4.580 (1)	10.96**	36.77	0.390	0.108	5.87
						–7.952 (3)	11.16**		–0.390		3.41
						2.605 (11)	2.74**		0.71		0.77
6.	19	0.371	0.138	15.36	39.19**	2.862 (8)	3.49**		0.091		1.44
					(6,1437)	3.596 (16)	5.65**		0.144		0.21
						4.644 (1)	11.12**		0.395		5.96
						–8.198 (3)	11.28**	36.63	–0.394	–0.031	3.44
						2.521 (11)	2.65**		0.69		0.74
						–1.502 (19)	2.64** (1437)		–0.068		0.21

The partial regression coefficient (b) presented in the column 7 is 4.991. This value indicates that ATS value would change by 4.991 units for every one unit of change in ME. The '*t*' value for *b* is 6.09 which is highly significant at 0.05 level. The value of the constant that could be written to predict ATS at this stage is 38.42.

The general form of multiple regression equation may be written as :

$$Y = A + b_1 (X_1) + b_2 (X_2) + b_3 (X_3) + \ldots + b_n (X_n)$$

where Y is predicted score on the dependent variable, b_1, b_2, $b_3 \ldots$ b_n are partial regression coefficients X_1, X_2, $X_3 \ldots$ X_n are scores on different independent variables and A is constant.

Thus the multiple regression equation at the end of this step, could be written as ATS = 38.42 + 4.991 (ME)

Study Hours at Home (SHH) is entered into the step-wise regression analysis as the second most significant variable. The multiple correlation (R) between ATS on one side and ME and SHH on other side is 0.205. Thus the strength of the relationship between ATS and the two independent variables put together is 20.50 per cent. R is significant at 0.01 level (F = 31.42, df 2, 1441)

The value of R^2 is 0.042. This shows that the two variables put together could explain 4.20 per cent of variance in the dependent variable (ATS). Out of this 2.50 per cent of variance is explained by ME. The remaining 1.70 cent of variance is accounted for by SHH (Table 5.37 Col 12).

The regression equation to predict ATS with these two variables (ME and SHH) as predictor variables is:

ATS = 30.71 + 4.788 (ME) + 3.241 (SHH)

Where 30.71 is the constant to be considered at this step and 4.788 and 3.241 are the partial regression coefficients, and ME and SHH are scores on Mother's education and study Hours at home. The 'b' values for the variables are significant at 0.01 level.

There would not be much increase in R^2 after the 6th step.

The regression equation at the end of 6th step could be written as

$$ATS = 38.63 + 2.862\ (ME) + 3.596\ (SHH) + 4.644\ (M) - 8.198\ (L) + 2.521(FO) - 1.502\ (TSM).$$

It is observed from the Table 5.37 that it could be possible to explain 13.80 per cent of variance in the dependent variable ATS, with the above six variables.

There are 11 steps in this regression analysis. The summaries of the last step (11) of stepwise multiple regression analysis with achievement test score as dependent variable and nineteen (1-19) socio-demographic variables as independent variables are presented in the Table 5.38. The value of R^2 is 0.148. This shows that these eleven variables put together could explain 14.80 per cent of variance in the dependent variable (ATS). The regression equation at the end of 11th step could be written as;

$$ATS = 36.853+2.544\ (ME) + 3.294\ (SHH) + 4.619\ (M) - 7.854\ (L) - 2.451\ (FO) -1.363\ (TSM) + 1.391\ (C) - 2.668\ (A) + 1.151\ (RN) + 1.496(S) - 1.492\ (WH)$$

From the above discussion, it is clear that the multiple regression equation at the end of 6th step would be the best to predict ATS. Hence it is concluded that Achievement Test Score in mathematics could best be predicted with the help of 1. Mother's Education, 2. Study Hours at Home, 3. Management of the school, 4. Locality, 5. Father's occupation and 6. Time spent for mathematics Daily among the nineteen (1-19) socio-demographic variables.

Prediction of Scholastic Achievement in Mathematics with the help of 14 personality Factors (HSPQ)

The Achievement Test score in mathematics the variable number 53 in the Table 5.36 is predicted with the help of HSPQ (VN 20 to 33) using step-wise multiple regression analysis. The results of the regression analysis are presented in the Table 5.39.

Table 5.38: Summary of the Last Step (11) of Step-wise Regression Analysis with Achievement in Mathematics as Dependent Variable and 19 socio-demographic values as Independent variables

Step No.	IV (VN)	R	R^2	SER	F value for R	b (VN)	't' value for b	Constant	B	r	% of variance
1.	ME (8)	0.158	0.025	16.30	37.09** (1,1442)	2.545 (8)	3.093**	36.853	0.081	0.158	1.28
2.	SHH (16)	0.205	0.042	16.17	31.42** (2,1441)	3.294 (16)	5.135**		0.132	0.137	1.80
3.	M (1)	0.237	0.056	16.05	28.65** (3,1440)	4.619 (1)	10.795**		0.393	0.151	5.92
4.	L (1)	0.359	0.129	15.43	53.18** (4,1439)	-7.854 (3)	10.762**		-0.386	-0.087	3.37
5.	F.0 (11)	0.365	0.133	15.39	44.24** (5,1438)	2.451 (11)	2.580**		0.067	0.108	0.72
6.	TSM (19)	0.371	0.138	15.36	38.19** (6,1437)	1.363 (19)	2.394*		-0.061	-0.031	0.19
7.	C (5)	0.374	0.140	15.34	33.49** (5,1436)	1.391(5)	2.493*		0.063	0.053	0.34
8.	A (4)	0.378	0.143	15.32	29.92** (8,1435)	-2.668(4)	2.494*		-0.062	-0.041	0.26
9.	RN (12)	0.380	0.145	15.31	26.94** (9,1434)	1.151(12)	1.742@		0.043	0.072	0.31
10.	S (2)	0.382	0.146	15.30	24.57** (10,1433)	1.496(2)	1.768@		0.045	0.074	0.33
11.	WH (18)	0..384	0.148	15.29	22.62** (11,1432)	-1.492(18)	1.678@		-0.042	-0.065	0.28

Table 5.39: Prediction of Scholastic Achievement in Mathematics with the help of 14 personality factors (HSPQ).

Step No.	IV (VN)	R	R^2	SER	F value for R	b (VN)	't' value	Constant for b	B	r	% of variance
1	2	3	4	5	6	7	8	9	10	11	12
1.	FB	0.279	0.078	15.85	122.29**	2.611 (21)	11.06**	28.82	0.260	0.280	7.82
	21				(1,1442)		(1442)				
2.	FG	0.300	0.090	15.76	71.41**	2.405 (21)	10.05**		0.258		7.20
	26				(2,1441)	0.605 (26)	4.36**	23.17	0.112	0.163	1.82
							(1441)				
3.	FI	0.315	0.099	15.686	52.62**	2.329 (21)	9.74**		0.249		6.97
	28				(3,1440)	0.623 (26)	4.51**	17.74	0.115	0.111	1.87
						0.499 (28)	3.71**		0.093		1.04
							(14.40)				
4.	FQ_3	0.326	0.106	15.633	42.49**	2.179 (21)	8.99**		0.233		6.53
	(32)				(4,1439)	0.545 (26)	3.92**		0.101		1.64
						0.491 (28)	3.67**	14.03	0.092	0.160	1.02
						0.427 (32)	3.32**		0.086		1.38
							(1439)				

5.	FH	0.333	0.111	15.593	35.80**	2.049 (21)	8.32**	11.71	0.219	0.163	6.14
	(27)				(5,1438)	0.504 (26)	3.60**		0.093		1.51
						0.482 (28)	3.61**		0.090		1.00
						0.375 (32)	2.89**		0.075		1.21
						0.371 (27)	2.86**		0.075		1.21
						(1438)					
6.	FO	0.336	0.113	15.582	30.399**	2.036 (21)	8.27**	14.96	0.218		6.10
					(6,1437)	0.466 (26)	3.29**		0.086	–0.024	1.40
						0.486 (28)	3.63**		0.091		1.01
						0.335 (32)	2.55**		0.067		1.08
						0.338 (27)	2.58**		0.068		1.10
						–0.245 (30)	1.77@		–0.047		0.58

It could be seen from Table 5.39 that the first independent variable that entered into the step-wise regression analysis is 'Factor B' (FB) The multiple correlation R obtained is 0.279. It indicates that the strength of the relationship between the two variables (ATS and FB) is about 27.9 per cent. From Table 5.39 it is clear that R is significant (F=122.49) beyond 0.01 level of significance for 1 and 1442 df. The coefficient of R^2 is 0.078. This shows that 7.8 per cent of variance in ATS is accounted for by FB.

The standard error of multiple R (SER) is 15.85. From this it can be inferred that nearly 68 percent of the actual value of ATS would lie within M±15.85 of ATS value predicted with the help of this variable.

The partial regression coefficient (b), presented in the column 7 is 2.66. This value indicates that the value of ATS would change by 2.611 units for every one unit of change in FB. The 't' value for 'b' is 11.06 (Col 8) which is significant beyond 0.01 level of significance. The value of the constant that could be written to predict ATS at this stage is 28.82.

The multiple regression equation at the end of this step could be written as:

ATS = 28.82 + 2.611 (FB)

The second most important predictor variable that entered into the step-wise regression analysis is 'Factor G' (FG). The values of R and R^2 at this stage from the Table 5.39 are 0.300 and 0.090. Thus the amount of variance in ATS contributed by these two variables in combination is 9.00 per cent. Out of this the contribution of FB is 7.20 per cent and the remaining 1.82 per cent of variance is contributed by FG (V.N=26)

The multiple regression equation with these two predictor variables FB and FG could be written as

ATS = 23.17 + 2.405 (FB) + 0.605 (FG)

There are 6 steps in this regression analysis. The value of R^2 at the end of 6th step is 0.113. This shows that these six variables put together could explain 11.3 per cent of variance in the dependent variable i.e., ATS. The regression equation at the end of 6th step could be written as

$$ATS = 14.96 + 2.036\,(FB) + 0.466\,(FG) + 0.486\,(FI) + 0.335\,(FQ_3) + 0.338\,(FH) - 0.245\,(FO)$$

The above multiple regression equation at the end of 6th step would be the best equation to predict ATS. It is concluded that the scholastic achievement in mathematics could best be predicted with help of:

1. Factor-B,
2. Factor-G,
3. Factor-I,
4. Factor-Q_3,
5. Factor-H and
6. Factor-O among

14 personality factors.

It is possible to explain 11.26 per cent variance in the dependent variable with the help of the above 6 variables.

Predication of Scholastic Achievement in Mathematics with the Help of Study Habits

Prediction of Achievement Test Score (ATS), the variable 53, in the Table 5.36 (VN-53), is predicted with the help of study habits (VN 34 to 41), using step-wise multiple regression analysis, in this part. The results of the regression analysis are presented in Table 5.40.

It could be seen from Table 51 that the first variable entered into the step-wise regression analysis is 'Study Habits Total' (SH_T-41). The multiple correlation R obtained is 0.348. It indicates that the strength of the relationship between the two variables (ATS and SH_T) is about 34.8 per cent. It could be seen that R is significant (F=198.57) beyond 0.01 level of significance for 1 and 1442 df. The coefficient of multiple R^2 is 0.121. This shows that 12.1 per cent of variance in ATS is contributed by SH_T.

The standard error of estimation (SER), as seen from the Table 5.40 is 15.48. From this, it may be inferred that nearly 68 per cent of the actual ATS value would lie within M±15.48 of ATS value, predicted with the help of this variable (SH_T).

The partial regression coefficient presented in Column 7 of Table 5.40 is 0.305. This value indicates that the value of

Table 5.40. Prediction of Scholastic Achievement in Mathematics with the Help of Study Habits

Step No.	IV (VN)	R	R^2	SER	F value for R	b (VN)	't' value for b	Constant	B	r	% of variance
1	2	3	4	5	6	7	8	9	10	11	12
1.	SHT (41)	0.348	0.121	15.48	198.57** (1,1442)	0.305 (41)	14.09** (1442)	–4.30	0.348	0.303	12.10
2.	SH_5 (38)	0.383	0.147	15.26	123.75** (2,1441)	0.232 (41)	9.615**		0.264	0.206	9.19
						0.738 (38)	6.57** (1441)	–4.97	0.181		5.47
3.	SH_4 (37)	0.387	0.150	15.23	84.79** (3,1440)	0.196 (41)	6.96**	–4.13	0.223	0.206	7.77
						0.720 (38)	6.41**		0.176		5.34
						0.368 (37)	2.45* (1440)		0.074		1.91
4.	SH_7 (40)	0.389	0.151	15.23	64.19** (41,439)	0.230 (41)	6.33**		0.262	0.260	9.11
						0.680 (38)	5.89**		0.166		5.04
						0.324(37)	2.12*	–4.36	0.065		1.68
						0.186 (40)	1.48@ (1439)		–0.048		0.70

ATS would change by 0.305 units for every unit of change in SH_T. The 't' value for b is 14.09 (col.8) which is significant at 0.01 level. The value of constant that could be written to predict ATS at this stage is – 4.30.

The multiple regression equation at the end of this step could be written as

$$ATS = -4.30 + 0.305 (SH_T)$$

There are four steps in this regression analysis as shown in the

Table 5.40. The regression equation at the end of 4th step would be the best to predict the dependent variable ATS (VN-53) and could be written as:

$$ATS = -4.36 + 0.231 (SH_T) + 0.680 (SH_5) + 0.324 (SH_4) + 0.186 (SH_7)$$

With the help of above four variables namely:

1. Study Habits total Scores,
2. Preparation for examination,
3. Habits of concentration and
4. Social environment,

it is possible to explain 15.14 percent of variance in the dependent variable i.e. scholastic achievement in mathematics.

Prediction of Scholastic Achievement in Mathematics with the Help of Self-concepts.

This part deals with the prediction of ATS (dependent variable, VN 53 in the Table 5.36 with the help of 10 areas of self-concepts and self-concepts total score. (Independent variables, VN-42 to 52 in the Table 5.36), using stepwise multiple regression analysis. The results of regression analysis are presented in the Table 5.41.

As seen from the Table 5.41 the most important independent variable that entered first into the step-wise regression analysis is 'self concepts total' (SC_T). The multiple correlation R obtained is 0.255. It indicates that the strength of the relationship between the two variables ATS and SC_T is about 25.5 per cent. It could be seen that R is significant ($F = 100.54$) beyond 0.01 level of significance for 1 and 1443df. The coefficient of R^2 is 0.065. This shows that 6.5 per cent of variance in ATS is accounted by SC_T.

Table 51. Prediction of Scholastic Achievement in Mathematics with the help of self concepts

Step No.	IV (VN)	R	R^2	SER	F value for R	b (VN)	't' value for b	Constant	B	r	% of variance
1	2	3	4	5	6	7	8	9	10	11	12
1.	SCT	0.255	0.065	15.97	100.54**	0.275	10.027**	–0.15	0.255	0.111	6.52
	(52)				(1,1442)		(1442)				
2.	SC_2	0.265	0.070	15.93	54.36 **	0.219 (52)	6.39**		0.203		5.17
	(43)				(2,1441)	0.301 (43)	2.78**	0.71	0.088	0.085	1.84
							(1441)				
3.	SC_9	0.268	0.072	15.92	37.09**	0.231 (52)	6.59 **		0.215		5.49
	(50)				(3,1440)	0.278 (43)	2.54*	2.33	0.081	0.209	1.70
						–0.271 (50)	1.56@		–0.041		0.01
							(1440)				
4.	SC_1	0.270	0.073	15.91	28.53 **	0.251 (52)	6.77**		0.233		5.95
	(42)				(4,1439)	0.265 (43)	2.42*		0.078		1.62
						–0.288 (50)	1.65@	3.99	–0.043	0.069	– 0.01
						–0.211 (42)	1.65@		–0.045		– 0.21
							(1439)				

5.	SC_8	0.276	0.076	15.90	23.64**	0.292 (52)	6.87**	3.07	0.271	0.046	6.91
	(49)				(5,1438)	0.238 (43)	2.15*		0.069		1.45
						–0.321 (50)	1.84@		–0.048		–0.01
						–0.267 (42)	2.05*		–0.057		–0.26
						–0.261 (49)	1.96*		–		–0.49
							(1438)		0.058		
6.	SC_6	0.281	0.079	15.88	20.47**	0.330 (52)	7.14**	4.02	0.306	0.255	7.82
	(47)				(6,1437)	0.219 (43)	1.98*		0.064		1.34
						–0.356 (50)	2.03*		–0.054		–0.02
						–0.296 (42)	2.26*		–0.063		–0.29
						–0.305 (49)	2.27*		–0.068		–0.57
						–0.310 (47)	2.09*		–0.059		–0.41
							(1437)				

The standard error of estimation (SER) is 15.97. From this it can be inferred that nearly 68 per cent of the actual ATS value would lie within M ± 15.97 of ATS value predicted with the help of this variable (SC_T).

The partial regression coefficient (b) presented in column 7 of Table 5.41 is 0.275. this value indicates that the ATS value would change by 0.275 units for every unit of change in SC_T. The 't' value for 'b' (col 8) is 10.027 which is significant beyond 0.01 level of significance for 1 and 1442 df. The value of constant that could be written to predict ATS at this stage is -0.15. The multiple regression equation at the end of this step could be written as:

$$ATS = -0.15 + 0.275\ (SC_T).$$

The second important predictor variable that entered into the step-wise regression analysis is SC_2 (VN 43). The value of R and R^2 at this stage from the Table 5.36 are 0.265 and 0.070 respectively. Thus the amount of variance in ATS contributed by these two variables in combination is 7.00 per cent out of which SC_T has contributed 5.17 per cent of variance and the remaining 1.84 per cent of variance is contributed by SC_2 (VN 43).

The multiple regression equation with these two predictor variables SC_T and SC_2 could be written as

$$ATS = 0.71 + 0.219\ (SC_T) + 0.301\ (SC_2).$$

There are six steps in this regression analysis. The value of R^2 in the 6th step from the Table 5.41 is 0.079. This shows that these six variables put together could explain 7.90 percent of variance in the dependent variable (ATS). The regression equation at the end of 6th step could be written as :

$$ATS = 4.02 + 0.330\ (SC_T) + 0.219\ (SC_2) - 0.356\ (SC_9) - 0.296\ (SC_1) - 0.305\ (SC_8) - 0.310\ (SC_6)$$

With the help of the above six variables namely

1. self concept total score,
2. Abilities,
3. Sociability
4. Health and Sex appropriateness,
5. Feelings of shame and Guilt, and
6. Past, Present and future, it is possible to explain,
7. 87 per cent of variance in the dependent variable.

Prediction of Scholastic Achievement in Mathematics with the Help of all 52 Independent Variables in the Study

In this part, the relative contribution of all 52 independent variables, (VN 1 to 52) in the Table 5.36 to the scholastic achievement in mathematics (VN 53) in the Table 5.36 is predicted with the help of step-wise multiple regression analysis. The results of the regression analysis are presented in the Table 5.42.

It could be seen from the Table 5.42 that the first variable entered into the stepwise multiple regression analysis is 'study Habits Total' (SH_T) among the 52 variables.

The multiple correlation R obtained is 0.348. This value shows that the strength of the relationship between the two variables, namely 'scholastic achievement and 'study habits total' is about 34.8 per cent. It could also be seen from the Table 5.42 that R is highly significant (F = 198.55) at 0.01 level for 1 and 1442 df. The coefficient of multiple R^2 is 0.121. This shows that 12.10 percent of variance is accounted for by this variable, to the achievement test score (ATS)

The standard error multiple R (SER) is 15.48. From this it may be inferred that nearly 68 percent of the actual ATS value would be within

M ± 15.48 of ATS value predicted with the help of this variable (SH_T).

The partial regression coefficient (b) presented in column 7 is 0.305. This value indicates that the ATS value would change by 0.305 units for every unit of change in SH_T. The 't' value for 'b' is 14.09 which is highly significant at 0.01 level. The value of the constant that could be written to predict ATS at the end of this stage is –4.30.

Thus the multiple regression equation at the end of this step could be written as:

$$ATS = -4.30 + 0.305 (SH_T)$$

The results of the regression analysis upto 9th step are presented in the Table 5.42. It is seen from the Table 5.42 that there is no much increase in R^2 from 9th step onwards.

Table 5.42. Prediction of Scholastic Achievement in Mathematics with the Help of all Independent Variables

Step No.	IV (VN)	R	R^2	SER	F value for R	b (VN)	't' value for b	Constant	B	r	% of variance
1	2	3	4	5	6	7	8	9	10	11	12
1.	SHT	.348	.121	15.48	198.55**	0.305	14.09**	–4.30	0.348	0.348	12.10
	(41)				(1,1442)						
2.	FB	.396	.157	15.16	134.37**	0.256 (41)	11.62**		0.293		10.18
	(21)				(2,1441)	1.849 (21)	7.86**	–7.91		0.280	5.54
							(1441)				
3.	SH_5	.422	.178	14.98	104.14**	0.193 (41)	7.95**		0.220		7.64
	(38)				(3,1440)	1.737 (21)	7.45**	–8.31	0.186	0.303	5.20
						0.672 (38)	6.08**		0.165		4.99
							(1040)				
4.	I	.444	.197	14.82	88.03**	0.193 (41)	8.04**		0.220		7.54
	(13)				(4,1439)	1.721 (21)	7.47**		0.184		5.15
						0.654 (38)	5.98**	–16.72	0.160	0.149	4.85
						8.156 (13)	5.73**		0.135		2.01
							(1439)				

5.	L (3)	.468	.219	14.61	80.82** (5,1438)	0.199 (41)	8.43**		0.227		7.90
						1.775 (21)	7.81**		0.190		5.32
						0.656 (38)	6.08**	–13.77	0.160	–0.087	4.86
						10.133 (13)	7.05**		0.168		2.50
						–3.156 (3)	6.48** (1438)		–0.155		1.35
6.	M (1)	.508	.258	14.25	83.38** (6.1437)	0.205(41)	8.88**		0.234		8.13
						1.566 (21)	7.02**		0.168		4.69
						0.525 (38)	4.94**		0.128		3.89
						6.225 (13)	4.23**	–6.24	0.103	0.151	1.54
						–7.153 (3)	10.81**		–0.351		3.07
						3.515 (1)	8.68** (1437)		0.299		4.51
7.	FI (28)	.515	.265	14.19	73.96** (7,1436)	0.206 (41)	8.96**	–	0.235		8.17
						1.508 (21)	6.77**		0.162		4.52
						0.516 (38)	4.88**		0.126		3.83
						6.214 (13)	4.24**	10.87	–.103	0.111	1.53
						–7.149 (3)	10.85**		–7.149		3.07
						3.487 (1)	8.64**		0.297		4.47
						0.442 (28)	3.64** (1436)		0.083		0.92

...(Contd.)

1	2	3	4	5	6	7	8	9	10	11	12
8.	SHH	.521	.271	14.13	66.75**	0.193 (41)	8.32**	−13.88	0.220	0.137	
	(16)				(8,1435)	1.477 (21)	6.65**		0.158		
						0.533 (38)	5.05**		0.130		
						5.951 (13)	4.07**		0.099		
						−7.115 (3)	10.84**		−0.349		
						3.526 (1)	8.77**		0.300		
						0.461 (28)	3.80**		0.086		
						2.010 (16)	3.49**		0.080		
							(1435)				
9.	SCT	.525	.276	14.09	60.77**	0.168 (41)	6.89**	−22.75	0.192	0.255	
	(50)				(9,)1434	1.415 (21)	6.36**		0.192		
						0.513 (38)	4.87**		0.152		
						5.932 (13)	4.07**		0.126		
						−6.983 (3)	4.07**		0.099		
						3.489 (1)	10.65**		−0.343		
						0.451 (28)	8.70**		0.297		
						1.878 (16)	3.73**		0.084		
						0.084 (52)	3.27**		0.075		
							3.12**		0.078		
							(1434)				

Therefore, the regression equation at the end of 9th step would be the best to predict the dependent variable ATS and it could be written as

$$ATS = -22.75 + 0.168\,(SH_T) + 1.415\,(FB) + 0.513\,(SH_5) + 5.932\,(I) - 6.983\,(L) + 3.489\,(M) + 0.451\,FI) + 1.878\,(SHH) + 0.084\,(SC_T)$$

With the help of above nine variables it is possible to explain 27.6 per cent of variance in dependent variable i.e. scholastic achievement in mathematics.

There are 18 steps in this regression analysis. The summary at the end of 18th step is presented in the Table 5.43.

From the value of R^2 in 18th step, it is inferred that 29.6 per cent of variance in ATS is, contributed by all these 18 Predictor variables put together.

The regression equation at the end of 18th step could be written as.

$$\begin{aligned} ATS = {} & -2875 + 0.119\,(SH_T) + 1.314\,(FB) + 0.507\,(SH_5) \\ & + 3.600\,(I) - 7.026\,(L) + 3.515\,(M) + 0.483\,(FI) \\ & + 1.690\,(SHH) + 0.097\,(SC_T) + 0.411\,(SH_4) \\ & + 1.538\,(C) - 0.253\,(SC_8) + 1.438\,(RN) \\ & + 1.385\,(ME) - 1.693\,(A) + 1.402\,(S) \\ & + 0.183\,(FQ_3) + 1.330\,(FO) \end{aligned}$$

SUMMARY TABLE OF THE FINAL STEP

Table 5.43. (18) of Regression Analysis with Scholastic Achievement in Mathematics as Dependent Variable and Remaining 52 Variables as Independent Variables.

Step No.	IV (VN)	R	R^2	SER	F value for R	b (VN)	't' value for b	Constant	B	r	% of variancc
1	2	3	4	5	6	7	8	9	10	11	12
1.	SHT (41)	0.348	0.121	15.48	198.55** (1,1442)	0.119	4.241**	–28.75	0.136	0.348	4.71
2.	FB (21)	0.396	0.157	15.16	134.37** (2,1441)	1.314	5.888**		0.141	0.280	3.94
3.	SH_5 (38)	0.422	0.178	14.98	104.14** (3,1440)	0.507	4.805**		0.124	0.303	3.76
4.	I (13)	0.444	0.197	14.82	88.03** (4,1439)	3.600	2.292*		0.060	0.149	0.89
5.	L (3)	0.468	0.219	14.61	80.82 ** (5,1438)	–7.026	10.463**		-0.345	-0.087	3.01
6.	M (1)	0.508	0.258	14.25	83.38** (6.1437)	3.515	8.581**		0.299	0.151	4.51
7.	FI (28)	0.515	0.265	14.19	73.96** (7,1436)	0.483	3.977**		0.090	0.111	1.00

8.	SHH (16)	0.521	0.271	14.13	66.75** (8,1435)	1.690	2.933**		0.068	0.137	0.92
9.	SCT (52)	0.525	0.276	14.09	60.77** (9,1434)	0.097	3.195**		0.090	0.255	2.29
10	SH_4 (37)	0.529	0.280	14.05	55.78** (10,1433)	0.411	2.968**		0.082	0.260	2.13
11	C (5)	0.533	0.284	14.02	51.68** (11,1432)	1.538	3.005**		0.070	0.053	0.37
12	SC_8 (49)	0.536	0.287	14.00	47.99** (12,1431)	–0.253	2.214*		–0.057	0.084	–0.47
13	RN (12)	0.538	0.289	13.98	44.79** (13,1430)	1.438	2.381*		0.055	0.072	0.39
14	ME (8)	0.539	0.293	13.96	41.99** (14,1429)	1.385	1.821@		0.044	0.158	0.70
15.	(A) (4)	0.541	0.293	13.96	39.39** (15,1428)	–1.693	1.732@		–0.040	–0.041	0.16
16.	(S) (2)	0.542	0.294	13.95	37.11** (16,1427)	1.402	1.770@		0.042	0.074	0.31
17	FQ_3 (32)	0.543	0.295	13.94	35.09** (17,1426)	0.183	1.536@		0.037	+0.160	0.59
18	FO (11)	0.544	0.296	13.94	33.29** (18,1425)	1.330	1.473@		0.036	0.108	0.39

Summary, Findings, Conclusions, Recommendations and Suggestions

This chapter deals with the summary, major findings, conclusions, recommendations and suggestions for further research.

SUMMARY

Mathematics plays a very important role in the life of all human beings. Every body needs the knowledge of mathematics in one way or other. Importance of mathematics is very clear, from its wide applications ranging from daily uses of even a common man, to its applications for the development of science, Engineering and Technology and even social sciences including languages. Former President of India A.P.J. Abdul Kalam called upon the universities to turnout a global cadre of skilled professionals in Science and Technology to make India to realize its dreams of a developed nation by 2020. Mathematics plays a key role for the development of Science and Technology. National Education commission observed "proper foundation in the knowledge of the subject should be laid down at the school level itself".

The achievement in mathematics is related to various factors. The present investigation is to find out the relationship between achievement in mathematics of 10th class students and various socio-demographic and Psychological variables.

Introduction

Education is found to be an effective tool to bring the required changes in the society. The National Education Commission

(1964-66) has emphasized that education is the one and only instrument that can be used to bring about a change towards the social and economic betterment of India. Further, the Commission quoted: "India is now being shaped in her class rooms". It is not only a saying but also a reality. In the world, based on Science and Technology, it is the education that determines the level of prosperity, welfare and security of the people.

The present day modern world is witnessed with unprecedented growth of Science and Technology and the life style of the people has been constantly changing accordingly. Mathematics can be considered as the back-bone for the development of Science and Technology. Mathematics plays a very important role in the development of the country. Napoleon said:

> "the progress and improvement of mathematics are linked to the prosperity of the state."

In view of the important role that Mathematics plays in the modern world, it has been imperative for any nation or the world to promote mathematics education, in their respective countries. It is not possible for us to expect improved mathematics education, in the higher education, unless, we succeed in providing a sound mathematics education at the school level.

Secondary education has been considered as the weakest link between lower and higher education levels, in view of the low standards and more failures and dropouts after the secondary level of education. In this aspect, an achievement of the students in all the subjects is the most significant factor, in educational system. Among the different areas of research in education, academic achievement, is one of the most extensively investigated phenomena. The standards of education at schools and colleges would be reflexed by the performance of pupils in their academic subjects. Academic achievement is the main concern of our educationists and the government. Achievement of the students, depends upon several Sociological, Psychological and environmental aspects. This fact was established by several investigations, in our country and aboard. The present study is aimed at establishing a meaningful relationship between achievement in mathematics and various psychological and demographical variables.

Statement of the Problem

The present study is concerned with the scholastic achievement of 10th class students in mathematics. It examines the main effect of management, sex and their interaction effect on the scholastic achievement. It also examines the main effects of locality, caste and their interaction effect on the achievement. It establishes the relationship between the scholastic achievement and other variables, personality factors, study habits and self-concepts. It also predicts the scholastic achievement with the help of different sets of psycho-sociological variables.

Title of the Problem

The title of the problem is "Performance in School Mathematics."

Scope of the Study

The main intention of the study is to find the relation of scholastic achievement of 10th class-students with socio-demographic variables, personality factors, study habits and self-concepts. The marks obtained in an objective test, in mathematics are taken as scholastic achievement in mathematics which is regarded as dependent variable in the present study. The objective achievement test is developed and standardized by the investigator. The socio-demographic variables personality factors, study habits and self concepts are measured by using the relevant instruments. The study is confined to, only 22 schools of Chittoor District, under the managements of Zilla Parishad, Government, Municipalities, A.P. Social Welfare Department and Private. As already described in the earlier chapters, only a few variables have been included in this study. A number of factors will have their impact on the achievement, in mathematics. Each and every variable having its influence on the achievement could not be included in this study.

The study also attempts to predict the scholastic achievement with the help of different sets of psycho-sociological variables.

Need for the Study

In one's life, the intellectual capacities and capabilities are assessed by his/her achievements in various subjects. In the present educational system, the various programmes are not confined, only to the text books. Using of libraries and laboratories for additional information, making arrangements for workshops, seminars, various competitions, have come into school life. The unprecedented expansion of educational system, the enormous financial investments, made in educating the children, by individuals and governments, and the need to point out the priorities of educational expenditure, necessitate the identification of various factors, contributing most, for student learning and achievement levels. The achievement in various subjects, of learners, is the result of combined efforts of teachers, parents, managements of schools and students. Again there is an effect of various Psycho-sociological factors, on the achievement of students.

There is an urgent educational and social need to study and identify the influence of various factors, on the achievement of high school pupils, to draw up the conclusions for high/low achievements.

Scholastic achievement, continues to be one of the most important variables, held in high esteem in all cultures, countries and times. Hence, the research related to the area of academic achievement, is ever growing concern of the researchers, educationists and educational administrators.

In the present day, education is viewed seriously that there is every need to raise the standards of the pupils at all levels. A concerted effort is to be made to identify some of the significant socio-psychological factors that influence the academic achievement of the student and to explain the contribution of these factors.

An interesting feature observed is that majority of the studies in the area of scholastic achievement were confined to the simple correlational analysis between predictors and criterion variables. Individual and cumulative effects of several independent variables on the scholastic achievement could be assessed more accurately by employing regression analysis. Therefore the main aim of the present study is to identify, the influence of independent factors and to predict the multiple effect of independent factors on the achievement of 10th class students, in mathematics, with the help of various socio-psychological factors and further to suggest suitable regression equations, in the prediction of scholastic achievement. The study also aims at making some recommendations for further study in the field and some suggestions for teachers.

The above crucial conditions lead the investigator to make an attempt in this area of scholastic achievement of 10th class pupils in mathematics in relation to certain psycho-sociological factors.

Objectives of the Study

The following are the objectives of the study:

1. To understand the present status of 10th class students with regard to their achievement in mathematics.
2. To study the impact of management and sex and their interaction effect on the scholastic achievement.
3. To study the impact of locality and caste their interaction effect on the scholastic achievement.
4. To study the influence of socio-demographic variables on the scholastic achievement.
5. To study the impact of personality factors on the

scholastic achievement of 10th class students in mathematics.

6. To study the impact of self-concepts on the scholastic achievement of 10th class students in mathematics.
7. To predict the scholastic achievement of 10th class students in mathematics, with the help of socio-demographic variables, personality factors, study habits and self-concepts.
8. To predict the scholastic achievement of 10th class students, in mathematics, with the help of all the independent variables in the investigation.
9. To develop mathematical equations for predicting the scholastic achievement of 10th class students in mathematics.
10. To summarize the findings of the present investigation.
11. To make appropriate recommendations on the basis of present findings.
12. To provide suggestions for further research.

Hypotheses to be Tested

In the light of the above objectives, the following major null hypotheses have been formulated for the purpose of investigation.

1. All the 10th class students would not have the same scholastic achievement abilities in mathematics.
2. Management, sex and their interaction would not have significant influence on the scholastic achievement of 10th class students in mathematics.
3. Locality, caste and their interaction would not have significant influence on the scholastic achievement of 10th class-students in mathematics.
4. Socio-Demographic variables would not have any significant influence on the scholastic achievement of 10th class students in mathematics.

5. Personality factors would not have any significant influence on the scholastic achievement of 10th class students in mathematics.
6. Study habits would not have any significant impact on the scholastic achievement of 10th class students in mathematics.
7. Self-concepts would not have any significant impact on the scholastic achievement of 10th class students in mathematics.
8. It would not be possible to predict the scholastic achievement with the help of all independent variables.
9. It would not be possible to develop mathematical equations with the help of different sets of independent variables.

Variables Included in the Study

The review of related literature in the field of scholastic achievement reveals the fact that the scholastic achievement of students has been influenced by a number of psycho-sociological variables. Hence the following psycho-sociological variables are included in the study

Dependent Variables

Achievement in objective Achievement Test (OAT) consisting of 100 multiple choice questions.

Independent Variables

I. Socio-Demographic Variables (1-19)

1. Management of the School
2. Gender
3. Locality
4. Age
5. Caste
6. Birth order

7. Number of members in the family
8. Mother's education
9. Father's education
10. Mother's occupation
11. Father's occupation
12. Religion
13. Income of the family
14. Economic Status
15. Separate room for study
16. Study hours at Home
17. Help from family members
18. Works at home
19. Time spent for mathematics

II. Personality Factors HSPQ (20-33)

20. Factor-A
21. Factor-B
22. Factor-C
23. Factor-D
24. Factor-E
25. Factor-F
26. Factor-G
27. Factor-H
28. Factor-I
29. Factor-J
30. Factor-O
31. Factor-Q_2
32. Factor-Q_3
33. Factor-Q_4

III. Study Habits (34-41)

34. Home environment for study
35. Reading and note taking

36. Planning for reading subjects
37. Habits of concentration
38. Preparations for examinations
39. General Habits and attitudes
40. School Environment
41. Study Habits total score

IV. Self-Concepts (42-52)

42. Health and sex Appropriateness
43. Abilities
44. Self-confidence
45. Self-acceptance
46. Worthiness
47. Self-Concepts about present, past, future
48. Beliefs and convictions
49. Feelings of shame and guilt.
50. Sociability
51. Emotional Maturity
52. Self-concepts total score.

Research Tools

1. The investigator has developed Objective Achievement Test (OAT) and standardized to measure the achievement in mathematics of 10th class students.
2. Cattle's 14 personality factors, Form-A (HSPQ) is adopted to measure the personality traits of the students.
3. Study-Habits inventory developed and standardized by Dr B.V.Patel, is adopted to study the influence of study habits of the pupils on the dependent variable, (Achievement in mathematics).
4. Dr (Miss) Mukta Rani Rastogi's (1974) self-concept scale is adopted to measure the self-concepts of the students.

5. Personal Data Questionnaire is developed by the investigator with the help of experts in the field of education, to measure the socio-economic and demographic variables.

Sample Selected

For the present study, the sample consisting of 22 schools under different managements namely Zilla Parishad, Government, Municipalities, A.P Social Welfare Department and private management have been selected. Geographically the Chittoor District is divided into four revenue divisions, namely Madanapally, Tirupati, Chittoor and Palamaner. Keeping in view the number of schools, existing in each revenue division, ten Zilla Parishad high schools, three Government high schools, three Municipal High Schools, three Andhra Pradesh Social Welfare Residential Schools and three private unaided schools under different managements are selected. The sample selected consists of 650 boys and 794 girls (N=1444)

Collection of Data

The investigator personally visited all the schools selected for the study and explained the heads of the institutions, the purpose of collecting the data. The students were given necessary instructions and motivated to respond genuinely. Advance intimation about the visit of the investigator was provided to the Headmaster and the students. The students, who attended the schools, on the days of collecting data are considered for the purpose of investigation. All the necessary data was collected with the help of the data gathering instruments and teachers of the concerned schools.

Scoring and Analysis

1. The objective achievement test consists of one hundred multiple choice questions and each correct response is awarded with one mark.
2. For the 14PF personality questionnaire, the scoring key prepared by th author is employed.

3. The study habits inventory is scored on a five point scale by giving weightages 5,4,3,2 and 1, for positive items and 1, 2, 3, 4, and 5 for negative items to the five alternatives; always, often, some times, rarely and never respectively. The self concept scale is scored in a similar manner to the five alternatives strongly agree, agree, undecided, disagree and strongly disagree.

   The total scores for each area of respective inventories are entered and grand total is obtained by adding all the weightages, on all the statements and marked them on the top right corner of the inventory.

4. The information furnished by the students on socio-demographic variables is numerically coded in order to suit for the computer analysis.

The analysis is carried out on the basis of objectives of the study and hypotheses formulated, by employing appropriate statistical techniques.

Frequency distribution tables are prepared for the total sample, for different types of schools, for boys and girls, for different localities and different castes.

Measures of central tendency, measures of dispersion, skewness, Kurtosis, coefficient of variation and standard error of mean, are computed and used wherever necessary.

The inferential Statistical Techniques 't' test and 'F' test are employed to test the different hypotheses. Multiple 'R' is computed for carrying out stepwise regression analysis, for predicting the scholastic achievement with the help of different sets of independent variables. The services of S.V. University computer centre are also utilized.

The levels of significance employed with respective symbols are given below.

** Indicates significant at 0.01 level

* indicates significant at 0.05 level

@ indicates not significant at 0.05 level

MAJOR FINDINGS OF THE STUDY

The statistical analysis of the data reveals the following broad findings of the investigation:

Distribution characteristics of scholastic achievements scores

1. The mean scholastic achievement score of 10th class students in mathematics for the whole group is 44.97. Hence the performance of the students is poor. Median is 41.00 and mode is 33.06. Hence, the distribution is not normal. It is more peaked than the normal distribution.
2. The values of skewness and Kurtosis are 0.82 and 3.39 respectively. Hence, the distribution of the scholastic achievement scores for the total sample is positively skewed and leptokurtic.
3. It is found that the mean scholastic achievement score for the pupils of private schools is the highest (53.78) among all the groups namely (*i*) whole groups (*ii*) Zilla Parishad schools (*ii*) Government Schools (*iv*) Municipal Schools (*v*) A.P. Social welfare Residential schools (*vi*) Private schools (*vii*) males (*viii*) females (*ix*) rural (*x*) semi urban (*xi*) urban (*xii*) schedule caste/tribes (*xiii*) Backward castes and (*xiv*) other castes. The mean scholastic achievement score for the students of government schools is the least (38.10), as compared with other groups. The performance of males (46.31) is better than that of females (43.86). It is also observed that the rural pupils' performance (47.26) is better than semi urban (44.39) and urban (43.63). The performance of the urban students is the least (43.63). Also it is noticed that the performance of O.C. students (46.81) is better than SC/ST (44.54) and BC (44.00) students. For all the distributions, the value of skewness is positive. Hence, all the distributions are positively skewed. The values

of kurtosis for A.P. Social Welfare Residential School students (2.58) and private school students (2.30) are less than 3.00. Hence, these two distributions are leptokurtic. The value of kurtosis for OC students is 3.00. Hence the distribution for OC students is mesokurtic and all the remaining distributions are platykurtic.

Factorial Designs

4. There is a significant influence of 'Management' on the scholastic achievement of 10th class students in mathematics at 0.01 level of significance.
5. Sex has no significant influence at 0.05 level, on the scholastic achievement of 10th class students in mathematics.
6. There is, significant interaction effect of management and sex at 0.01 level, on the scholastic achievement of 10th class students.
7. 'Locality' has significant influence at 0.05 level on the scholastic achievement of 10th class students in mathematics.
8. The variable 'caste' has significant influence at 0.05 level on the scholastic achievement of 10th class students.
9. There is significant interaction effect of locality and caste at 0.01 level on the scholastic achievement of 10th class students in mathematics.

Influence of Socio-Demographic and Personal Variables

10. 'Age' has no significant influence at 0.05 level on the scholastic achievement of 10th class pupils in mathematics.
11. 'Birth order' has no significant influence at 0.05 level on the scholastic achievement of 10th class students in mathematics.

12. 'Number of members in the family' has no significant influence at 0.05 level on the scholastic achievement of 10th class students in mathematics.
13. 'Mother's education' has significant influence at 0.01 level, on the scholastic achievement of 10th class students in mathematics.
14. 'Father's education' has significant influence at 0.01 level, on the achievement of 10th class students in mathematics.
15. Mother's occupation has significant influence at 0.01 level on the scholastic achievement of 10th class students in mathematics.
16. 'Father's occupation' has significant influence at 0.01 level on the scholastic achievement of 10th class students in mathematics.
17. 'Religion' has significant influence at 0.01 level on the scholastic achievement of 10th class students in mathematics
18. 'Annual income of the family' has significant influence at 0.01 level on the scholastic achievement of 10th class students in mathematics. Better the income, better is the academic achievement.
19. 'Economic status of the family' has significant influence at 0.01 level on the scholastic achievement of 10th class students.
20. It is observed that 'separate study room' has significant influence at 0.05 level on the scholastic achievement in mathematics. Students with separate study room will have better achievement.
21. 'Study Hours at Home' has significant influence at 0.01 level on the scholastic achievement of 10th class students in mathematics. It is clear that more the number of study hours, at home, better is the scholastic achievement.
22. 'Help from the family members' has no significant influence at 0.05 level on the scholastic achievement of 10th class students.

23. 'Works at home' has significant influence at 0.05 on the scholastic achievement of 10th class students in mathematics. Hence more the works at home, less would be the achievement in mathematics.
24. 'Time spent for mathematics daily' has no significant influence on the achievement of 10th class students in mathematics. Hence it is clear that the time spent on mathematics, is not the criterion for better achievement. Better achievement in mathematics may depend upon so many other factors, like interest, attitude, intelligence etc.

Influence of Personality Factors (HSPQ)

25. It is found that students who are having personality characteristics of (i) More intelligent (*ii*) Emotionally stable, (*iii*) Obedient, (*iv*) Super-ego strength, (*v*) venturesome, (*vi*) Tense – minded, (vii) placid, and (*viii*) controlled have significantly better scholastic achievement in mathematics than the students who are having the personality characteristics of (*i*) Less intelligent (*ii*) Emotionally less stable, (*iii*) Assertive, (*iv*) Moral standards, (*v*) Shy (*vi*) Though minded, (*vii*) Apprehensive and (*viii*) Undisciplined.

    The remaining personality factors do not have significant influence on the scholastic achievement in mathematics.

Influence of Study Habits

26. It is found that the students, who have better study habits achieved significantly better in mathematics. Therefore 'Study habits' have significant influence on the achievement of 10th class students in mathematics. Developing proper study habits is desirable.

Influence of Self-Concepts

27. It is found that self-concepts like (*i*) Abilities (SC_2), (*ii*) Self-confidence (SC_3), (*iii*) Self-Acceptance (SC_4),

(*iv*) Worthiness (SC_5), (*v*) present-past-future (SC_6), (*vi*) Beliefs and convictions (SC_7), (vii) Feelings of Shame and Guilt (SC_8), (*viii*) Emotional Maturity (SC_{10}) and (*ix*) Self-concepts total score (SC_T), have significant influence on the achievement of 10th class students in mathematics.

28. The areas of self-concepts namely
    (*i*) Health and sex appropriateness (SC_1) and
    (*ii*) Sociability (SC_9) do not have significant influence on the achievement of 10th class students in mathematics.

Step-wise Multiple Regression Analysis

29. It is found that the best regression equations for predicting the scholastic achievement in mathematics of 10th class students are:
    (*i*) With the help of 19 socio-demographic variables
    ATS = 3863 +2.862 (ME) + 3.596 (SHH) + 4.644 (M) – 8.198 (L) + 2.521 (F.0) – 1.502 (TSM).
    The variance explained with the help of the above 6 variables is 13.80 per cent.
    (*ii*) With the help of 14 personality factors.
    ATS = 14.96 + 2.036 (FB) + 0.466 (FG) + 0.486 (F((I) + 0.335 (FQ_3) + 0.338 (FH) – 0.245 (FO)
    The variance explained with the help of the above 6 variables is 11.26.
    (*iii*) With the help of 7 areas of study habits.
    ATS = –4.36 + 0.231 (SH_7) + 0.680 (SH_5) + 0.324 (SH_4+) + 0.186 (SH_7)
    The variance explained with the help of the above 4 variables is 15.14 per cent.
    (*iv*) With the help of 10 areas of self-concept scale.
    ATS = 4.02 + 0.330 (SC_T) + 0.219 (SC_2) – 0.356 (SC_9) – 0.296 (SC_1) – 0.305 (SC_3) – 0.310 (SC_6)

The variance explained with the help of the above 6 variables is 7.87 per cent.

(*v*) With the help of all independent variables in the study

$$ATS = -22.75 + 0.168\ (SH_T) + 1.415\ (FB) + 0.513\ (SH_5) + 5.932\ (I) - 6.983\ (L) + 3.489\ (M) + 0.451\ (F(I) + 1.878\ (SHH) + 0.084\ (SC_T)$$

With the help of the above nine variables, it is possible to explain 27.6 per cent of variance in the dependent variable.

It is concluded that the achievement in mathematics could be best predicted with the help of (*i*) study habits total scores, (*ii*) Personality Factor-B, (*iii*) Preparation for examinations (*iv*) Income of the family, (*v*) Locality, (*vi*) Management of the school, (*vii*) Personality Factor-I, (*viii*) study hours at home and (*ix*) self-concepts total score.

30. A model of relationship between independent variables and dependent variables is shown in Fig. 6.1.

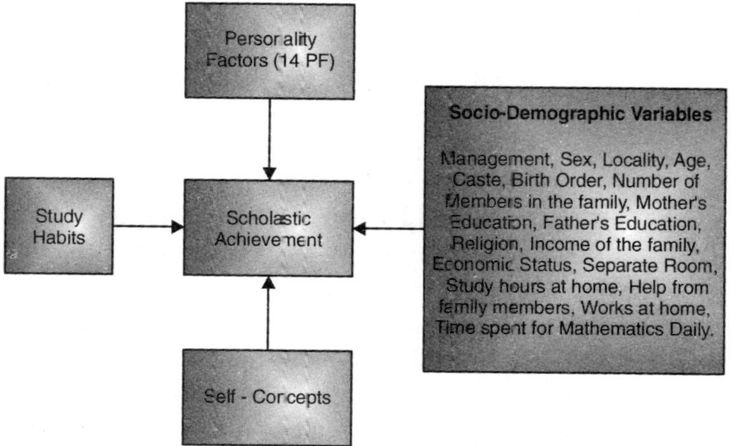

Fig. 6.1. Model of Relationship Between Independent and Depenent Variable

CONCLUSIONS

On the basis of the findings in the preceding pages, the following conclusions are drawn:

1. The frequency distributions of the scholastic achievement of 10th class students for the whole group is not normal. It is more peaked than the normal distributions.
2. All the 10th students do not have the same scholastic achievement abilities.
3. There is a significant influence of 'Management' on the scholastic achievement of 10th class students in mathematics.
4. 'Sex' has no significant influence on the scholastic achievement of 10th class students in mathematics.
5. There is significant interaction effect of management and sex on the scholastic achievement of 10th class students in mathematics.
6. 'Locality' and 'Caste' have significant influence on the scholastic achievement of 10th class students in mathematics.
7. There is significant interaction effect of 'Locality' and 'Caste' on the scholastic achievement of 10th class students in mathematics.
8. The socio-demographic and personal variables viz., (*i*) Mother's education, (*ii*) Father's education, (*iii*) Mother's occupation, (*iv*) Father's occupation, (*v*) Religion, (*vi*) Annual income of the family, (*vii*) Economic status, (*viii*) Separate Room for study, (*ix*) study hours at home and (*x*) works at home have significant influence on the scholastic achievement of 10th class students in mathematics.
9. The following socio-demographic and personal variables, viz., (*i*) Age, (*ii*) Birth order, (*iii*) Number of members in the family, (*iv*) Help from family members and (*v*) Time spent for mathematics, do not

have significant influence on the scholastic achievement of 10th class students in mathematics.

10. The personality Factors B, C, E, G, H, I, O and Q_3 have significant influence on the achievement of 10th class students in mathematics.

    The personality factors namely A, D, F, J, Q_2, and Q_4, do not have impact on the scholastic achievement of 10th class students in mathematics.

11. All the seven areas of SHI and the total score of SHI have significant influence on the scholastic achievement of 10th class students in mathematics. Better study habits, is associated with better scholastic achievement of 10th class students in mathematics.

12. The self-concepts (I) Abilities, (II) Self-onfidence, (III) Self-acceptance, (V) Worthiness, (V) Present-past-future, (VI) Beliefs and convictions, (VII) Feelings of shame and guilt, (VIII) Emotional Maturity and (IX) Self-Concepts total score, have significant influence on the scholastic achievement of 10th class students in mathematics. The self-concepts namely 'Health and sex appropriateness' and 'sociability' have no significant influence on the scholastic achievement in mathematics.

13. It is possible to predict the scholastic achievement of 10th class students in mathematics, with help of different sets of independent variables.

14. It is possible to develop, the regression equations for predicting the achievement in mathematics of 10th class students with the help of different sets of independent variables.

EDUCATIONAL IMPLECATIONS AND RECOMMENDATIONS

After analyzing the results of the study carefully, the following implications can be drawn. It is seen from the study that the general performance in mathematics of 10th class pupils is poor namely, below 50 per cent. Mathematics plays a crucial role in the life of students. To improve the achievement in mathematics at 10th class level, efficient, dedicated, honest and committed teachers of mathematics are to be recruited. Plans are to be made to design more Para-mathematical activities, as curricular inputs, to eliminate the fear of mathematics in children. The knowledge of mathematics at secondary level forms the basis for mathematics at higher education and hence, combined efforts by mathematics teachers, parents, educational administrators, inspecting authorities and government, may be made for ensuring the quality of school mathematics for all the children up to the collective level (say 10th class). Special programmes such as providing additional information, encouragement to participate in competitive tests and providing suitable study material etc may be taken to safeguard the interests of those students, who want to specialize, in the area of mathematics and related branches. The teachers in general should posses the knowledge of results of research findings. They must know which of the psycho-sociological factors that influence the achievement in mathematics and act accordingly to improve the achievement in mathematics.

On the basis of the results of this investigation, the following recommendations are made:

1. As the achievement in mathematics of 10th class students is very poor in government, Municipal and Zilla Parishad schools, special attention should be paid to improve the achievement in mathematics by parents, teachers, managements, administrators and Government.
2. Proper positive attitude towards the subject must be laid down by the concerned teachers. Without positive attitude, it is rather difficult to raise the standards.
3. Fear of the subject, test-anxiety and tension should be removed by proper counselling and guidance by the teachers.

4. Pupils must be made aware of the importance of the subject, uses of the subject in daily life, its correlation with other subjects and thereby interest in the subject must be aroused by the teachers.
5. More importance is to be given for making the concepts in the subject clear, understanding of the formulae and applying the formulae.
6. Pupils must be encouraged to solve at least 50 per cent of the problems in each topic and in each exercise.
7. Sufficient number of oral questions on the subject are to be put and answers my be elicited from the pupils, while teaching.
8. More number of tests, with objective questions namely multiple choice, filling up the blanks, matching type and true or false, are to be conducted.
9. Special training must be given to the students to face different competitive examinations and the students must properly be encouraged to face such examinations.
10. It is observed that the performance of the students belonging to the government schools is very less. This may be due to the vacant post of mathematics teachers, lack of proper supervision, lack of commitment on the part of the teachers and lack of proper infrastructural facilities in the schools. Parents, teachers, administrators and government have to put up a combined effort to raise the standards in government schools, there by creating confidence among the parents and avoiding mad rush for private schools. More competitive, highly qualified and dedicated teachers are to be recruited for the post of mathematics teachers in Government Schools.
11. It is observed from this study that the performance of rural students is some what better than semi-urban and urban students. This may be due to lack of proper study habits and wasting of time in other

activities than studies by students of urban and semi urban areas. Students of semi urban and urban areas should be properly motivated and proper study habits may be developed among them to improve their standards.

12. It is also observed from this study that the achievement of SC/ST and BC Students is less, when compared with OC Students. Therefore special attention should be paid towards SC/ST and BC students. Extra classes and suitable remedial measures for SC/ST and BC students, are to be taken by all the concerned teachers, to raise their achievement levels.
13. It is observed that performance of male students is slightly better than female students. Healthy and proper competitive spirit may be developed among male and female pupils, in their academic activities.
14. Mother's and Father's education is positively related to the achievement in mathematics. Hence steps may be taken to encourage the parents to improve their qualifications through distance mode of education. [Directorates of Distance Education (D.D.E)].
15. It is observed that the students of Hindu religion have performed better than the students of other religions. The Muslim and Christian students may be properly motivated to improve their achievement.
16. Annual income of the family is positively related with achievement. Hence, more number of scholarships, loan facilities for school education may be provided to the pupils by the government and other funding agencies. Special care must be taken by parents to see that children must be kept in dark about the financial burdens of the family.
17. Students may suitably be provided with proper study facilities at home and at school, by the concerned.
18. It is observed that number of study hours at home is

positively related with achievement. Hence the pupils may be encouraged by parents to study at least three to four hours daily at home.

19. Works at home, is negatively related with achievement. Hence the students may not be assigned with other works, other than studies, at home, by the parents. Here parents' co-operation is needed.
20. The following personality characteristics may be developed among the 10th class pupils, through counselling and guidance for better scholastic achievement in mathematics: (i) More-intelligent, (ii) Emotionally stable (iii) Assertive, (iv) Super-ego strength, (v) Venturesome, (vi) Tens-minded, (vii) Placid and (viii) Controlled.
21. It is found that all the seven areas of study habits are positively related with the scholastic achievement of pupils. Hence proper study habits may be developed in the pupils for better achievement both at home and at school.
22. The following self-concepts among the pupils may be developed through guidance and counselling for better scholastic achievement in mathematics. (i) Abilities, (ii) Self-Confidence, (iii) Self-Acceptance, (iv) Worthiness, (v) Present-Past-Future, (vi) Beliefs and Convictions, (vii) Feelings of Shame and Guilt, (viii) Emotional Maturity, (ix) Self-Concepts Total score.
23. Kothari Commission (1964-66) observed.
    1. Special attention should be given to the study of mathematics in view of the importance of quantification and advent of automation and cybernetics.
    2. The curriculum in mathematics need to be modernized and brought uptodate at all stages, with necessary emphasis on laws and principles of mathematics and logical thinking.

In view of the present unprecedented development of science and technology, the extensive use of computer knowledge, in all the fields of education, mathematics assumes a special significance and hence raising the standards in mathematics at primary and secondary levels of education is the primary duty of teachers, parents, educational managements, administrators and governments;

24. The investigator, has been associated, with the teaching profession for the last 35 years at different levels of education namely : 1. Upper primary level, 2. Secondary level, 3. Intermediate level, 4) Degree level and 5. B.Ed level and has been associated with teaching of mathematics, in the above levels of education.

    The investigator, with the present scientific investigation, combined with his vast experience feels that proper commitment on the part of the teacher, handling of the subject, his potentialities and humour, his efforts in developing positive attitude towards the subject, his motivational efforts, his efforts in making the students to realize the importance of the mathematics and its usefulness, its relation with other subjects and its practical values in the daily life of human-beings; lowest or highest class of the society and narrating often and often some interesting and important events from the life history of famous mathematicians would help create interest in the subject and thereby improvement in achievement of mathematics can be made possible.

    The combined efforts of teachers and parents in developing good study habits at the early stage of a child, would be fruitful.

    The pupils must be made to solve at least fifty per cent of the problems, in each exercise after the concepts, pertaining to every principle, have been made clear, by the teacher.

Mathematics is a different subject when compared to other subjects, in the sense that, the pupils seem to understand the subject well, while listening to the teaching, but face difficulty to solve the problems independently, in different situations. Therefore pupils must be made to solve as many problems as possible to gain perfection.

Further majority of the students have test-anxiety in mathematics and hence this anxiety is to be removed by proper guidance and counselling and also by involving them in solving the more number of problems.

The pupils must be made, to be thorough with each and every formulae and must be so trained as to apply them systematically, wherever necessary.

Parents must constantly encourage the children towards their education, know their interests and aptitudes and safe guard their interests.

LIMITATIONS OF THE STUDY AND SUGGESTIONS FOR FURTHER RESEARCH

The following limitations and suggestions are considered for further investigation:

1. The present study is confined only to 1444 students. Future researchers may undertake studies with large samples.
2. This study is confined only to Chittoor District. It may be extended for other districts of Andhra Pradesh and other states of the country.
3. This study is confined only to 10th class students. It may be extended to other classes, lower or higher viz 6th, 7th, 8th and 9th classes, Intermediate course and Degree levels.
4. This investigation is limited to mathematics subject only. This kind of research in different school subjects can be planned to plug the weak areas in the respective subjects.

5. The tool used for measuring the achievement in mathematics is developed and standardized by the investigator. Therefore, it is suggested that standardized tools, for measuring the achievements in different subjects should be developed for repeated use, by different researchers, keeping in view, the existing syllabus in school subjects.
6. Only very few socio-demographic variables and psycho-sociological variables are used in the present study. Some other variables such as attitude of teachers towards the subject, attitude of students towards mathematics, facilities in the school, parental involve-ment in the education of their children, teachers qualifications and merits, regularity of students etc may help to know their impact on achievement in mathematics.
7. Studies to estimate the influence of course content, books available, availability of guide material for teachers, laboratory facilities for mathematics, may be under taken.
8. A longitudinal study may be conducted in order to prove that good scholastic achievement, in secondary level, will lead to the corresponding success in higher levels.
9. Studies to estimate the influence of medium of instruction may be under taken.
10. Studies related to the 'Commitment of Mathematics Teachers' may be under taken, keeping in view their teaching style, completion of syllabus on time, taking special classes for backward students, conducting of periodical tests and evaluating them, maintaining cordial relations with students and parents etc.
11. Studies related to the teacher-pupil ratio may be under taken to know the impact of this ratio on the achievement in mathematics at 10th class and higher levels.

12. The government is spending huge amounts of money on in-service training programmes of mathematics teachers and other subject teachers. Hence, studies may be under taken to know the impact of these in-service training programmes on the achievement of students in mathematics at 10th class level or other levels or other levels.
13. Studies may be conducted to know the impact of higher qualifications of mathematics teachers on the achievement in mathematics of 10th class students.
14. Studies may be conducted to know the various causes for under-achievement in mathematics at 10th class level, so as to enable school administration to take suitable remedial measures.

Bibliography

Agarwal, Archana (2002): "Some correlates of Academic Achievement", *Indian Journal of Educational Research*, Vol.21(2): 75-76, *Educational Abstracts*, pp.47-48.

Aggarwal, P.C. (1974): "A study of the correlation of Achievement Motivation" unpublished Ph.D. Dissertation, Kurukshetra University.

Aggarwal, Y.P. and Saini V.P. (1969): "Pattern of Study Habit and its Relationship with Achievement and Parents economic and educational status", *Journal of Educational Research and Extension* vol. 5. No.4, April 1969, pp. 1593169.

Aggarwal, Y.P. (1990): "Statistical Methods", a textbook, Sterling Publishers Pvt. Ltd., New Delhi-16, pp.131-139.

Ahuja, Malvinder (2006): "Parental Involvement and academic achievement across various SES levels", *Recent Researches in Education and Psychology,* Vol. II, No. 3, p. 84-93.

Alam, A.M (2001): "A Comparative study of Academic Achievement, Self-concept and Alienation of Hearing impaired and Normal Students", *Educational Abstracts*: Vol. 4, No. 1, Jan 2004, Abstract No. 23, p. 24

All Port, G.W. (1949): "Personality-psychological interpretation": A Text Book, London-Constable and Co.

Anand : 1973' "A study of Relationship Between certain Psych-sociological Factors and Achievement of Students-Teachers in Teacher Training Institutions of Andhra

Pradesh" by R.V.V. Gopala charyulu: Ph.D in Education, S.V. University, Dec 1983.

Annakodi, R (2008): "Study of Scientific Attitude of pupils of class XI and Their Achievement In Science". *Miracle of Teaching – A quartly Journal* – January – February, March – April, 2008, Vol. VIII, No. 1, Published by Asian Academy of Education and Culture, pp. 39-41.

Archana and Mona Sharma (2002): From "Study Habits of Intermediate Students in Relation to Certain Psycho-Sociological Factors", by Rajni (2004) Ph.D., Thesis, SVU, Tirupati, p.53.

Arockiadosis (2005): "Study Habits and academic performance of college students", *Experiments in Education*, Vol.33, No.33, pp.77-79.

Aruna, N.S. (1981): " A study of the Factors influencing the achievement of standard VIII students Belonging To scheduled and scheduled Tribes Whose medium of instruction is Kannada" Ph.D in Education: Mysore University.

Arya, Kalpana and Kistwaria (2002), "Effect of Employment of Home-makers on Academic Performance of Adolescent Daughters". *Indian Journal of Psychometry and Education*, Vol. 33(2), 151-154, *Indian Educational Abstracts*, p. 48.

Ayishabi, T.C. and Moly Kuruvilla (1998): "Achievement Motivation of secondary School children of working and Non working Mothers of Kerala". *Experiments in Education* Vol. 26, No. 12. Dec 1998, pp. 203-205.

Ayodhya, P. (2007): "Emotional problems in Secondary School children and its Relation to Life Events and Scholastic Achievement", Abstract: *Journal of Community Guidance and Research*: November 2007, Vol. 24, No. 3, pp. 347-355.

Balasubramanian, T. and Feroze, M. (1966): "A Comparative Study of the Academic Achievement in Mathematics of Urban and Rural Students of Standard X in the High Schools of Coimbatore", *Journal of Educational Research and Extension*, Vol. 3, No. 1, p. 25.

Basantha, J.M. and Mukhopadyaya, D. (2001): "Effect of Environmental Factors on Achievement: a study on Rural Students", *The Educational Review*, Vol. 44, No. 11, Nov. 2001, pp. 201-204.

Behera, Laxmidhar and Sushanta Kumar Roul (2004): "Trainees performance of BEd in Relation to their Gender, Academic Back Ground and Type of Institution". *The Educational Riview*: Vol. 47, No. 11, Nov. 2004, pp. 206-211.

Bellingham, John (2004): "Academic's Dictionary of Education" Academic (India) Publishers, New Delhi, p. 4, 70, 83, 228, 252, 260, 261, 265, 269, 333.

Bernstein, B. (1968): "Some Sociological Determinants of Perception – An enquiry in to sub-cultural Differences" *British Journal of Sociology*, Vol : 9, p. 159.

Best, J.W (1977): *Research in Education*, Prentice-Hall Inc Englewood Cliff, USA-31.

Bhaskara Rao, D. Somasurya Prakash Rao. A and Bhuvaneswara Lakshmi G (2004): *The Educational Review*, Jan-2004, cross, Mahalakshmi Layout, Bangalore.

Bhatnagar, Asha (1980): "A study of some Factors Affecting student Involvement in studies" *Journal of Education Research*, Vol.15, No.3, pp.70-75.

Borbora and Rupa Das: "Influence of Parental Literacy on the Academic Achievement of children Belonging to the Backward classes: A study of Kamrup District". *Journal of Indian Education*, vol.27(1), 59-65 from *Indian Educational Abstracts,* Vol. 2. No. 2 July 2002 *Abstract* No. 141; pp. 13-14.

Bose, S. and Joshi, V. (2004): "Effect of Involvement of Parents in the education of children: An exploration", *Educational Abstracts:* Vol 5, No: 1 and 2, Jan and July 2005, 88 Abstract No: 111, p. 87.

Britannica Word Language Dictionary (1961): A Dictionary, Funk & Wagnall's Company, New York: Vol. 2, p. 1126

Brown, F.G. and Dubois (1964): "Study Habits and attitudes, college experience and college success" *Personal and Guidance Journal*, Vol. 43, pp. 287-292.

Brown, W.F. and Holtzman. W(1955): " A study of attitude question for Predictor Academic success." *Journal of Education Psychology*, Vol.46, pp.75-84.

Brownell W.A. (1947): "The place of meaning in the teaching of arithmetic". *Elementary School Journal*, 47, 256-65.

Brownell, W.A. (1945): "When is arithmetic meaningful". *Journal of Education Research*, 38, 481-98.

Burnet, C.W.(1951): "Study Skills and chancellor Training – A, Two way Teaching programme". California Journal of Educational Research. Vol. 2, pp. 18-21.

Cattell R.B. (1950). "The main personality factors in questionnaire, Self estimated material", *Journal of Social Psychology*, Vol.31, pp.3-38.

Cattell RB (1970): *'Theories of Personality'*, John Wiley & Sons, Inc (2nd ed), p. 386.

Cattell, R.B. (1969): "Handbook for Junior Senior High School Personality Questionnaire": Ellinois, Institute of Personality and Ability Testing.

Chadha, N.K. and Sunanda Chandana (1990): "Creativity, intelligence and Scholastic achievement – A Residential study" *Indian Educational Review, Quarterly*, Vol.25, No.3, July-1990, pp. 81-85.

Chakrabarthi, Bhupal Prasad (2002): "Experiments in using comprehension Type Tests with Multiple choice Type Items In Primary Mathematics". *Vigyan Shikshak*, Vol.46(3), 5-9. Indian Educational Abstracts, p.33-34.

Chakrabarthi, Sharmistha (2002): A critical study of Family Problems faced by the Learners, Socio-Economic status Physical facilities Available in Literacy centres, organizational and Instructional Aspect as Literacy Programme and their Relation with Literacy Achievement of Female Learners in West Bengal" Research Project, University of Culcutta; NCERT,-(ERIC Funded) from

Indian Educational Abstracts, Vol.2. No.2, July 2002. Abstract, No. 128, p. 3.

Chauhan, S.S. and Singh H. (1982): " An Investigation into the study Habits of 10 to 12 years of children with regard to their parental Profession". *Indian Education Review NCERT*. New Delhi, Vol. 22, No. 1, pp. 92-96.

Chel, Madan Mohan. D. (1990): "Diagnosis and remediation of under achievement in compulsory mathematics of Mathematic examination in west Bengal". Ph.D Thesis in education, University of Calcutta, India.

Chopra R.K (1982), "A study of organizational climate in school in Relation to job satisfaction of Teachers and students Achievement". Ph.D in Education Agra University. Third Survey of Research in education (1987): *Abstract* No. 1133, pp. 796-797.

Cobb, P *et al.* (1991): "Assessment of a problem centred second-grade mathematics project", *Journal for Research in Mathematics Education*, 22, pp. 3-29.

Corter, H.D (1955): Development of a Diagnostic scoring scheme for a study method test". *California Journal of Educational Research* Vol. 6, pp. 26-32.

Darlene, Gordan (1988): "The Relationship among Academic Achievement self-concept, Academic Achievement and persistence with self Attribution, Study Habits and perceived school Environment". *Dissertation Abstracts International*, Vol. 58, No. 12, p. 26.

Dash J (2002): Trends and problems of Higher Education of Scheduled Tribes in Orissa" D.Litt in Education, UKal University, from *Indian Educational Abstracts*. Vol. 2. No.2: July 2002, *Abstract* No. 142, pp. 14-16.

Davidson, G.W. Seaton, MA; and Simpson, J. (1998): "*Chambers Concise 20th century Dictionary*", Allied Publishers Pvt Ltd., pp. 336, 889.

Davidson, N. (1985): "Small group cooperative learning in mathematics" in R. Slavin (Ed) "Learning to co-operate - cooperating to learn", pp. 211-30, NY: Plenum.

Deb, M. and Gravel, H.P. (1990): "Relationship between study habits and Academic Achievement of under Graduate Home Science Final year students" *Journal of Educational Research*, Vol. 25, No. 3, pp. 71-74.

Della, Thompson (1996) (Ed): "The concise Oxford Dictionary of Current English" Ninth Edition, Oxford University Press; p. 12-35.

Derek, Rowntree (1981): *A Dictionary of Education*. Haper & Raw Publishers London, pp, 16, 41, 65, 75, 89, 126, 214, 236, 244.

Desai, H.G. (1979): "Under achievement syndrome among high ability High school boys". In M.B. Buch(ed), *Second Survey of Research in Education*, Baroda, p. 579.

Devi, S and Mayuri K (2000): "The Effects of family and school on the Achievement of Residential School Children", *Educational Abstracts*: Vol. 4, No:2, July 2004: p.35; Abstract No: 154

Dhalakia, J.V. (1980): "Effects of observers and feed back upon changing the classroom Performance of Public Teachers" Ph.D. in Education, M.S University, Baroda, in third Survey & Research in Education (1987). *Abstract* No., 1138, p.799.

Dhall, G.D.J. Gautam, SKS; Avtar, Ram and Sankar M (2000): "Effect of using Remedial Materials in Mathematics on Achievement of Slow Learners", *Educational Abstracts*: Vol. 2, No.1, Jan 2002, p.70; *Abstract* No. 97.

Diener, C.L. (1960): " Similarities and differences Between over achieving and under Achieving students". *Personal Guidance Journal*, Vol. 38, No.5, pp. 396-400.

Drapper, N.R. and Smit, A.H. (1981): "Applied Regression Analysis", A textbook, Second Edition, John Wiely and Sons, New York.

Dubey, S.N. and Mishra (1999): "Psycho-Social Determinants of Academic Success in Rural Boys", *Prospectives in Education* Vol. 15, No. 3, July 1999 pp. 157-164.

Ediger, Marlow (1999): "Parents, the teacher and Mathematics", *Experiments in Education*, Vol.XXVII, No.6, June pp. 93-103.

Edwards, A.L. (1969): "Techniques of Attitude Scale construction". A textbook, Vikas, Feffer and Simmons Pvt. Ltd., Bombay.

Ekanadha, N.K. and Sunanda Chandana (1990): "Creativity, intelligence and scholastic achievement - A residential study", *Indian Educational Review Quarterly*, Vol 25, No.3, July 1990, pp. 81-85.

Esther, Mary St(1945): "An Analysis of Study Habits and catholic high school students". Catholic Education, London, pp. 542-549.

Farquhar, W.W. (1963): "A comparative study of Motivational Factors underlying Achievement of Eleventh Grade High school studies" Columbia University Team Library pp. 44

Fisher R.A. (1950): "Statistical Methods for Research Workers", A text book, Hafner Publishing Co., New York.

Ford, Dawson (1970): "An Analytical study of the Effects of Maternal Employment of some sex Denials In Pre-adolescence and of Residential Mobility on self Actualization-Achievement in a Sample of Adolescents", *Dissertation Abstracts International*, Vol. 3, p. 924.

Fraser, E.(1959): Home environment and school London, University of London Ltd.

Gakhar S.C. (1982): "A Study of Acquisition of Mathematical concepts among 8th Grader of different types of schools experiments in education", Vol.II, No.9, pp. 164-167.

Gakhar, S.C. and Assema (2004): "Social stress, Locality and Gender Affecting Academic Achievement and Reasoning Ability", *Journal of Educational Research and Extension*, Vol. 41, No. 4, Oct-Dec 2004, pp. 60-66

Garrett, H.E. (1973): "Statistics in Psychology and Education" A text book Valiks, Feffer and Simons Pvt Ltd; Bombay, India: pp. 213-215, 337-370.

Garrett, H.E. (1973): "Statistics in psychology and Education", Bombay, Vikalls Feffer and Simon Pvt. Ltd.

George, A.A (2003): "Mathematical backwardness and its Remediation in Goa" - *Educational Abstracts*: Vol. 4, No: 2, July 2004, p.10. Abstract No. 113.

George, Neetha, Anitha Ravindran (2005): "Academic Achievement in Relation to Time Perception and Coping Styles" Abstract: *Journal of Community Guidance & Research,* Vol.22, No.1, March 2005, pp. 55-65.

Gilson, Judith. E. (1999): "Single Gender Education versus Co-education for Girls: A study of Mathematics Achievement and Attitude Towards Mathematics of Middle – School students": *ERIC*, Vol. 34, No.9, Sep. 1999 ED 430011, p. 56.

Girija, P.R. Bhadra, B.P. and Ameerjan, M.S.(1975): "The Relationship of study Habits with study skills, academic Achievement Motivation, and Academic Achievement", *Journal of Educational Psychology*, Vol.33, No.1, pp. 47-53.

Gnanaguru. and A. Suresh, M. (2008): "Under achievement B.Ed students in relation to their home environment and Attitude towards Teaching". *Edu Tracks*: Vol. 7, No:12, August 2008, Neelkamal Publications Pvt. Ltd., Koti, Hyderabad, August, 2008, p. 20.

Gnanasundaratharasu, A. and Vincent, De Pauls (2002) "Effectiveness of video Assisted Instruction in Teaching and Learning Social Science at Primary Level" *Experiments in Education*; Vol. 30, No. 5. May 2002, pp. 98-101.

Goel, Swami Pyari (2002): "Feeling of Security, Family Attachment and values of Adolescents Girls in Relation to their Educational Achievement" *Indian Journal of Psychometry and Education*, Vol. 33(1), 25-28, *Indian Educational Abstract*, p. 51.

Golden and will B. (1978): "A profile of high and low achievers is Mathematics among 6th grade students" *District. Abst. Int.* Vol. 38(8), p. 4639

Golden, H.P.(1941):"Study Habits Inventory score and scholarship". *J. of Applied Psychology*, Vol. 25, pp. 101-107.

Good .C.V. (1973): "Dictionary of Education" McGraw-Hill Book company, New Delhi, pp. 2333, 441, 464, 464.

Gopal Rao, D. (1965): "A Study of some Factors Related to Scholastic Achievement", Ph.D Thesis, University of Delhi.

Gopala Charyulu R.V.V (1984): "A study of Relationship Between certain Psycho-sociogical Factors and Achievement of student Teachers Training Institutes of Andhra Pradesh", Ph.D Thesis in education; SVU in Fourth survey of research in education (1991), *Abstract* No. 1069, p. 940.

Gorden and Will, B. (1978): "A profile of high and low achievers in Mathematics among 6th grade students" *Dissr. Abst. Int.* Vol.38(8), p. 4639A.

Gorden, H.P. (1941): "Study Habits Inventory Scores and Scholarship". *Journal of Applied Psychology*, Vol. 25, pp. 101-107.

Goswamy, Meenakshi (2000): "Achievement Motivation and Anxiety among children of working Mothers studying in Secondary schools of Shillong". *Educational Abstract*, Vol. 2, No.2, July 2002, pp. 54-55.

Goswamy, Minakshi (2002): "Achievement Motivation and Anxiety Among children of working and Non working Mothers studying in Secondary Schools of Shillong: *Journal of All India Association for Educational Research.* Vol. 12. (1 & 2) 25-28 from *Indian Educational Abstracts* Vol. 2 No. 2 July 2002. *Abstract No*: 187, pp. 54-55.

Guilford J.P. (1954): "Psychometric methods" A text book,

McGraw-Hill Publishing Company-New York, pp: 47, 373, 37, 4, 378, 417.

Guilford, J.P. (1950): "Fundamental statistics in psychology and Education: International student Edition, New York, McGraw Hill.

Gupta, Har Govinda (1968) "A study of the Relationship Between some environmental Factors and Academic Achievement", *Journal of Educational Research and Extension.* Vol. 5, No. 1, July 1968, pp. 17-23.

Gupta, Naresh Kumar (2002): Need to Boost Primary Pupils' Achievement – A Strategy of Education for All", *Indian Educational Review,* Vol. 38. No. 1, Jan 2002, pp. 115-138.

Gupta, P.L. (1983): "A study of personality characteristics of Ninth Grade over and under Achieving Boys and Girls at Different levels of Achievement Motivation". Ph.D Thesis Panjab university.

Gupta, S.P. (1974): "Statistical Methods" A text book, Sultan Chand and Sons, New Delhi.

Gupta, V.P (1968): "Intelligence, Economic status, sex, and Academic success" *Journal of Educational Research and Extension* Vol. 5, No. 2.

Guravaiah, K. (2004), "Study Habits of Residential and non-Residential pupils of Xth class in Relation to certain Psycho-sociological Factors" Ph.D in education, SVU Tirupati.

Harbans Singh (1989), "An Investigation in to the study habits of scheduled caste Adolescent in Relation to their sex and Achievement Motivaiton" *Journal of Education and Psychology*; Vol. 47, No.1-2 April-July 1989; pp.21-25.

Head, John (1981): "Personality and learning of Mathematics". Educational Studies in Mathematics, p. 339-350.

Hembree, R and Dessart, D.J. (1986): "Effect of hand – held calculators in pre-college Mathematics Education: A meta-analysis", *Journal of Research in Mathematics Education*, 17, pp.83-99.

Husen, T. (1967): "International study of achievement in mathematics", Vol.2, NY: Wiley.

Jagannadhan, K. (1983): "The Effect of certain socio-psychological Factors of Academic Achievement of children studying in class V to VII" Ph.D Thesis in education, SVU, pp. 212-216.

Jagannadhan, K. (1986): "Socio-Economic Status and Academic Achievement": *Journal of Educational Research and Extension*, Vol. 22, No. 3, pp. 141-149

Jain, J.R. (1990): "A study of self concept of socially disadvantaged adolescent girls and identification with parents as contributing to realization of academic goals" – in fifth survey of Educational Research, New Delhi, NCERT *Quest in Education*, Vol. XXVIII, No.41, October, 2004, pp. 22-33.

James, Anice (2005): A Text Book: '*Teaching of Mathematics*', p. 21.

James, Anice and Marice PV (2004): "Achievement in Science as Related to Scientific Aptitude and Scientific Attitude Among XI Standard Students in Tamil Nadu", Journal of *Educational Research and Extension*, Vol. 41, No. 2 April- June 2004, pp. 13-16

Jammu, K.K. (1958): "Study Habits and Achievement" *Psychological Studies*, Vol.3, No.1, pp.37-42.

Jammur, K.K. (1971): "Study Habits and some back ground factors". *Psychological Studies*, Vol.17, No.2, p.14-18.

Jayachandrarama Naidu, K (1998): "A Comparative Study of Academic Achievement of Formal and Non-Formal Education", *Indian Educational Review*, Vol. 33, No. 1, Jan 1998, pp.152-158.

Kapoor J.N. (1993): "Some Aspects of School Mathematics", Arya Book Depot, Karol Bagh; New Delhi, pp.15-16, 79-83.

Karl R and Pyari A. (2004): "Family climate and Income as determinants of educational Achievement", *Educational Abstracts:* Vol. 4, No. 2, July 2004, p.38 *Abstract No:* 159

Kennedy (1975), From "Influence of certain psycho-sociological Factors on scholastic Achievement of DIET students" Ph.D Thesis by Govinda Reddy. V (2002) S.V.U. p. 74.

Khalid, Mohd Nasin (1997): "Factors affecting Mathematics achievements in Malasian Schools", *Dissertation Abstracts International*, Vol. 58, No.7. p. 34-49.

Khan, Asud Ulla Sudha, B.G. and Lalitha V. Tirth (1982): "Scholastic Achievement as a Function of Aspiration, Religion and socio-economic status" *Journal of Education and Psychology*, Vol. 39, No. 4, Jan 1982, pp. 218-223.

Khanna, M.(1980): "A study of Relationship Between students of Socio-Economic Back ground and their Academic Achievement at Junior Level", Ph.D in Education, Kanpur University.

Khayyer, Mohammad and Philip R. DeLacey (2005): "Prediction of academic achievement from some demographic, family background and locus of control variables".

Kobal-Palcic-Darya Musek and Janek (1999): "Self concept and Academic Achievement of central and western European Groups of Adolescents", *ERIC* Vol. 35, No. 4, Oct-Dec 1998, pp. 29-35.

Krishnamoorthy S, and Rao, T.R.S. (1969), "A comparative Investigation of study Habits of Sub- Urban and urban children in some high school incompitiable". *Journal of Education Research and Extension,* Vol.6, No. I, pp. 32-41.

Krishnamoorthy, S. (1999): "Achievement as Related to Academic Achievement Motivation and Attitude Towards Study of History", *The Educational Review.* Vol. 42, No. 5&6, May- June 1999, pp. 95-99

Kumar, Anil (1998), "Academic self-concept, study Habits, Attitude towards Distance education and Academic performance of Distance Learners" Staff and Educational Development International Vol. 2, pp. 167-173.

Kumar, S and Anita (2004): "Effectiveness of self-learning Module in Mathematics in Relation to class-room environment", *Educational Abstracts;* Vol.4, No, 2, July 2004, p.51. Abstract No.180.

Kumar, Salim C. (1998): Impact of Select Factors on Academic Achievement", *Experiments in Education.* Vol. 26, No. 1, Nov. 1998, pp. 194-197.

Kumara Swamy, T(1992): "A study of certain Factors Related to achievement of Adult learners". Ph.D in Adult Education, SVU., pp. 335-338.

Lakshmi Devi, S (2004): "Vidya Jyoti (DIET Calendar): Bukkapatnam : DIET Hand Book, p. 42-43.

Lalithamma, K.N. (1975): "Some factors affecting achievement of secondary school pupils in mathematics", *Second Survey of Educational Research*, No. 2, p. 349.

Lalithanhawla (1983): "An investigation into the causes of failures in science and Mathematics in high school certificate examination in Mizolam, Aizwal"; Northeastern Hill University Campus, unpublished M.Ed Dissertation.

Lavanya, T (2000): "A study of Personality development and study skills for Scholastic Achievement" *Journal of Psychological Researches*, Vol. 44, No. 1, pp. 47-58.

Leef, Ruth (1992), "Development of Study skills pocket to improve Grades of IX and X students" *ERIC*, Vol. 281, No. 3, p.137.

Lidhoo, M.L. and Khan, M.A. (1990) "Bright under Achievers Among the Socially Backward counselling and Remedial measures", *Indian Journal of Clinical Psychology*. Vol.17, pp. 28-32.

Lincoln H. Hall (1969): "Selective variables in Achievement of Junior college students"—, *Journal of Educational Research*, 63, 2. pp.61-63.

Mac Aulay, Dolina J. (1990): "Classroom Environment: A Literature review" *Educational Psychology*, Vol. 10, No. 3, pp. 239-253.

Majolribanks, K (1982): "Family Environment and Children's Academic Achievement": Sex and Social group difference, *Psychological Abstracts*, 68(1), 2096. *Quest in Education*, Vol.XXVIII, No.4, October 2004, pp.22-33. A quarterly Journal.

Manchala (2007): "Achievement of B.Ed Students" published Ph.D Thesis in education S.V. University Tirupati, pp. 50-52, 270.

Mangal, S.K. (2002): "Statistics in Psychology and Education", A Text book of second edition, Prentice-Hall of India Pvt. Ltd., New York.

Manjuvani and Mohan (2002): Adjustment Problems and Academic Achievement of Adolescent Boys and Girls studying in single sex schools and Co-Education Schools, *Experiments in Education,* Vol. 30, No.4, April 2002 pp. 86-90.

Marcon, Rebecca A. (1999): "Demographic and Educational Influences on Academic Motivation, Competence and Achievement in Minority urban students". *ERIC*. Vol.34, No.9, Sep., 1999, Ed 430061, p. 162.

Marrow and Williamson R.R. (1961): "Family relationship of school children, Child Development, 32, 501-521. Quest in Education, Vol.XXVIII, No.4, October, 2004. *A Quarterly Journal Published.*

Martin (1995): "Achievement of B.Ed students": A Ph.D Thesis by Dr. C. Manchala, SVU., Tirupati, p.103.

Mc Robbie and Fraser (1993): "Achievement of B.Ed Students" From the Ph.D Thesis by Dr. C. Manchala (2007) Published by Discovery Publishing House, Delhi, p. 103.

Mehara, M. (1992):"Level of School Performance of Backward and Non Backward Rajasthani Higher Secondary Boys", *Journal of Psychological Researches*, Vol. 36. No. 2, pp. 64-67.

Mehera, C. (2004): "A study on the Achievement at the Secondary Level and Some of its Determinants" Educational Abstracts: Vol. 5, No. 1 and 2, January and July 2005, pp. 10-11.

Mennon, (1973) : From " A study of relationship Between Certain Psycho-Sociological Factors and Achievement of Students- Teachers in Teacher Training Institutes of Andhra Pradesh" by R.V.V. Gopala charyulu; Ph.D in Education S.V.U 1983; pp. 69-70.

Mishra, B.N. *et al.* (1960): "An Investigation into the influence of Home Environment on the School Achievement", *Journal of Educational and Vocational Guidance*, 7, 72-76, *Quest In Education*, Vol. XXVIII, No. 4, October, 2004.

Misra, Rajendra (1980): "A study of attitude towards mathematics of secondary school students". (Thesis submitted to Patna University (1978), *Indian Educational Review*, pp. 91-94.

Molia M.S (1999): "A study of the effectiveness of Inductive Thinking Model of Retentional Indices in Mathematics of class VIII", *Educational Abstracts,* Vol 2, No.1 Jan 2002, p. 35. Abstract No: 47

Murphy G. (1947) "Public Opinion and the individual", Harper & Co, New York.

Nagalakshmi, R.S. (1995): "Construction of problem solving ability test in mathematics for secondary students and study of problem – solving abilities of X class in Twin Cities of Hyderabad", Ph.D. Dissertation, Osmania University, Hyderabad.

Nagaraju, M.T.V (2001): "Study Habits of high school pupils in Relation to certain Psycho-sociological Factors".Ph.D in education, SVU Tirupati.

Narayana, Koteswara, M. and Rama Chandra Reddy, B. (1998): "A study of reading Achievement in Relation to Demographic variables": *Experiments in Education,* Vol. 26, No.11, Nov 1998, pp.180-200

Natesan, N. and Susila, C. (2000): Personality Factors and Achievement in Environmental science of V standard students", *Experiments in Education* Vol.28, No. 12, Dec 2000, pp. 188-192

Nayar, Padmanabhan, K and Visveswaran. H (1966):"A Comparative Study the Achievement in General Science of Urban and Rural Students Studying in X class in the High Schools in Coimbatore District", *Journal of Educational research and Extension,* Vol. 2, No. 3, p. 20.

NCERT (2008): "Mather's Education is important than Father's Education – A mid term National Survey". Published in *"The Hindu"*, Chennai Edition, October 2008, p. 5.

Nortan, D.F. (1959): "The Relationship of study Habits and other measures of Achievement to IX Grade Science". *Journal of Experiments in Education,* Vol.27, pp. 211-217.

On Tsk Ka and Wat Kins, D. (1994): "Doing Living and Study Habits and Academic Achievement of Secondary School Students in Hong Kong", *Perpectual and Motor Skills*, Vol.79, No.1, pp.231-234.

Panchalingappa, S.R. (2004): Study Habits, Family Climate, Adjustment and Academic Achievement of Children of Devadasis", Quests in Education, *Quarterly Journal*, Vol. 28, No. 4, Oct 2004, pp. 22-23

Panchalingappa, Shahpur Nagappa (1995): "An Investigation into the causes of under achievement in secondary school Mathematics", *Educational Abstracts*. Vol. 2, No.1, Jan 2002. p. 37, Abstract No: 50

Panchanathan, N. and Shanmuga Ganesan V (1992): "The Effect of Psychological Stress on Academic Achievement", *Journal & Community Guidance and Research* Vol. 9, No. 2.

Panda, B.N. (2002 a): "A study of Factors Affecting Pupils Achievement in primary schools of Orissa". Research project. RIE, Bhubaneswar, (NCERT, ERIC funded): *Indian Educational Abstracts*: Vol.2, No.2, July 2002, Abstract No: 185, PP 52-53

Panda, Bhujendra Nath (1991): "Academic Achievement and selected Demographic Factors-A study on Urban-Rural High School Adolescents" *Journal of Education and Psychology*; Vol. 49, No:1-2, April-July 1991, pp. 49-54.

Panda, Manoranjan (2002): "Analysis of Relationship between Academic Achievement and school Interventions of Class IX students". *Journal & Educational Research and Extension* Vol. 37, No. 4, Oct-Dec. 2000 pp.1-8.

Panda, Manoranjan (2005): "Correlation between Academic Achievement and Intelligence of Class IX Students" Edu Tracks, September 2005, Vol. 5, No. 1 Neel Kamal Publications. Pvt. Ltd., Koti, Hyderabad, pp. 36-38.

Panday, S.N. and Md. Faiz Ahmad (2008): "Significance of Difference Between Male an Female Adolescents on Academic Motivation, Intelligence and Socio-economic Status", Abstract : *Journal of community Guidance & Research, March* 2008, Vol. 25, No. 1, pp. 34-39.

Pandey, S.N. and Md Faiz Ahmad (2008): Significance of Difference between Male and Female Adolescents on Academic performance, Achievement motivation and Socio-Economic status, Abstract: *Journal of Community Guidance & Research*, March 2008; Vol. 25, No. 1, pp. 34-39.

Panigrahi, Manas Ranjan (2005): "Academic Achievement in Relation to Intelligence And Socio-economic Status of High School Students", Edu tracks, October-2005, Vol.5, No.2, pp.26-30, Suresh Chandra Sarma Koti, Hyderabad.

Patel, B.V. (1975): "Study Habits Inventory, Ludiana: Psychological Laboratory.

Patel, DN (1981): "The impact of study Habits of Intellectually Backward pupils upon their academic Achievement". *The Progress of Education*, Vol. 56, No. 2, pp. 33-37.

Patel, MR (1996): "Study Habits of Pupils and it's impact upon their Academic Achievement", *Indian Educational Abstracts*; Vol. 3, No. 1, Jan 2003, Abstract No. 73, p. 57.

Pattison P. and Grive, N (1984): "Do spatial skills contribute to sex differences in different types of mathematical problems"; *Journal of Educational Psychology*, 76, p. 678-689.

Pavithran, A.N and Feroze M (1965): "Influence of socio-economic Factors on the scholastic achievement of Tenth standard of Pathanamthitta educational District" *Journal of educational Research:* Vol. 1, No. 4, pp. 6-12.

Ponnuswamy and Sudharsan. S (2001): "Students Achievement and Cooperative Learning Method in Mathematics at Upper primary Level", *Educational Abstracts:* Vol. 5, No.1 and 2, Jan and July 2005, p. 36-37. Abstract No. 43.

Prahallada (2004): "Teachers as inspiring Agents" Edu. Tracks. April, 2004, Neelkamal Publications, Koti, Hyderabad, Vol.3, No.8, pp. 19-20.

Prakash .S (2000): "A Study of Mathematical Creativity and Achievement of Elementary School Students in Relation to Problem solving Ability, Anxiety and Socio-Demographic Variables". Ph.D in Education Punjab University; Chandigarh.

Prakash, S. (2003): "Temperament and Memory as Determinants of Mathematics of Achievement of Intermediate Students" Educational Abstracts, Vol.3, Number 2; July 2003, pp. 50-51.

Prakash. S. (2000): "A study of Mathematical creativity and Achievement of Elementary school students in Relation to problem solving Ability, Anxiety and Socio-Demographic Variables", Ph.D. in Education, Punjab University, Chandigarh.

Premalath sarma: (1986), "Study Habits and Academic achievement Among Rural Girls' Journal of educational Research and Extension, Vol. 22, No. 4, pp. 220-224.

Quraishizm and Bhat VD (1986): "Academic Achievement in Relation to socio economic status, Age and sex" Indian Journal of Psychometric and education, Vol. 7, No. 1 and 2, pp. 57-66.

Radhamohan (1998): "Academic Achievement and certain selected variables: A suggested discriminate Function model" Prospectives in Education Vol. 14. No. 3, pp. 161-171.

Rahaman MH (2003): "A study of Achievement in Mathematics of Eighth Grade Students of Different Ethnic Groups of Nepal", Educational Abstracts: Vol. 5, No: 1 and 2, Jan and July 2005, p. 35. Abstract No. 41.

Raj, Madhu (1996): "Encyclopedic Dictionary of Psychology and Education", New Delhi, Vol. 1, 2 and 3, p. 18, 510, 588, 658, 740, 742, 842, 972, 1168, 1528.

Rajani M. (2004): "Study Habits of inter mediate students in relation to certain Psycho-sociological factors". Ph.D in Education, SVU, Tiurapti.

Rama Rao, G. and Sinha, R.K. (1993): "Female Education and Achievement in Higher Education". *Journal of Higher Education* Vol. 16, No. 2, spring 1993, pp. 293-302.

Ramana, Sood and Dalvinder Kumar, (2007): "Study habits and Academic Achievement of First Generation Learners and Second Generation Learners" MERI *Journal of education,* Vol.II, No.II, October, 2007, p.45.

Ramaswamy, R. (1990): "Study Habits and Academic *Achievement Experiments in Education*; Vol. 18, No.10, pp. 225-259.

Rangaswamy, S.P. and Visveswaran (1977): A comparative study of Academic Achievement of High school sports Men and other students in Coimbatore District", *Journal of Educational Research and Extension*: Vol. 13, No: 4, pp. 230-240

Rastogi, M. Rani, (1974): "Manual for Self-concept scale", Agra Psychological Research Agra-282004, India.

Rathore, Jyoti (2000): "A study of Scholastic Achievement of children studying at Primary level in Environmental studies with special Reference to MLL and Development of remedial Teaching strategies", *Journal & Educational Research and Extension* Vol. 37, No. 4, Oct-Dec 2000, pp. 9-13.

Ravindra, G. Basavaiah D and Basti. B.E (2000): "Gender Difference in Mathematical Abilities", *Educational Abstracts:* Vol.4, No.1, Jan. 2004, p. 61. Abstract No. 61.

Reddy, G.L.; and Jeevanantham M. (2004): "A Study on school effectiveness Factors (Physical, Curricular and Administrative Factors) and their contribution towards

Enhanced Learning Achievement at Primary Stage" *Educational Abstracts:* Vol. 5, No. 1 and 2, Jan and July 2005. p: 8-9: Abstract No. 6.

Reddy, Govinda, (2002): "Influence of certain psycho-sociological Factors on scholastic Achievement of DIET students"; Ph.D Thesis, S.V.U. Tirupati.

Reddy, Naveen Kumar K. (2003): "An Investigation into study Habits of Secondary School Children" MEd Dissertation, SVU., Tirupati, p.48.

Regnerus, Markd. (2000): "Shaping school success: Religions Socialization and Educational out comes in Metro Politan Public Schools". *Journal for Scientific Study of Religion* Vol. 39, pp. 363-370.

Richard G.W and Virginia (1967): "The Relation ship of knowledge and usages of study skill Techniques to academic performance". *Journal of Educational Research* Vol. 61, No. 2, pp. 78-80.

Roach, DA. (1979): "Effects of conceptual style Preference, Related cognitive variables and sex on Achievement in Mathematics" *British Journal of Educational Psychology*, Vol. 49, pp. 79-82.

Rossi, P. H. (1950):"Social Factors in Academic Achievement- a Brief Review"- as Quoted in "educational, Economy and Society", the Free Press-New York Collien- Mac Millan Ltd p. 47.

Saakshi, Daily Newspaper, Telugu: June I (2008), "Girls are also great in Mathematics", p. 31.

Salvin, R.E. (1990): "Student team Learning in mathematics" Boston: Allyn & Bacon, pp.69-102.

Sam, Sananda Raj and Sreethi S (2000): *Journal of Psychological Research* Vol. 44, No. 2, pp. 82-87.

Samantray, Jayasree (2008): "Inculcation of values through education" *Edu Tracks:* Vol. 7, No:12, August 2008, Neel Kamal Publications Pvt. Limited Koti Hyderabad, p. 11-12.

Samuel, TM and Rao, TRS (1967), "An Investigation of study Habit of the Pre-university colleges students in Coimbatore". *Journal of Educational Research and Extension,* Vol. 5. No. 4, pp. 18-28.

Sanders, Mavis and Jerald R. Herting (2000): "Gender and Effects of School, Family and Church support on the Academic Achievement of African American urban Adolescents".

Satyanandam, B.D. (1969): "A study of Socio-Economic Status and Academic Achievements" Govt College of Education, Kurnool; AP. State: India.

Saxena, S.K. (2001): "Self-concept as function of socio economic and cultural setting in First Divisioners of High School Students". *Indian Journal of Educational Research,* Vol. 20, No. 2, pp. 53-58.

Selvam, M. and Sundara Valli S (2002): "An Empirical Study of Problems of Higher Secondary Students and their Achievement", *Recent Researchers in Educational Psychology,* Vol. 7, No. 324, pp. 102-104.

Sethi, Vijay Kumar (1990): "Personality Patterns of High Achieving and low Achieving students in professional courses" *Indian Educational Review Quarterly,* Vol. 25, No:1 Jan 1990. PP: 92-94

Sharama K.K. (1977): "The effect of different Techniques of feed back upon the attainment of Teaching skills Related to stimulus variation, Reinforcement, silence and non-verbal cues in the student Teachers". Unpublished Doctoral Thesis, M.S. University of Baroda.

Sharma, S. Nidhi (2002): "A study of the Effect of Parental Involvement and aspirations and Academic Achievement of + 2 Students", *Indian Educational Abstracts,* Vol. 3, No: 1, Jan 2003, Abstract No.78, p. 61

Sharma, V.P. and Bhargava M. (1980): "Academic Achievement and Prolonged Deprivation" *Journal & Education and Psychology,* Vol. 37, p.4.

Sidhu, Kulbir (1995): Teaching of Mathematics", A Text Book, Sterling Publishers Pvt. Ltd., L-10-Green Park extension, New Delhi – 110016, p. 1-2.

Siegel, Sidney (1956): "Non Parametric Statistics for Behavioural Sciences", A text book of McGraw-Hill Book Co., Inc, New York.

Singh P. (1993): "Academic Achievement motivation of the SC and upper caste Boys" Paper Presented at 8th Science congress, Goa.

Singh, Lal (1984): "Effect of socio-economic Status on the Academic Achievement of XI Grade Students", *Journal of Education and Psychology.* Vol. 42. No. 4, Jan 1984. pp. 223-228

Singh, S.K (2002): *Encyclopedic Dictionary of Education*, Vol. 1, pp.11, 132, 215, 219, 243, 283, 478, 526.

Singh, Suneel Sumar, Shaheen Malik and Dr. A.K. Sing (2003): "Achievement difference in class II students in Maths, with regard to Area, Gender, and social grounds during B.A.S and M.A.S in Gonda District". *The Educational Review,* March, Vol. 46, No. 3, pp. 55-57.

Sinha, Sudha R. (1980): "Effect of school system on the competence of secondary school students", *Indian Educational Review* January, pp. 62-77.

Sirohi, V. (2004): "A study of under Achievement at secondary level" *Educational Abstracts*. Vol. 5, No.1 and 2, January and July 2005, pp. 12-13.

Sood, Ramana (1990): "A Study of Academic Achievement of Pre-Engineering Students in Relation to Socio-Economic Status". *Journal of Educational Research and Extension*, Vol. 26, No. 4, April 1990, pp. 223-230.

Sood, Ramana and Dalvinder Kumar (2007): "Academic Achievement of First Generation Generation learners and Subsequent Generation Learners M.E.R.I, *Journal of Education* Vol. II, Number II. October (2007), pp. 45-49.

Sood, S. (1999): "A study of creativity, Problem solving Ability and personality characteristics as correlates of

Mathematical Achievement of students of Residential and Non-Residential schools" Ph.D in Education, Panjab, University; Chandigarh.

Srinivasan, T. and Arivudayappan, A. (2004): "Interest and Achievement of Eighth Standard Pupils in Social Sciences in Nilgiri District" *Experiments in Education*, Vol. 32, No.1, Jan 2004, pp. 8-12.

Srivastava S.N, Singh, J, and Thakur, G.P (1980): "Examination Anxiety and Academic Achievement as a function of socio Economic Status" *Psychological Studies* 25, 2, pp. 108-110.

Stella and Purushiotham (1993), "Study Habits of under Achievers", *Journal of educational Research and Extension,* Vol.29, No.4, pp. 206-214.

Subramanyam, K. and K. Sreenivasa Rao (2008): Academic Achievement and Emotional Intelligence of Secondary School Children. *Journal of Community Guidance & Research* 2008, Vol. 25, No. 2, pp. 224-228.

Sudamma, GR (1973): A study of the Effect of Library use on Academic Achievement of Post graduate students" Ph.D. Thesis, MSU, Baroda.

Sukhia. S.P., Mehrotra, PV and Mehrotra, R.N. (1980): "Elements of Educational Research". A text book, Allied publishers, Bombay India, pp. 101-102.

Sumangala, V. (1998): "Effect of tutoring at home on achievement in Mathematics of secondary school pupils", *Experiments in Education*, September, Vol. 26, No. 9, pp. 155-158.

Sundararajan, S and Dhandapani B (1991): "Attitude of higher secondary students of Pondchery Territory towards the study of mathematics and their achievement in it". Experiments in Education, Vol. XIV, No. 9, September, pp. 249-260.

Suneetha, B. and Mayuri, K. (2002): "A study on Age and Gender Differences on Factors Affecting High Academic Achievement", *Journal of community Guidance and*

Research, Vol.18 (2); 197-208-from *Indian Educational Abstracts,* Vol. 2, July 2002, Abstract No. 199, p. 64

Suydam, MN and Higgings, J.L. (1977): "Activity based learning in elementary school mathematics: Recommendations from research" Columbus, OH: *ERIC* Clearing House for Science, Mathematics and Environmental Education.

Taneja, R.P. (1991): *Dictionary of Education*, Anmol Publications, New Delhi, pp. 3, 4, 224.

Thorndike (1952): From "A study of Academic achievement of pre-engineering students in Relation to socio-economic status" by Ramana Sood,; *Journal of Educational Research and Extension,* Vol. 26, No. 4, April 1990, pp. 223-230.

Tuilford, J.P. (1950): "Fundamental Statistics in Psychology and Education: International student Edition, New York McGraw-Hill.

Uma, S. (2004): "Learning of Science and Maths through computers" Edu tracks, April, 2004, Vol. 3, No. 8.

Upadyaya, H.P. (2003): "Effect of Constructivism on mathematics Achievement of Grade V students in Nepal", *Educational Abstracts*: Vol. 4, No.1, Jan 2004, Abstract No. 27, p. 28.

Vamadevappa, H.V. (2002): "An Investigation in to Factors causing under achievement in Biology among pre-university students". Ph.D in education, Kuvempu university; from Indian educational Abstracts Vol:2 No:2 July 2002, Abstract. 175, p. 43.

Varghese, N.V. (1995): "School facilities and Learner achievement : Towards a Methodology of Analysing School Facilities in India". *Perspectives in Education*, Vol.11(2), 97-108, Indian Educational Abstracts, p. 29-30.

Varma, B.P. (1996): "Test Anxiety and study Habits; A study of the main and interaction Effects on Academic Achievement" *Journal of Applied Psychology*, Vol. 33, No. 2, pp. 55-61.

Vasantha, Ram Kumar (1969): "Self-concept and Achievement on school subject of prospective university entrants". Ph.D Thesis, Kerala university

Vasanthi, R and Ms Bhama Lalithambika (1997): "Interest of High School Students in Mathematics".

Venkataiah, N and Jayachandrama Naidu K. (1990): "Who are better non-starters in non-formal education centres in India". *Educational Review Quarterly*, Vol. 25, No. 3, July 1990, pp. 32-39.

Verma, B.P and Gupta, CK (1990): "Influence of home Environment on children's Scholastic Achievement". Journal of Education & Psychology; Vol. 47, No. 3-4 Oct-Jan 1989-90, pp. 159-164.

Verma, S. and Kumar, R. (1999): "A correlation study between study habits and Achievement in different school courses", *Educational Abstracts*: Vol 3 No: 2 July 2003. p.82. Abstract No: 206

Vijaya Lakshmi, O and Hemalatha Natesan (1992): "Factors Influencing Academic Achievement", Research High lights, *Journal of Avanashilingam Institute of Home Science and Higher Education for Women, Quarterly,* Vol. 2, No. 1, Jan 1992, pp. 62-67.

Vyas, R.P (1982): "Relationship of selected factors with Teaching success of prospective teachers of Rajasthan" Ph.D. in Education, Rajasthan University, from fourth Survey of Research in Education: Abstract No. 1239, p. 854.

Webster's' New Dictionary and Treasures (1995): A Dictionary, Promotional Sales book, Inc; Printed in U.S.A., pp. 337- 421.

Winner, B.J. (1971): "Statistical Principles in Experimental Design", New York, McGraw-Hill.

Wiseman, S. 1967: "The Manchester survey in children and other primary schools": The plowder Report: Vol. 2, London: Her Majesty's' Stationary Office, p. 90.

Wiseman, Stephans (1964): "Education and Environment" University Press: Manchester. p. 89

Wiseman-Stephany (1964): "Education and Environment", University Press: Manchester, p. 89.

Wood, T. (1999): "Creating a Context for Argument in Mathematics Class" *Journal for Research in Mathematics Education:* 30, pp. 171-91.

Woodruf (1940): "Study Habits of Intermediate students in Relation to certain psycho-sociological Factory" by M. Rajani Nov.2004 Unpublished Ph.D Thesis, Dept of Education, SVU., Tirupati, p. 47.

Wrenn, C.G. and Hamber, W.J. (1941): "Study Habits Associated with High and low senolarhisp. J. Edu. Psy, Vol:32, No. 8, pp. 611-615.

Yasoda, R. (2003): " An investigation into the problems relating to Teaching – Learning Mathematics at Secondary level". Ph.D in education, S.V.U. Tirupati, pp. 58-61.

Yate, N.W. (1965): "Statistics in Education and Psychology", New York. The McMillan.

Yeng, Yeh-Hsiang (1991): "Achievement in History as Related to Academic achievement Motivation". By Dr. S. Krishna Moorthy, *Experiments in Education*, Vol. 28, No.3, March 2000, pp. 47-52.

Young, Deirdre J. (1999): "Self-esteem in rural schools. Dreams and Aspirations" *ERIC* Vol. 34, No. 9, Sep 1999. Ed. 429789, p. 117.

Index

T

U

V

Z